SWEET AND DEADLY

SWEET AND DEADLY

HOW COCA-COLA SPREADS DISINFORMATION AND MAKES US SICK

MURRAY CARPENTER

THE MIT PRESS CAMBRIDGE, MASSACHUSETTS LONDON, ENGLAND

The MIT Press
Massachusetts Institute of Technology
77 Massachusetts Avenue, Cambridge, MA 02139
mitpress.mit.edu

The MIT Press would like to thank the anonymous peer reviewers who provided comments on drafts of this book. The generous work of academic experts is essential for establishing the authority and quality of our publications. We acknowledge with gratitude the contributions of these otherwise uncredited readers.

This book was set in ITC Stone and Avenir by New Best-set Typesetters Ltd. Printed and bound in the United States of America.

Library of Congress Cataloging-in-Publication Data

Names: Carpenter, Murray, author.
Title: Sweet and deadly : how Coca-Cola spreads disinformation and makes us sick / Murray Carpenter.
Description: Cambridge : The MIT Press, 2025. | Includes bibliographical references and index.
Identifiers: LCCN 2024024721 (print) | LCCN 2024024722 (ebook) | ISBN 9780262049504 (hardcover) | ISBN 9780262381789 (epub) | ISBN 9780262381796 (pdf)
Subjects: LCSH: Coca Cola (Trademark) | Cola drinks—Health aspects. | Selling—Cola drinks.
Classification: LCC HD9349.C6 C34 2025 (print) | LCC HD9349.C6 (ebook) | DDC 659.2/966362—dc23/eng/20241125
LC record available at https://lccn.loc.gov/2024024721
LC ebook record available at https://lccn.loc.gov/2024024722

10 9 8 7 6 5 4 3 2 1

EU product safety and compliance information contact is: mitp-eu-gpsr@mit.edu

publication supported by a grant from
The Community Foundation for Greater New Haven
as part of the *Urban Haven Project*

This book is dedicated to the scientists, doctors, and nurses working to understand chronic disease and protect human health. And to all Americans, who deserve to get the facts to support their health, unfettered by corporate disinformation.

CONTENTS

PROLOGUE: SENDING THE MEMO

In every case of corporate disinformation, there's a similar pattern. First come the zealots shouting from the rooftops that Corporation X is killing us with Product Y. But they are easily dismissed as crazy activists. Then the academics and researchers come along, some years later, and say, "You know what, guys, that actually might be true." But they say this gently, and their thoughts are easily drowned out by waves of corporate propaganda.

"Y is not harmful," say the reassuring voices, often doctors in lab coats who are well paid by Corporation X. "I mean, that would be crazy, right? A little Y won't kill you. It's all about moderation. What will they come after next—mother's milk and apple pie? Anyway, Americans just want choice."

Finally, many years later, the balance tips, and it becomes conventional wisdom that Corporation X has been lying and Product Y is harmful. This happened for Philip Morris, of course, and Exxon, and Purdue Pharma.

In each case, scientists raised red flags. In each case, very reasoned voices allied with industry reassured American consumers that there was nothing to worry about. It's always a long game, hard-fought and scrappy. But science bats last.

Science has shown that smoking tobacco is exceedingly harmful to human health. Science has shown that Oxycontin use leads to opioid addiction. It's shown that emissions from burning fossil fuels are changing the planet dramatically and harming human health. In each instance, corporations have profited wildly while society has picked up the tab.

Eventually, all of this is accepted as common knowledge. Over time, we forget the yearslong battles before the balance tipped and the messages were received by the American public.

The strange thing is this: even as the significant health risks posed by sugar-sweetened beverages have become ever clearer, the balance has never tipped for Coca-Cola.

The zealots have been shouting for a century, academics and researchers nodding agreement for seventy years, and the health science has become ever more compelling. Coca-Cola has countered its critics better than any other major corporation. The brand seems ever enshrouded in an aura of goodness and happiness. Its public relations campaigns are so effective that many Americans still have not gotten the memo about the health risks posed by sodas.

Sweet and Deadly considers the questions of why the balance has not tipped for Coca-Cola, and how it has so long avoided a reckoning. It makes two arguments: Coca-Cola significantly contributes to chronic disease, and the corporation's sophisticated shadow network has masterfully spread disinformation for decades to hide the health risks from its consumers.

These claims may seem, at first glance, hyperbolic. But research shows that sugar-sweetened beverages are not just unhealthful elements of American diets; they are uniquely unhealthful. Some scientists say they are the single item that most contributes to obesity and maladies such as type 2 diabetes and cardiovascular disease. And Coca-Cola is America's favorite sugar-sweetened beverage, by a long shot.

Put another way, one of the greatest threats to public health in the United States, and around the world, is the consumption of Coca-Cola and other sugar-sweetened beverages. The inverse is also true—research shows that ditching sugar-sweetened beverages is nearly a silver bullet for killing chronic diseases.

Coca-Cola is at the forefront of growing concerns about changing dietary patterns. Increasingly, health professionals are raising concerns about the proliferation of hyper-palatable, ultra-processed beverages and foods, and about the pattern of eating known as the Western diet, which includes an abundance of pre-packaged foods, refined grains, and sugary drinks.[1] Coke is often a key component of the dietary pattern.

This book focuses on the decade from 2010 to 2020, and takes this on from several angles. Part I discusses the beverage Coca-Cola, its enduring, even addictive, appeal, and the early indicators of its role in promoting chronic disease. Part II shows how just as the health science became more compelling, Coca-Cola dramatically ramped up its disinformation campaigns. In part III, you'll see how Coke and its allies fought back against soda taxes and regulatory efforts. Part IV will consider soda's disproportionate impact on communities of color, partly through the lens of a revealing court case. And part V will show that even as the science firmed up and Coke's disinformation tactics were exposed, its business model appeared stronger than ever.

Along the way, we'll see, in internal documents and court testimony, exactly what Coke's staff and allies were saying about the health risks. We'll see how well-established, mainstream nonprofit organizations and academic institutions lined up eagerly to do Coke's bidding. And we'll see just how close and friendly Coke executives were with obesity researchers, influential politicians like Bill and Hillary Clinton, and policy makers including the head of the Centers for Disease Control.

Regarding the book's scope, the focus is on Coke as opposed to the soda industry writ large, because it is not only the world's biggest beverage company, but has also been the most aggressive at spreading health disinformation. But that is not to suggest that the sugar-sweetened beverages produced by Pepsi or Dr Pepper are somehow more healthful than Coke products. The assumption here is that if the balance of public opinion tilts away from Coke, it will do the same for these other companies producing sugar-sweetened beverages.

By hewing closely to the themes of the health impacts of sugary beverages, and related disinformation, this book will omit some other controversial aspects of the corporation, such as its water use in India, anti-union practices in Colombia, and its role in plastic pollution. These are beyond the scope of this book, as is the growing body of research showing the metabolic effects of no-calorie sweeteners and diet soft drinks. And a note on nomenclature: the terms "Coke" and "Coca-Cola" will be used to refer to both the beverage and the eponymous corporation.

* * *

The health statistics are dramatic. More Americans are battling chronic diseases—the so-called diseases of lifestyle—than are healthy.[2] These include heart disease, cancer, lung disease, stroke, Alzheimer's disease, type 2 diabetes, and chronic kidney disease, and they are often linked to diet. Chronic disease kills about 1.7 million Americans annually, twenty-one times more than opioids.[3]

"Chronic disease" is a fairly anodyne term for a cluster of health problems that often develop into a positive feedback loop of diminishing health and increasing medical costs, a vicious circle. For example, the condition known as metabolic syndrome, which is associated with sugary drinks, includes increased abdominal fat, high blood sugar, high blood pressure, and high triglyceride levels. Eventually, this can lead to type 2 diabetes, kidney failure, and dialysis. Those who suffer from chronic disease can wind up on a treadmill of debt-inducing medical interventions and prescriptions.

Americans are among the heaviest people on the planet; two-thirds live with overweight or obesity.[4] In the fifty years that soda consumption spiked, so did obesity. From 1961 to 2016, American men gained thirty pounds, on average, and American women twenty-six pounds. This boom in obesity came just as high-fructose corn syrup oozed into American diets. It is as cheap as it is sweet, and has flooded food markets since the early 1980s to the extent that it's now hard to avoid. Sodas are the largest source of these sugars in the American diet.

The science of obesity has advanced dramatically in recent years, with greater discussion of the roles of hormones like ghrelin and leptin, and the understanding that body fat is not inert but is an organ with active metabolic functions.[5] A newer twist in the discussion is the growing popularity of weight-loss drugs like semaglutide, marketed as Wegovy or Ozempic.

Regarding obesity, it's emphasized here not to suggest that there is a perfect body type, or that the conditions of overweight and obesity are anything more than they are—physical conditions resulting from metabolic processes. As a culture, Americans are slowly moving toward body positivity—a long-overdue embrace of the many and varied natural shapes of human bodies. It's also important to understand that obesity is associated with a wide variety of chronic health challenges. This book's discussions of sugar-sweetened beverages and metabolism are offered while understanding the complexities of health, happiness, and personal choice.

* * *

Coca-Cola's health disinformation campaigns were already quite aggressive by the 1940s. In fact, that's when the sugar industry, with Coca-Cola's support, developed the strategies that the tobacco industry would so successfully adopt in the 1950s, now known as "the tobacco playbook." But in the decade from 2010 to 2020, Coca-Cola took its obfuscation campaign to the next level.

In one instance, the corporation got caught red-handed while trying to hide its fingerprints on a sprawling front group it created. The Global Energy Balance Network was a campaign to promote the concept of energy balance. This is the notion that maintaining a healthy body weight is simply a matter of ensuring that you burn as many calories as you consume. If the equation is in balance—the same number of calories in as calories out—you will not gain weight. In some cases, its proponents argue that it matters not if the calories come from yogurt, oats, or Coca-Cola, as long as the equation balances. As we'll see, this is inaccurate.

Still, the corporation spent millions to fund researchers and academics to promote this concept. Its allies in this campaign were not second-tier wannabes, but high-profile scientists at major North American universities.

This will lead us to an investigation of the front groups that Coca-Cola and other corporations have developed to carry their water. In a strategy that pushes the bounds of corporate cynicism, we'll see that Coca-Cola and its allies even created a statewide referendum campaign, run through several opaque front groups, to preempt a wave of municipal soda taxes in California.

We'll also listen in on a court case, because when the balance of public opinion does tip for a corporation, it's often due to a lawsuit. For years, critics of the soda industry have wondered when the big one might come along—a court case that would change the perception of sugar-sweetened beverages from benign treats to malign health risks, akin to the legal actions that finally succeeded against the tobacco industry in the mid-1990s. So some health advocates had high hopes in 2017, when pastors Delman Coates and William Lamar filed suit in DC Superior Court, alleging that Coca-Cola was hiding the health risks of its sodas.

The pastors claimed their congregants were suffering the health consequences of sugar-sweetened beverages and were being deceived by Coke's advertising and public relations campaigns. "I believe we're losing as many, if not more, people to sweets as we are to the streets," said Coates.[6]

In addition to the pastors' lawsuit, obesity specialists such as Dr. Yolandra Hancock, a pediatrician and assistant professor of public health at George Washington University, were calling attention to soda's disproportionate health impacts in communities of color. Dr. Hancock's concerns would soon take on greater urgency as the COVID-19 pandemic cut a tragic path through these communities and the Black Lives Matter movement began to amplify their long-muted voices.

If ever there was a moment of inflection, a tipping point for the soda battle, it looked like this might be it. But it would not be simple.

One challenge is that Coca-Cola's wholesome image is burnished by cheerleaders like Warren Buffett, the All-American billionaire known as the Oracle of Omaha. The bigger challenge is Coca-Cola's long-term strategy of obfuscating and spinning science in order to hide soda's health costs from the public and boost its sales. The campaigns have been very effective in attaining their objective: sowing doubt in consumers' minds about the growing body of sugar science.

All of the disparate parties working to inform Americans about the health risks posed by Coke are up against a foe as fierce as it is sweet. They are engaged in a tug-of-war over nutrition science and Americans' health.

* * *

This book is the story of a decade in the soda wars, but it is not a simple one. The health risks of sodas are inherently complex, as are the shadow networks Coke has built to mislead its consumers.

The health risks of sugar-sweetened beverages are not as straightforward as those posed by tobacco, or even opioid abuse. Sugar-sweetened beverages attack the body incrementally, through widely varied metabolic mechanisms. It's not a blitzkrieg, but a death by a thousand cuts, a long, grinding ground war with odds heavily stacked against the soda drinker. For this reason, it's important to understand not only that sodas pose greater health risks than other items in the modern diet, but also precisely how they inflict the damage on the human body. This is, at times, complicated.

More complicated still are the strategies Coke has used to confuse consumers about the dangers of sodas, in order to maximize its profits. Like the tobacco companies, Coke has developed a grand, overarching scheme. To simplify the scheme is to serve Coke's purposes, to make it appear less cynical and sinister. Again, this complexity will challenge the reader, but only in the details will the full picture emerge.

A spoiler: Public opinion did not reach a tipping point in the decade we detail. Neither the pastors' lawsuit nor the growing body of research was enough to prompt major shifts in the public perception of the product Coke or the corporation Coca-Cola.

Like the mastermind in a heist film, Coke got away with the loot. Coke stole America's health and cashed it in for billions of dollars, privatizing the profits while socializing the costs, and leaving in its wake many unhealthy citizens, often with massive medical bills. It retained its caramel-colored halo and its exalted position in society, rubbing elbows with politicians and captains of industry and continuing to make its shareholders happy and rich.

This story starts with an odd blend of chemicals and sugar, lots of sugar. It is the most appealing, most profitable beverage yet concocted by humanity. It is also among the most harmful.

It is Coca-Cola.

I

CARB-O-NATION

1

There is nothing quite like an ice-cold Coke. The sharp crack when the can pops open, followed by the subtle hiss of carbonation. The way the bottle feels in your hand. And that promising deep caramel color, effervescent and dark.

That first sip! It's sweet, yes, but that's just a part of it. The sweetness is tempered with tartness, a tang from the phosphoric acid. It passes smoothly over your tongue. Exquisite mouthfeel. Thicker than water. Thinner than whole milk. A tingly little wave of refreshment, cold and bubbly.

Penn State food scientist John Hayes described it well in the Michael Moss book *Salt Sugar Fat*:

> But in terms of flavor, there is that third leg of the stool that everyone forgets about, and that is the somatosensory, or the touch component, and this includes things like the tingle from the carbon dioxide bubbles, or the bite from the chili peppers, or the creaminess. In the case of Coca-Cola, what's so interesting about it is you're really activating *all* of these modalities. You have those nice aromas from the vanilla and the citrus and the whole family of brown spices, like cinnamon and nutmeg. Then you have that sweetness. And there's the bit of phosphoric acid, the tingle of the carbon dioxide. You end up stimulating all the different parts of the flavor construct that we experience.[1]

Downing the Coke, you can anticipate its metabolic boost. It's a two-stage rocket. The sugar will quickly course through your bloodstream. Then the caffeine—a modest but essential dose—will kick in within twenty minutes. The best way to describe the combined effect: it just makes you feel good.

But why bother discussing its attributes? Because if it is not the perfect beverage, it will do until a better one comes along. We know this because the marketplace has spoken. Coca-Cola is far and away the most popular soft drink on the planet. It is the cornerstone of a diversified global corporation selling more than two billion servings of drinks in two hundred countries every day.[2]

From time to time, you'll see a news story suggesting that Coca-Cola is no longer the world's most recognizable brand. The story will suggest another brand—say, Apple or Microsoft—is better known than Coke. And it may be true. In 2023, Interbrand ranked Coca-Cola eighth among the top global brands.[3] But it's an academic distinction. If you even have to discuss whether or not you're the world's most recognizable brand, you've already won.

2

In downtown Atlanta's Centennial Park, near the Georgia Aquarium, the National Center for Civil and Human Rights, and the CNN Center, sits another popular tourist attraction. It's a museum called World of Coca-Cola. In the plaza by the entrance is a bronze statue of Coca-Cola inventor John Pemberton, holding a glass aloft. Visitors, including many international tourists, pay $21 for a tour that includes a short film that's essentially a high-energy Coke ad, along with nostalgia-heavy exhibits of Coca-Cola history and paraphernalia.

The tour is sandwiched between sugar-sweetened beverages. Visitors get a complimentary can of Coke at the start of the tour, then finish up in a taproom where they can sample dozens and dozens of Coke products from all over the world, with limitless refills. The last stop is the gift shop, full of Coke-branded products, from infant onesies to boxers to hoodies to backpacks. Anyone not yet fully whacked out on sugar can purchase an ice-cold 500-milliliter bottle of Mexican Coca-Cola for $3.

One of the museum's primary attractions is a stylized high-tech vault door, in a dark room with red lighting that could be the set for a heist film. It's the Vault of the Secret Formula. A plaque nearby reads, "The secret recipe for Coca-Cola became the most sought after—and closely guarded—trade secret in American history." The secret is locked behind the massive door.

Much has been made of Coca-Cola's secret formula over the years. But it's really no secret. The ingredients are listed on the label: "Carbonated water, high fructose corn syrup, caramel color, phosphoric acid, natural flavors, caffeine." It's an unnatural slurry of chemicals, and a lot of hype.

Though it has been modified over the years, Coca-Cola still approximates the concept that Doc Pemberton had in mind in 1884. That's when he formulated French Wine Coca, to imitate the French patent medicine Vin Mariani, which was then all the rage. A blend of soothing alcohol and stimulating caffeine and coca extract, it may have been the ultimate feel-good drug. Imagine a Jägerbomb with a small bump of cocaine.

By 1888, Pemberton had eliminated the alcohol in favor of carbonated water and was marketing the product as a temperance beverage. Pemberton settled on a catchy name: Coca-Cola.

Already, in those days, it was sweet and tart. "Pemberton had come up with the perfect sugar delivery system, one that made people feel good without overwhelming the tongue," Bartow Elmore wrote in *Citizen Coke*. By the 1910s, Elmore wrote, "Coke was the single largest industrial consumer of sugar in the world, funneling roughly 100 million pounds annually into customers' bodies."[1]

The formula was tweaked a few times along the way. In the early 1900s, Asa Candler, who had wrested control of the company from Pemberton, decided to remove the cocaine from the blend. (Though he did insist on keeping "decocainized coca-leaf extract," an ingredient to this day.)

The other stimulating drug, caffeine, stayed in the formula. The caffeine was extracted from waste tea leaves by a fledgling chemical company in St. Louis: Monsanto. Coca-Cola and Monsanto grew symbiotically for decades. In that era, Coke was often served in eight-ounce servings, which contained eighty milligrams of caffeine. That's the size and caffeine content of a can of Red Bull. Put another way, Coca-Cola invented the energy drink eighty years before Red Bull.

The caffeine levels were tweaked and lowered over the years. But Coca-Cola settled on its modern formula sometime after World War II. Now it's usually made with synthetic caffeine, produced in overseas pharmaceutical plants that are under-regulated and sometimes filthy. A 2009 US Food and Drug Administration (FDA) inspection of Jilin Shulan Synthetic Pharmaceutical Co. found equipment rusting and peeling, and workers using "mops soaked in dirty water" to clean within the production area. After the inspection, but before FDA banned imports from the company, Coca-Cola bought enough caffeine powder from the Chinese plant to produce more than a billion cans of Coke.[2]

There are other synthetic chemicals in the recipe. Ascorbic acid from a chemical factory in Shijiazhuang, China. Monopotassium phosphate shipped from Dublin, Ireland, and Antwerp, Belgium. Citric acid from Santos, Brazil. Gum rosin from Mexico. Phosphoric acid solution, in plastic jerrycans, from Thailand, via Ireland; and caramel color, in tankers, from Cork, Ireland. "Extracts, flavouring," from Jiutepec, Mexico, via Cartagena. One shipment from Mexico City via the port of Veracruz is labeled: "Liquid flavor dangerous goods as per attached shipper."[3] These are some of the ingredients shipped to Caribbean Refrescos, Coca-Cola's blending plant in Cidra, Puerto Rico, in the mountains above San Juan.

Coca-Cola opened the plant in 1978, as part of a deal that allowed Puerto Rican subsidiaries of American corporations to forgo millions in federal income tax. (Pepsi built a plant on the other side of town, but closed it abruptly in 2018.) That tax benefit has gone away, but the Coca-Cola plant remains, with its four hundred employees and a payroll of $30 million.

Now, this factory is the nexus of global trade routes that funnel the chemicals into cans and bottles of Coca-Cola. In all, more than six thousand shipping containers move to and from the plant annually.[4] They are trucked through the congestion of San Juan, then up the winding two-lane roads, past almond, mango, and papaya trees and small banana groves, and an endless line of roadhouses bearing Coca-Cola banners reading "La esquina del sabor," the corner of flavor. Finally, the trucks ascend to Cidra, which one reporter called "an obscure little mountain town."

In the square downtown, old men play dominoes in the shade. But half a mile away, global commerce is being done. More than one hundred thousand tons of goods flow through the plant annually. Some is blended with high fructose corn syrup for consumption in Puerto Rico. But most is blended into a powdered concentrate, then shipped to the United States.

At this point, the Coca-Cola ingredients scarcely resemble a food product. The concentrate is just a powdered blend of flavoring, coloring, and the world's most popular psychoactive drug, caffeine. It seems odd that this chemical amalgamation is needed to produce a tasty soda, but it is.

One key ingredient is phosphoric acid, and Coca-Cola has, helpfully, described its purpose. "The Coca-Cola Company uses phosphoric acid in some of its products to provide a pleasant tartness. The acid in these beverages does not contribute to dental erosion in the course of normal beverage consumption. Nor does it make a significant contribution to the total daily intake of phosphorus."[5]

Part of the challenge of blending the chemicals, and then adding the water and sugar, is the challenge of consistency. To handle this, the company employs teams of sensory scientists to ensure that one Coke tastes just like the next Coke, anywhere from Atlanta to Zanzibar.

At the plant in Cidra, these powdered ingredients are mixed together into a powerful concentrate—one gallon of concentrate will produce five hundred gallons of Coca-Cola.[6] Most of the sodas in the United States are produced from this concentrate. All you have to do is add carbonated water and high-fructose corn syrup.

That's the secret formula.

The ingredients in a modern Coca-Cola do not even remotely resemble food, but it is not the powders from overseas chemical plants that are the primary concern to health researchers. It's the ingredient from the heartland of the United States—sugar, usually in the form of high-fructose corn syrup—that looks worse with each passing day. And sugar is especially harmful when served in liquid form.

3

Before dawn every morning, in a large parking lot squeezed between the Bruckner Expressway and the East River in the Bronx, dollies clatter over the asphalt, as delivery crews ferry freshly bottled cases of Coca-Cola to a waiting fleet of trucks. They load each truck with hundreds of cases of Coke and other beverages. Then dozens of diesel engines cough and rumble to life.

Soon, a fleet of long red trucks bearing that recognizable white script logo fan out to deliver Coca-Cola to thousands of bodegas, grocery stores, and restaurants throughout New York City. This is part of the Liberty Coca-Cola bottling network, one of the nation's largest. At similar bottling facilities nationwide, concentrate from Caribbean Refrescos is blended with high-fructose corn syrup and water to make Coke.

The same process is repeated in every corner of the country—more than six thousand Coca-Cola trucks,[1] among the world's largest truck fleets, are dispatched from hundreds of nodes, in an elaborate circulatory system, efficiently delivering more than one hundred million servings of Coca-Cola products daily onto cooler shelves, and then into the hands, guts, and arteries of its thirsty consumers.

The capillaries reach so far that in every retail environment—chain drug stores in big cities, dollar stores along the highways, and little country stores in rural corners of America—you have to slalom through displays of Coca-Cola products as you do your shopping.

Coca-Cola is unparalleled in its ubiquity. On urban thoroughfares and rural back roads, the Coca-Cola sign is omnipresent. In small towns the red-and-white signs illuminate the sidewalks at night. It's virtually impossible to walk twenty feet on a city sidewalk without seeing a Coke sign.

Every grocery store, every corner store and gas station, every drug store, every bus, train, and airport terminal has a Coca-Cola machine or a Coca-Cola sign. (As an indication of their marketing savvy, the Coke logo on store signs is often larger than the name of the store.)

The familiar Coca-Cola signs are so common that it's easy to overlook them. They are just part of the landscape. It's the culmination of a strategy that began when Robert Woodruff, then Coca-Cola's chairman, stated in 1923 that a Coca-Cola should always be "within arm's reach of desire." Arm's reach soon morphed into ubiquity, even in schools.

"Our strategy is ubiquity," Coca-Cola spokesman Randal W. Donaldson said in 1994. "We want to put soft drinks within arm's reach of desire. We strive to make soft drinks widely available, and schools are one channel we want to make them available in."[2]

Coca-Cola is ubiquitous not just in the United States, but all over the world. In developing countries, Coca-Cola is often seen as a symbol of wealth, sophistication, a Western lifestyle. From Beijing to Bogota, and along all the tiny little back roads in the hinterlands of the developing countries of the world, Coca-Cola truly is everywhere. It sells its products in more than two hundred countries, and international sales account for two-thirds of its annual revenues of $46 billion.[3]

As it grew internationally, Coca-Cola became a symbol of everything that America represents. When Coca-Cola entered Burma in 2012, the BBC interviewed author Mark Standage. "The moment Coca-Cola starts shipping is the moment you can say there might be real change going on here," Standage said. "Coca-Cola is the nearest thing to capitalism in a bottle."[4]

4

It's hard to say precisely when Americans became fully immersed in sodas, but World War II marked a significant turning point.

Coca-Cola's wartime marketing was unparalleled. War correspondent Gordon Frazer recounted the moment ten cases of Coke reached a gun pit on the front lines in Italy: "Jack was already pouring his down and some of it was drooling off his chin. He stopped for just long enough to say it was the first Coke he'd had in a year and a half, and then took to the bottle again. Shorty Brockman took a couple of healthy swigs, looked up, and with a big grin on his face, said it sure tasted like the States."[1]

Coca-Cola flooded America during the postwar economic boom. Partly, the soda was displacing coffee. Coffee consumption peaked in 1946, when Americans were drinking nearly a gallon a week. By 2005, Americans were drinking about half that amount.[2]

Sodas displaced more than coffee. Milk also fell out of favor as a regular beverage, with an even more abrupt decline than coffee—from forty-two gallons per American in 1945 to just twenty gallons in 2012.[3] In 1945, Americans drank more than four times as much milk as soft drinks; by 1997, they drank more than twice as much soda as milk. Tap water also went into the gutter.

In *For God, Country, and Coca-Cola*, Mark Pendergrast reported on a dramatic scene featuring Coca-Cola's chairman and CEO, on the occasion of Coca-Cola's one hundredth anniversary in 1986:[4]

> "Right now," Roberto Goizueta informed the assembled bottlers at the centennial, "in the United States, people consume more soft drinks than any other liquid—including ordinary tap water." The Coke CEO then painted a glorious scenario. "If we take full advantage of our opportunities," he said, "someday,

not too many years into our second century, we will see the same wave catching on in market after market until, eventually, the number one beverage on earth will not be tea or coffee or wine or beer. It will be soft drinks. *Our* soft drinks."

Coke was determined to further tip the balance away from ordinary tap water. In cooperation with Olive Garden, it even developed the H_2NO campaign. With the catchy slogan "Just say no to H_2O," it was an effort to steer patrons of the restaurant chain away from water and toward soft drinks and other beverages.[5]

As these other beverages dried up, soda consumption increased fivefold, from eleven gallons per person in 1947 to fifty-two gallons per person in 2005. That's about enough soda to fill a bathtub.

"For Coca-Cola stockholders, the years from 1980 to 1997 were especially sweet," Michael Moss wrote in *Salt Sugar Fat*. "Sales more than quadrupled from $4 billion to $18 billion. The per caps were equally impressive. By 1997, Americans were drinking 54 gallons of soda a year, on average, and Coke controlled almost half of the soda sales, with a 45 percent share. The rising consumption, which had more than doubled from 1970, also had staggering implications for the nation's health. With diet sodas accounting for only 25 percent of the sales, the sugary soda that people drank each year—more than 40 gallons—delivers 60,000 calories and 3,700 teaspoons of sugar, per person."[6]

By 2011, most Americans drank at least one sugar-sweetened beverage per day.[7] The average person was getting 145 calories daily from sodas, a bit more than the 140 calories in a twelve-ounce can of Coke. The pattern of consumption was not evenly distributed, however. Soda consumption was higher among young men, African Americans, and people with less education.[8]

Starting in the late 1960s, another phenomenon was occurring just as soda consumption spiked. Americans began developing obesity at unprecedented rates. The diseases associated with obesity—especially type 2 diabetes—skyrocketed.

Part of the story was anecdotal. Clothing manufacturers needed to make ever-larger sizes. Airlines began providing extension belts for travelers with obesity. Vacationers at the beach looked remarkably different than thirty years earlier. The story was also statistical. In 1960, American men weighed 166 pounds, on average, and women weighed 140.[9] Americans were, in those days, remarkably slender by modern standards.

Even in that era, Coca-Cola was trying to appease its customers' concerns about weight gain. A 1961 television ad featured actress Connie Clausen as she took a break from sewing. "Well, that's enough for today," she said to the camera. "Now for a lively lift—ice-cold Coca-Cola. There's no waistline worry with Coke, you know. Actually this individual-sized bottle has no more calories than half a grapefruit."

Things changed quickly after 1960. By 2016, American men weighed 197 pounds on average; thirty pounds more than fifty-five years earlier. The average woman weighed 164, twenty-six pounds more than her 1961 counterpart.[10] Obesity affected 40 percent of American adults, and nearly 20 percent of adolescents.[11]

But even as Americans became heavier and heavier, few people understood the role that sugar-sweetened beverages played in driving the epidemic. The tendency was to blame fatty foods for weight gain, not sweet drinks. And it was not just the epidemics of obesity, type 2 diabetes, and related diseases that were linked to sodas. The most common malady associated with sodas, and the most common chronic disease in America, is dental caries, better known as cavities. And the odds of getting cavities and losing teeth, even among young people, are higher among soda drinkers.[12]

Sure, many people, maybe most people, had an idea that Coke was not a health food and that it may harm your teeth, but few understood the degree to which it was unhealthful. This is partly because the body of research was not as robust before 2010 as it has become in the years since. So researchers could say soda consumption had spiked, and obesity and type 2 diabetes spiked concurrently, but that does not prove a link. Correlation, as careful scientists often point out, does not prove causation.

But these two trends—increased soda drinking and decreased health—are indeed linked. And the evidence is growing all the time. Writing for *JAMA Internal Medicine* in 2014, Quanhe Yang of the Centers for Disease Control and Prevention and colleagues surveyed the link between added sugars and cardiovascular disease death among US adults.[13] Their conclusion was straightforward: "A higher percentage of calories from added sugar is associated with significantly increased risk of CVD [cardiovascular disease] mortality. In addition, regular consumption of sugar-sweetened beverages is associated with elevated CVD mortality. Our results support current recommendations to limit the intake of calories from added sugars in US diets."

It sounded simple. Limit added sugars. Limit the largest source of added sugars—sugar-sweetened beverages. And health will improve. Simple, but difficult.

One reason it can be so difficult to change the behavior is due to the nature of chronic disease. Chronic diseases are also called diseases of lifestyle. These include heart disease, cancer, lung disease, stroke, Alzheimer's disease, type 2 diabetes, and chronic kidney disease. They can be caused, or exacerbated, by personal habits, particularly by diet and a lack of physical activity.

Chronic diseases creep up on you, incrementally. First, you'll gain a few extra pounds, often around the belly. And that extra weight makes exercising more difficult, and less appealing. Then a few more pounds, and a bit less enthusiasm for exercise. Soon this cycle can lead to insulin resistance and pre-diabetes. As the weight grows, it contributes to joint pain—knees that are perfectly happy carrying a 160-pound load get creaky ferrying 190 pounds around every day, just as they would if everywhere you went you carried a thirty-pound backpack, representing the extra pounds Americans have gained.

Somewhere along the way, elevated blood pressure might show up. Soon the trajectory of these preventable chronic diseases might lead to blood pressure medications, cholesterol medications, and the cancers that are associated with ill health.

It's a gradually growing metabolic storm that steals not only the health of millions of Americans but also their time and money, as they bounce from doctor to doctor and buy prescription upon prescription. Travel far enough down this road and somewhere near its terminus, you will find kidney failure waiting, and regular visits to a dialysis clinic. The latter comes at great expense, sometimes to the patient, but more often to American taxpayers through Medicare.

According to the Centers for Disease Control, 60 percent of Americans have one or more chronic diseases. The diseases account for the bulk of the nation's health care costs,[14] which reached $4.5 trillion by 2022.[15] A

2021 paper estimated the excess health care costs of overweight and obesity alone at $200 billion annually.[16]

Here's the thing about chronic disease—it kills 1.7 million Americans annually, twenty-one times as many as opioids. But the link, the cause of death, is far less apparent. Coca-Cola drinkers just grind themselves down, day after day, a liter of soda at a time. And when they die, people say it was heart disease that killed them. Or was it kidney failure, or maybe diabetes? They don't tend to link it back to the sugary drinks.

5

By 2020, when William E. Eubank II was sixty-seven, he had been a Coca-Cola addict for five decades. For many of those years he drank two or three two-liter bottles a day.

Eubank preferred the flavor of twelve-ounce bottles or, better yet, the ten-ounce glass bottles—"that is the best flavor there is"—but he did not often drink them because they were more expensive. And don't get him started on cans. "No Marine would drink out of a can," he joked. "Cans are nasty, they are nasty."

Eubank drank Pepsi when he was very young, but his older sister was his hero, and she was hooked on Coca-Cola. So he switched. And even in a very thirsty situation, he would not drink a Pepsi.

Eubank partly attributes his Coca-Cola loyalty to savvy ad campaigns that he felt were wonderful, sexy, and morally appealing. Like millions of Americans, he especially liked the "I'd like to buy the world a Coke" ad that debuted in 1971 and is widely considered one of the most effective ads in history.

"Let me tell you something, I thought that was wonderful. I really did. Because I'm one of those people drinking the Coke," Eubank said, in a phone interview from his home in Virginia. His story illustrates the allure of the beverage, the health risks it poses, and the cognitive dissonance some soda drinkers experience as they try to reconcile the two.

Eubank's father was very concerned about him and his sister drinking so much Coca-Cola, and even once sent Eubank a clipping about Coca-Cola working to make the drink addictive. But Eubank said he was young and not concerned about it.

Eubank is from a military family, and his own nearly twenty-year career in the US Marines took him all over the world. Coke was everywhere he went. "There was just no place that I could not get a Coke," he said. "Okinawa, Korea. All over the east and south of the US. If you asked someone if they wanted a soda, they didn't even have to tell you what it was. You knew it was a Coke."

Partly, the sodas were a spot of flavor in an otherwise drab military diet. "The C-rats [rations] were terrible, always have been. This was before they came out with MREs [meals ready to eat]. I would eat that soda in the morning for breakfast and go do what I had to do," Eubank said. "I didn't drink Coca-Cola, I ate it. I would look at it as something literally to eat. And I would feel better and everything else. And I'm paying for it now."

In late 2019, Eubank quit drinking soda. And he started doing something else. "Just Tuesday night I gave myself my first insulin shot," Eubank said in early 2020. "I've been type 2 for about two solid years. I've been pre-diabetic for many years, and I don't blame anyone. I'm not angry at Coca-Cola, it was my drug of choice. I'll tell you right now, there is nothing better to me than to wake up, and get a twelve-ounce soda, a Coca-Cola, out of the refrigerator, and chug it. And my day is lit up, I'm locked and cocked and ready to go, and everything's fine."

Eubank said his Coca-Cola habit probably led to his diabetes. "It's just one of those things," he said. "I'm not being cavalier about it, it's not like I went out there and got shot. I went out there and shot myself."

Eubank still keeps one twelve-ounce Coca-Cola in his home refrigerator, and one in his work refrigerator, in case he goes into insulin shock after taking his shots and needs to quickly boost his blood sugar.

When he had kids, he had a rule: "The last soda in the house is mine. The last soda is mine. And that's sad," Eubank said. "But it is a true addiction. And all the exercise and all the good food in the world won't help you if you're drinking soda the way I did."

Though the Coke formula has evolved since its origins as a patent medicine, it retains its intense, pharmaceutical allure. The cold, fizzy, sweet, lightly caffeinated beverage is more than appealing—it's mildly addictive. Eubank said the idea that Coke is addictive is more accepted than it once was.

Many people dislike using that term for products like Coke, because it is addictive on a different scale than, say, heroin or other opiates. However, the term "addiction" is useful in describing the pattern that Eubank and millions of other soda drinkers know so well: they feel good when they drink it, they feel lousy when they don't, and they feel driven to continue drinking it even though they are aware that it is unhealthful.

The addiction is driven, in large part, by the drug caffeine. Coca-Cola, Pepsi, and Dr Pepper blend pure, powdered caffeine into all of the top-selling soft drinks in the United States. There is some variation. Coca-Cola uses 35 percent more of the drug in Diet Coke than in Classic Coke. But all of the top sellers include caffeine.

As do energy drinks. In fact, it is sort of silly to consider energy drinks as distinct from sodas or so-called sports drinks. The caffeine, carbonation, and sugar levels vary. But these are all sugar-sweetened beverages.

Researcher Jennifer Temple of the University of Buffalo has studied the role of caffeine in driving soda consumption. One of Temple's studies showed that caffeine reinforces the soda drinking habit in teens, more for males than females.[1] This is important from a marketing standpoint, because it is the age at which soda companies are hoping to hook consumers for life.

Coca-Cola has vacillated in its promotion of caffeine. In its early days, Coke was clearly marketed as a stimulant, an invigorating tonic for fatigue, and the company boasted of its caffeine. By the middle of the last century, the company toned down these claims, and said that caffeine was merely a flavoring agent. But Roland Griffiths and colleagues at Johns Hopkins showed that most people were unable to distinguish the flavors of caffeinated and uncaffeinated sodas.[2] So why has the industry persisted in keeping low levels of caffeine in soft drinks?

An elegant study by an Australian team, published in 2015, provides the likely answer.[3] The researchers blended lemon-flavored sugar-sweetened beverages with and without caffeine. The subjects were unable to taste the difference. In a four-week trial, half of the one hundred subjects were issued the caffeinated beverages, to drink at will, and the other half got drinks without caffeine. The group with caffeinated drinks consumed significantly more than the group without: fourteen ounces daily versus nine ounces. The research suggests that caffeine is blended into

Coca-Cola and other sodas because it makes them more appealing and increases sales.

Looking beyond caffeine, there are those who think some beverages, especially those rich in sugar, can also drive addictive patterns. Laura Schmidt, professor of health policy at the University of California, San Francisco (UCSF) School of Medicine, describes the pattern in more academic terms: "Those who support bringing sugar and other foods under the addiction rubric note that, like addicts, binge eaters experience a lack of control, continue overeating despite harm to their health, experience social, legal, and financial problems, and are often unsuccessful at attempts to cut back or reduce their consumption."[4]

Part of the challenge is that eating triggers the same dopamine circuits as illicit drugs like cocaine, but to a lesser degree. Gene-Jack Wang, a senior clinician at the National Institute of Alcohol Abuse and Alcoholism, has spent more than ten years studying brain images to understand this behavior. He said the similarities between eating, even when people know it is harmful, and drug addiction are striking. In both cases, cues play a strong role. For a drug addict, it could mean meeting a friend who has a bindle of cocaine. For the Coca-Cola addict, it might be something as subtle and universal as a Coke sign or ad.

"The cue is very, very important," Wang said. "The cue makes you change your mind. You don't need it, but because you just pass by, and you see the symbol there, it makes you change your mind, and you cannot stop it."

In unhealthy eating, as in drug addiction, reinforcement plays a role—taking some of the substance makes you feel good, which reinforces the behavior, and makes you want to have more. In both cases, dopamine becomes down-regulated. This means you need more of a substance to get the same dopaminergic effect. And in both cases, impulse control is the most challenging aspect of managing the addiction.

Wang said many scientists don't like to use the term "food addiction," because it is too broad. The term usually refers to what he calls hyperpalatable foods, usually those with high levels of fat, salt, or sugar. Food companies know how appealing such products are. "They want you to come back," he said. "That is the purpose."

Coke and other sodas pack a one-two punch with their sugar-caffeine combo. Wang believes the two have a synergistic effect, though it's been little studied.

With a blend of two chemicals widely considered addictive, sodas are supremely attractive. But you don't need brain imaging to understand this. The marketplace is a better metric. The addictive allure has made Coke the best beverage the world has ever seen, from a commercial vantage, driving the corporation's $46 billion in annual revenue. It is as though all of the ingredients are working synergistically to make it appealing to consumers, even those, like Jane Grant, who'd rather not drink it.

Grant will only drink Coke over ice. That's the way she enjoyed it when she and her siblings would split a liter of soda when she was growing up in Brazil. Now living in Texas, she associates Coke with those happy times, joking around with her family. And there is that unparalleled flavor.

"You know how when you take that first sip, how it tastes so good, how it hits all the taste buds in your mouth, and you go 'Yeah, it tastes so good!'" said Grant. "Well, that's how I used to have Coke. The pouring in the cup. You hear the sound of the ice readjusting in the glass. And then I have to have a straw. And having the first sip, and then when it hits my tongue, and I can taste all the sweetness and deliciousness."

Around 1998, Grant went from drinking Coke socially to drinking it daily. "The caffeine, that's how the whole madness started," Grant said. "I thought the caffeine would help with my migraines. By the time I noticed it didn't work, I was already hooked."

These days, Coke doesn't taste so good to her anymore, and her relationship with Coke is not a happy one. When she is abstaining, Grant said something as benign as the sound of opening a can or bottle triggered the craving. It serves as the cue that Wang mentions.

"Everywhere you go, it is in your face," she said. "When you are trying to quit, everywhere you go, somebody is drinking a Coke. The sound is everywhere."

When Grant quits, she tapers from two twenty-ounce bottles daily to one bottle a day, to two twelve-ounce cans, to one twelve-ounce can. "And after that, it will be cold turkey," she said. "I know it sounds ridiculous. It sounds weird. But in order to quit drinking Coca-Cola, why is it so hard?

"I lose weight fast when I quit. I don't eat my calories, I drink my calories. It's a lot of empty calories," Grant said. "I used to think dieting was hard. But there is something worse—to quit an addiction that is not recognized as an addiction. It's supposed to be a refreshment."

Grant has worked as a medical interpreter, and often interpreted for people quitting smoking. While doing that work, she noticed that all addictions have their rituals. Smokers wake up in the morning and think about cigarettes; Coke drinkers think about Coke. In her case, Grant said it is a true addiction. She cannot drink Coke socially. She has seen a therapist to help her quit, and has been strongly supported by her doctor, Chrisette Dharmagunaratne.

"Some people are able to overcome the addiction," she continued. "Others say, 'I am so miserable, that's the only thing that brings me pleasure.' And they don't want to deal with it. . . . I wish there was a Coca-Cola anonymous, to deal with this stupid drink."

For Gail Mates, the addiction was Cherry Coke and plenty of it. At her peak, she was drinking three or four cans for breakfast, then often another three at lunchtime, and maybe a couple at bedtime.

Mates, who lives in northern Virginia and has a background in pharmaceutical marketing, became depressed when her father died. "And I started eating uncontrollably," Mates said. "I just ate and drank. I was drinking one Cherry Coke after another. I was just digging my grave with a knife and a fork and a Coke.

"I just really had a thing for that Cherry Coke," Mates said. "I was an addict. I really felt like I was an addict. When you keep putting that sugar into your system, it just wants more and more."

The unhealthy habits caught up with her, which was especially worrisome because she had a family history of heart disease. "Through doing all this I developed diabetes type 2, I had high blood pressure, I had high cholesterol," Mates said. "I had a waist circumference bigger than thirty-five inches, which gave me metabolic syndrome and it put me at the highest risk of heart disease, not to mention my family history. I also developed a horrible case of reflux, through drinking all of these sodas."

Mates also developed sleep apnea and her teeth became discolored and full of cavities. "It really does do a number on your teeth," she said. Mates understood that poor dental health is associated with increased risk for heart disease. She could see that her soda habit was contributing to her downward spiral through several metabolic pathways.

"I knew that the Coke had no nutritive value," she said. "And because I'd become a diabetic from all of this, I realized that I was literally killing myself with these Cokes, with the type 2 diabetes. It just could not keep going. Coke is so high in sugar."

Before her daughter went off to college, she begged her mother to improve her unhealthy lifestyle. Mates decided to work on it, but followed a philosophy that small, simple changes add up to big results. "Instead of cutting out all of those Cherry Cokes, I would cut out one can a week, and I would replace it with a water, and I would infuse it with some fruit or a tiny splash of pure fruit juice," Mates said. "And then I just kept knocking out the Cokes with the water, and I kept doing it and doing it. I believe that slow and steady wins the race. Too much, too soon sets you up for failure."

She also incorporated exercise into her lifestyle, but very slowly, just five minutes a day at first. She felt good about it and kept going. By 2021, at age sixty-four, Mates was far healthier than when she started her journey a decade earlier. "I lost sixty-five pounds, and I reversed my diabetes," Mates said. "I also have reversed my high blood pressure. And my cholesterol is perfect. My waist circumference is below thirty-five; metabolic syndrome is a thing of the past.

"This is definitely from cutting out all this sugar and these sodas and also eating much healthier," she said. "Because after you become healthier, you don't want all of these sodas."

Mates became a spokesperson for the American Heart Association, and has been featured in one of their videos. More than a decade after turning her health around, she finds it especially gratifying to have made her daughter happy. "The smile on her face now, knowing that I've got my life together, and I'm actually helping other people with this, has just made a world of difference," Mates said.

Her Cherry Coke habit is long gone. Once in a blue moon, Mates said, she will have a couple of sips for the taste of Coke, but not often. "I don't want that in my body," she said.

These accounts of Eubank, Grant, and Mates show just how appealing Coke is to the consumer. And they illustrate another odd truth about Coke. It is not only the perfect beverage from a sales perspective, but also a very effective poison, because its addictive allure keeps drawing consumers back until it's inflicted its damage.

6

"Is soda the new tobacco?" *New York Times* columnist Mark Bittman asked in a provocative essay in early 2010.[1] Bittman quoted Dr. Tom Frieden, the director of the Centers for Disease Control, describing the similarities: "There are aspects of the food industry that are reminiscent of tobacco—the sowing of doubt where there's no reasonable doubt, funding of front groups, use of so-called experts, claims that new products which are safer for consumers are available, and the claim that they are not marketing to children."

The column came at a moment of churn for the soda and sugar industries, as anti-soda forces were growing increasingly loud and forceful. A year earlier, Frieden, then leading the health department for New York City, had coauthored a *New England Journal of Medicine* article calling for soda taxes.[2] He and Kelly Brownell, of Yale's Rudd Center for Food Policy and Obesity, made a direct analogy to the tobacco taxes that helped reduce smoking rates. They also noted the astonishing cost of poor diets: "The contribution of unhealthful diets to health care costs is already high and is increasing—an estimated $79 billion is spent annually for overweight and obesity alone—and approximately half of these costs are paid by Medicare and Medicaid, at taxpayers' expense."

Their pitch was that a soda tax could improve health, while raising money. "A penny-per-ounce excise tax could reduce consumption of sugared beverages by more than 10%," they wrote. "It is difficult to imagine producing behavior change of this magnitude through education alone, even if government devoted massive resources to the task. In contrast, a sales tax on sugared drinks would generate considerable revenue, and as with the tax on tobacco, it could become a key tool in efforts to improve health."

An indication of the depth of the industry opposition to soda taxes had come the year before, when a federal soda tax was briefly discussed then killed. Coca-Cola, Pepsi, and the American Beverage Association spent more than $24 million in 2009 to fight the tax and other regulatory proposals.[3]

Besides the soda tax conversation, there were other ominous signs for the soda industry. "Sugar: The Bitter Truth," a wonky talk on sugar metabolism by UCSF professor Robert Lustig, had become an improbable YouTube hit.[4] Gary Taubes's 2007 book, *Good Calories, Bad Calories*, which challenged head-on the notion of all calories being equal, was selling well. And New York mayor Michael Bloomberg was preparing a proposal to allow New York City and the state of New York to ban the purchase of sodas with food stamps.[5]

Also, just days before Bittman's column was published, First Lady Michelle Obama had rolled out her "Let's Move" campaign to fight childhood obesity.[6] She specifically targeted sugar. "The truth is, our kids didn't do this to themselves," Obama said. "Our kids didn't choose to make food products with tons of fat and sugar and supersize portions, and then to have those foods marketed to them wherever they turn."

Taken together, the growing concerns about sugar, the increasing likelihood of soda taxes, and the steadily growing analogy to tobacco combined to make it a moment of great peril for Coca-Cola.

7

When Mark Bittman and others said soda is the new tobacco, they omitted a key chapter in history: tobacco was once the new soda. Or the new sugar, anyway. In the 1950s, the tobacco industry modeled its public relations efforts on work the sugar industry had begun a decade earlier.

The extent of the sugar industry's public relations campaigns and manipulation of consumers was not well understood until recently. Key parts of the sugar history would still be moldering in forgotten banker's boxes tucked away in archives but for an improbable twist of fate.

Dr. Cristin Kearns, a dentist and a dogged researcher, deserves much of the credit for unearthing the details. Her journey to the soda wars is a winding one, but one she seemed destined for. "It's been an evolution for me," Kearns said on a gray afternoon in her office at the University of California, San Francisco, where she is an assistant professor working in both the School of Dentistry and the Philip R. Lee Institute for Health Policy Studies.

After graduating from dental school, Kearns worked in private dental practice in Denver but grew frustrated with the industry's focus on cosmetic work. Then she worked for low-income dental clinics, which suited her better, but she eventually burned out. After earning an MBA, Kearns went to Oregon to work with Kaiser Permanente, managing dental clinics in the Pacific Northwest. There, she was able to do some of the work that appealed to her—integrating dental health with medical health. The two have been divorced for far too long, Kearns believes.

Cavities are the most common chronic disease in America, but oral health is often considered in isolation, as though it is somehow separate from other health matters. "Why aren't we looking at this as people's teeth are rotting out of their heads?" Kearns said. "You get a gangrenous toe and you have an amputation and that's a really big deal, but that's basically also happening in your mouth. Your teeth are rotting out of your body. This is a problem. But we just think, 'Oh, you go to the dentist, you get your teeth fixed.' You don't really think about what it means."

Soon an interaction about diabetes launched Kearns's career on a still another trajectory. "I went to a medical conference about the links between periodontal disease and diabetes, thinking that I could apply what I'm learning, and take it back to Kaiser," she recalled. Instead, she found misinformation. A keynote speaker from the National Diabetes Education Program of the Centers for Disease Control and Prevention (CDC) distributed handouts about type 2 diabetes. They recommended reducing saturated fats, increasing fiber, and decreasing calories. Notably, the literature said nothing about reducing sugar.

"At first, I was like, 'Did I miss something in what I learned about diabetes?'" Kearns said. "I got out my old biochemistry textbooks, I'm looking up glycolysis again, how it all works with glucose. Because here our national diabetes education spokesman is telling us this information, and I'm like, 'Am I getting this wrong?' And I realized, 'No, I'm not, clearly it's all connected.'"

Kearns started spending her evenings on the Internet, researching sugar. She began to see the outlines of the industry's campaigns to mislead the public about its health risks. "It was just sort of the wake-up call," she said. "I'd been trying to get to 'What is the root cause?' I kept going up and up, and then I realized, 'Oh, it's the industry. There's something much more sinister going on behind the scenes. And we have to take that on.'"

Kearns devoted herself to researching the sugar industry. "I ended up quitting my job," she said. "Because at some point I realized that there's a story here, I'm not sure what it is yet, but it's there. And nobody's talking about it, and somebody has to do it. I was like, 'All right, I'm going to do this.'"

She had moved back to Colorado, and one day she visited the Denver Public Library and typed "sugar" into the search box for the library catalog. "And that's when the Great Western Sugar Company archives popped up," she said. "That's how I found the first documents!"

Kearns called the archivist at Colorado State University to ask about the files. "Nobody had looked at this stuff," she said. "The archivist was like, 'I don't think you're going to find what you're looking for, but you should come up and take a look.' So I drove up to Fort Collins, photocopied everything, brought the papers home, had them spread out on my dining room table."

The papers were a treasure trove, revealing the sugar industry's early efforts to manipulate public opinion and nutrition policy.

Kearns had recently read Gary Taubes's book *Good Calories, Bad Calories*. So she sent him an email about her findings. When he ignored it, she thought maybe she didn't have anything good. Then Taubes showed up for a reading at a Denver bookstore and Kearns bent his ear. Soon they collaborated on an article for *Mother Jones*, outlining the untold history of the sugar industry's collusion with scientists and academics.[1]

"That's how it began," she said. "I didn't really know where I was going to go with it, I just knew I had to keep going. And wherever I could go that would help me to continue the work, that's where I was going to go."

The history of concerns over soft drinks and health extends as far back as 1909. That's when Coca-Cola got crosswise with Harvey Wiley. Wiley led the Bureau of Chemistry, the precursor to the FDA, and was a hard-charging advocate for healthy foods. He had his agents seize a load of Coca-Cola syrup en route from Georgia to Tennessee, and Wiley challenged the company in court. He claimed Coca-Cola was addictive, that it was adulterated with caffeine, and that it was marketed to children.

When the case went to trial in Chattanooga in 1911, Wiley opted not to testify, confident that his team of attorneys, doctors, and scientific experts could prove his allegations. Wiley was wrong. The court case—*United States v. Forty Barrels & Twenty Kegs of Coca-Cola*—took seven years to resolve, and eventually went all the way to the Supreme Court.[2] In a settlement, Coca-Cola admitted no wrongdoing but paid the court fees. Coca-Cola got off scot-free.

The medical community also fell in line. By 1932, Dr. Edward Cary, president of the American Medical Association, won the eternal gratitude of Coca-Cola with this statement: "It is enough to say, that we realize that carbonated beverages when properly made from pure ingredients, belong in the class of health foods."[3] Cary made the comment in a talk titled

"What the Medical Profession Thinks of Bottled Carbonated Beverages." The talk was printed as a brochure by the American Bottlers of Carbonated Beverages. And the brochure landed in the files of a grateful Robert Woodruff, president of Coca-Cola.

By 1942, though, the doctors' association was feeling less sanguine.[4] In a paper published by the American Medical Association, the Council on Foods and Nutrition noted the fast-rising rates of soda consumption, totaling eighteen billion six-ounce bottles in 1939.

"From such data it appears that the per capita consumption of soft drinks must be in the neighborhood of more than three bottles a week per capita," the authors wrote. Though the authors acknowledged the difficulty of quantifying the percentage of total sugar consumption represented by soft drinks, they said it was plenty.

"It seems obvious that, regardless of the method used to estimate the amount of sugar consumed as soft drinks," they wrote, "one obtains a result that is definitely undesirable from the standpoint of the nation's nutritional welfare."

They noted the soft drink companies' ads "usually make a play for sales to children." "It is obvious," they wrote, "that a school lunch suffers gross deterioration when the beverage chosen in place of milk is a solution of sugar in flavored water." The council concluded, "From the health point of view it is desirable especially to have restriction of such use of sugar as is represented by consumption of sweetened carbonated beverages and forms of candy which are of low nutritional value."

It was a strong summary. But it was no match for Coca-Cola's propaganda efforts that same year, in the middle of World War II. "To silence those individuals who questioned the company's scientific assertions about the benefits of soft drinks, Coke brought in a team of scientists to fight for its cause," Bartow Elmore wrote in *Citizen Coke*. "One passionate appeal came from US Surgeon General Thomas Parran, who exclaimed, 'In this time of stress and strain, Americans turn to their sparkling beverage as the British of all classes turn to their cup of tea and the Brazilians to their coffee. From that moment of relaxation, they go back to their task cheered and strengthened, with no aftermath of gastric repentance. There is no undue strain upon the purse; no physiological penalty for indulgence.'"

The very next year, the sugar industry kicked its public relations campaign into overdrive, forming the Sugar Research Foundation (SRF).[5] Kearns noted that the foundation was formed a decade before the Tobacco Industry Research Committee (TIRC). And when that committee was hiring someone to spin its science, it hired a sugar veteran. "In 1954, the TIRC hired SRF's first scientific director, Robert Hockett, to serve as the TIRC's associate scientific director," Kearns wrote in a historical analysis, "where he was positioned to help the tobacco industry learn key science manipulation tactics from the sugar industry."[6]

When Hockett had applied for his job with the nascent Tobacco Industry Research Committee in 1954, he described the work of the sugar foundation. "Ten years ago a very similar industry association, The Sugar Research Foundation, Inc., was formed to investigate charges that refined sugar is a primary cause of diabetes, tooth-decay, polio, B vitamin deficiencies, obesity, 'mid-morning hypoglycemia' and many other conditions," Hockett wrote.[7]

"During a period of nine years," he continued, "I organised and directed research projects in medical schools, hospitals, universities and colleges which exonerated sugar of most of the charges that had been laid against it. Methods were mapped out for modifying or mitigating such undesirable effects as were found to have basis in fact. In addition several new uses and values of sugar were discovered. The program also required me, as Scientific Director, to lead and to assist in public relations activities such as symposia, radio programs, preparation of moving pictures, publication of pamphlets etc. I delivered scores of talks and addresses before popular, industry and scientific groups." Hockett was describing what is now known as the tobacco playbook.

In *Merchants of Doubt*, Naomi Oreskes and Erik M. Conway detail the tobacco industry's strategy in 1953, as advised by the PR firm Hill and Knowlton: "They created the 'Tobacco Industry Research Committee' to challenge the mounting scientific evidence of the harms of tobacco. They funded alternative research to cast doubt on the tobacco-cancer link. They conducted polls to gauge public opinion and used the results to guide campaigns to sway it. They distributed pamphlets and booklets to doctors, the media, policy makers, and the general public insisting that there was no cause for alarm."[8]

As Hockett's application makes clear, the tobacco industry adopted the sugar industry's strategy, lock, stock, and barrel. The tobacco playbook, in other words, is really the sugar playbook.

The Sugar Research Foundation was working on Coca-Cola's behalf, using friendly academics, as far back as its first annual meeting in March 1944. One strategy involved Emory medical school physiology professor Dr. John Haldi.[9]

"Dr. John Haldi has aided the Coca-Cola Company in formulating replies to anti-sugar propaganda," Robert Hockett wrote. "We discussed the reasons for such propaganda and the methods of combatting it. I examined an elementary nutrition textbook designed for schools written by Dr. Haldi. Sugar is given its proper place in the book. The doctor is seeking an agency which might wish to print and distribute this book as a public relations undertaking."

Over the next few decades, Coca-Cola continued to push back waves of criticism, especially over the role of sugary drinks in promoting cavities. In 1951, Coca-Cola executive Felix Coste wrote a multi-page memo to company president Robert Woodruff, entitled "Proposed Program for Counter-Offensive Against Attacks on Coca-Cola on Dental and Nutrition Fronts."[10] Also that year, the corporation took great pains to avert any mention of the effects of sugar on dental health in the Boy Scout Handbook, which the American Dental Association had recommended.

In a letter to Coca-Cola's Roy Gentry, C. L. Emerson, the vice president of the Georgia Institute of Technology, wrote, "As a followup of the letter I recently wrote to you about the policy of the Boy Scouts of America in regard to their handbook, I attach hereto a confirming memorandum from Mr. Charles Heistand to the head of editorial service, putting them officially on notice in regard to the propaganda attempt about which we have corresponded. I think this fairly well closes the door to anything which might be harmful to the Boy Scouts of American [*sic*] and to the Coca-Cola Company."[11]

One persistent Coca-Cola critic was Cornell nutritionist Clive McCay, who proposed a soft drink tax in 1951 and urged that soda machines be banned from schools and replaced with milk machines.[12] In a memo to Coca-Cola president Robert Woodruff, public relations guru Steve

Hannagan offered an aggressive plan for responding to McKay, who he referred to simply as Cornell.

"The situation has grown worse," Hannagan wrote:

> It is high time it be met with vigor—instead of kicking it under the bed, hoping our 150,000,000 neighbors won't see it, at home, or that the erroneous whisperings won't be heard abroad. Already this false presentation hurts domestic business and gives our professional detractors in foreign lands a bucket of mud to sling in their nationalistic campaigns against our off shore progress. Leaving these Cornell and relative findings unanswered in the places they are preached, gives truth to falsehood by our very silence. Unequivocally, there must be a concerted, active campaign—already too long delayed—against these evil, untruthful, damaging presentations. But we can't use an ax to break through the wall because we are dealing with scientific groups. However, since these scientific groups are fostering only pseudo-scientific findings here, we can approach the problem more militantly than might otherwise be advisable.[13]

Among Hannagan's strategies was to target dietitians, to win their approval of soft drinks. "These approaches must be made scientifically, but with plenty of lay savvy too," Hannagan wrote. "In addition, I'd like to strike at the entire consumer mind."

As the public relations war flared up, scientists, too, fought over sugar. Some, like Ancel Keys, blamed most cardiovascular risk on fat. Others, like John Yudkin, said sugar was the bigger risk.

The man who emerged as the greatest asset to the sugar industry was a larger-than-life researcher named Fredrick Stare. He was the founder of the Department of Nutrition at the Harvard School of Public Health and an influential voice on nutrition. "Stare built his career attacking quack diets and health food advocates on television and radio and in his nationally syndicated newspaper column, 'Food and Your Health,'" reported the *Harvard Crimson* when Stare died in 2002 at ninety-one.

Stare was barely thirty and already had earned an MD and a PhD in 1941, when he was tapped to establish the nutrition program at Harvard. By 1950, he was working directly with Coca-Cola, advising the company on its booklet "Activities in Nutrition Education," aimed at high school biology students. Even then, there were hints that he and Coca-Cola saw eye-to-eye. In one phone call, he agreed to remove the sentence, "Recent studies indicate that soft drinks may be particularly harmful to teeth." But his bigger gift to Coca-Cola came later, and less directly.[14]

In 1967, Stare and his Harvard colleague Mark Hegsted published a two-part review on fats, carbohydrates, and cardiovascular disease in the *New England Journal of Medicine*. "The review concluded there was 'no doubt' that the only dietary intervention required to prevent CHD [coronary heart disease] was to reduce dietary cholesterol and substitute polyunsaturated fat for saturated fat in the American diet," Kearns and colleagues wrote in *JAMA Internal Medicine*. (Polyunsaturated fats are those found in foods such as olive oil, fish, and some nuts and seeds; saturated fats are found in animal products like meat and dairy.)

But Kearns, digging through long-forgotten files, noted that the researchers did not disclose funding they had received from the Sugar Research Foundation.[15]

In addition to funding research, the foundation worked to directly influence consumers. It even took the brazen step of pitching sodas in a diet ad campaign, in 1970. Full-page ads in *LIFE* and other magazines read, "Diet-hint: Have a soft drink before your main meal." Illustrated with a photo of a woman sipping a soda with a straw, the ad continued, "Sugar just might be the willpower you need to curb your appetite." It pitched the idea that "Sugar works faster than any other food to turn your appetite *down*, your energy *up*." "Sugar . . . only 18 calories per teaspoon, and it's all energy."

The ads triggered a Federal Trade Commission complaint, which ordered the Sugar Association and Sugar Information, Inc., to run a corrective ad.[16] "You want to lose weight?" that ad concluded. "Your doctor will tell you do exercise more and eat less, but stick with a balanced diet. And sugar, in moderation, has a place in a diet like that. Sugar. It isn't just good flavor; it's good food." Illustrated with a shot of a tasty-looking ice cream sundae, the ad looked rather saccharine, and hardly seemed a corrective.

In 1975, the Sugar Association funded a white paper written by Stare titled "Sugar in the Diet of Man." To this day, the association, the leading trade group for the American sugar industry, boasts about the paper on its webpage. Stare also cofounded and served as chairman of the board of the American Council on Science and Health. It touts itself as an independent research and education organization dedicated to fighting junk science, but it's earned a reputation as an industry front group that's been funded by Coca-Cola, tobacco conglomerate Altria, and others.[17]

Stare's legacy is still felt today. While some people understood as far back as the 1940s that sugar posed a risk, others, paid by the sugar industry, deflected blame onto fat. That led American dietary guidelines into the low-fat era, starting in the 1960s. This had the effect of shifting Americans' diet toward simple, highly refined carbohydrates, such as sugar. As that happened, the American crises of obesity, type 2 diabetes, and other chronic diseases gathered steam.

Kearns thinks the sugar industry's public relations campaigns had their intended effect, and are linked to the explosion in chronic diseases. "I'm not trying to convince people that sugar, the product sugar, is bad. We know that," Kearns said. "I'm trying to convince everyone that the industry is bad, and that they've been committing fraud for a very long time."

Taubes and Kearns's *Mother Jones* article caught the attention of Stanton Glantz, an icon of the anti-tobacco movement who was instrumental in collating a massive archive of tobacco industry documents at UCSF. Glantz invited Kearns out to San Francisco to talk about her research, and the university soon offered her a postdoctoral fellowship. Kearns moved to California, towing a U-Haul stuffed with her photocopies, and began digitizing her papers.

She started collaborating with other UCSF sugar researchers. Soon Kearns received a grant to develop a food industry archive in parallel with the tobacco papers. Now she was getting paid to do what she wanted to be doing: traveling around the country, finding archival documents, and evaluating them.

But even as Kearns was researching the historic campaigns to hide the health risks of sugar, Coke was formulating yet another project that was similar, but more ambitious.

8

In 2009, Rhona Applebaum had a problem. As more researchers were revealing the health risks of sugar-sweetened beverages, concerns about obesity were threatening the business model of her employer, Coca-Cola. Per-capita soda consumption had actually begun declining in the United States. Applebaum felt the diet side of the obesity equation had been getting too much attention, and the exercise side too little.

Applebaum had a plan. What if Coca-Cola designed a program to emphasize exercise over diet? What if the corporation designed and structured it, and partnered with the nation's largest physical fitness organizations—the American College of Sports Medicine and the National Strength and Conditioning Association—to promote it? Why not call it Exercise Is Medicine?

It would be an audacious scheme. Americans were surely savvy enough to know they should not be getting training information from a soda company. Or maybe not.

Applebaum was more than just another soda operative; she was a scientist with gravitas. She boasted a bachelor's degree from Wilson College, an MS in nutrition and food science from Drexel University, and a PhD in food microbiology from the University of Wisconsin.[1]

She had served on the Science Board—an advisory committee of the FDA—and chaired an influential panel in the FDA's Center for Food Safety and Applied Nutrition. All this was in addition to advisory work for the United States Department of Agriculture (USDA). Her scientific bona fides were impeccable, and she'd spent three decades in the food industry.

By 2009, she had risen to the post of vice president and chief scientific and regulatory officer for Coca-Cola. And she was leading the corporation's Beverage Institute for Health and Wellness, which it had established in 2004.[2] But there had been some bumps along the way.

Three years earlier, she had been pitching the company's new beverage, Enviga. It was a sparkling drink based on green tea. In a press release, Coca-Cola quoted Applebaum: "Enviga increases calorie burning. It represents the perfect partnership of science and nature. Enviga contains the optimum blend of green tea extracts (EGCG), caffeine and naturally active plant micronutrients designed to work with your body to increase calorie burning, thus creating a negative calorie effect."[3]

A "negative calorie effect" is a powerful sales tool. Americans spend tens of billions of dollars on diet aids annually. The calorie-burning claim was based on an unpublished study of thirty-two people funded by Coke and Nestlé that found that those who drank three cans of Enviga daily burned sixty to one hundred more calories than those who drank a placebo. (This also meant they were getting 300 milligrams of caffeine daily from the Enviga, a moderate dosage, roughly equivalent to sixteen ounces of strong coffee.)

Michael Jacobson of the Center for Science in the Public Interest (CSPI) filed suit. Jacobson was a crusading consumer advocate, armed with a PhD in microbiology from MIT. He had gone to work for consumer advocate Ralph Nader in 1970 because he was interested in corporate influences on society and government. And he soon cofounded the CSPI.

Over the years, Jacobson fought trans fats and food additives. But all along the way, his nutritional advocacy had a particular focus on sodas. Already in 1972, when he was not yet thirty, he gave this quotation to a *Wall Street Journal* reporter: "Soft drinks are just tasty garbage."[4] The paper misspelled his name. But he would become better known before long, and he would be a thorn in Coca-Cola's side for decades.

When he sued Coca-Cola over Enviga, he said, "It's ironic that Coke, a company that has been a major promoter of weight gain, is now pretending that it is coming to the rescue of overweight people. They should have called this drink 'Fleece,' since that's what they're trying to do to consumers. Plain old tap water has zero calories, five calories fewer than Enviga, but unlike Enviga, tap water doesn't cost 15 bucks a gallon."[5]

States' attorneys general filed a separate case, which they settled three years later. In the terms of the settlement, Coca-Cola paid $650,000 and agreed to stop making weight-loss claims. The drink soon faded into obscurity, and CSPI dropped its own lawsuit.

But by November 2009, Applebaum had bigger problems on her mind, as obesity science was catching up with Coca-Cola. A 2006 paper by Harvard researchers had hinted at the approaching wave of sugar research. "Sugar-sweetened beverages, particularly soda, provide little nutritional benefit, and increase weight gain and probably the risk of diabetes, fractures, and dental [cavities]," Frank Hu and colleagues wrote.[6]

Coca-Cola was quite disciplined in discussing obesity. But every once in a while, its worries slipped out. An unguarded comment by the company's global chief creative officer Esther Lee gave a glimpse behind the curtain. Speaking at an event in Venice in 2007, Lee said, "Our Achilles heel is the discussion about obesity. It's gone from a small, manageable U.S. issue to a huge global issue. It dilutes our marketing and works against it. It's a huge, huge issue."[7]

So Applebaum was working on several fronts to combat the bad press about sodas and obesity. On one front, she was pushing Coke's introduction of a 7.5-ounce mini can. "Research shows that calories count when trying to lose or maintain weight," Applebaum said, "so this 90-calorie mini can is another way for people who love Coca-Cola to get the taste they enjoy while managing their calories—taste, refreshment and hydration all in one can."[8]

Applebaum also signed Coca-Cola on with the American Academy of Family Physicians (AAFP) as its first corporate partner.[9] "We are proud to be the first company to partner with the AAFP and feature content on FamilyDoctor.org," said Applebaum. "Our partnership will help provide Americans with credible information on beverages and enable consumers to make informed decisions about what they drink based on individual need."

Dr. Lori Heim, president-elect of the AAFP, was excited about the partnership. "We look forward to working with The Coca-Cola Company, and other companies in the future, on the development of educational materials to teach consumers how to make the right choices and incorporate the products they love into a balanced diet and a healthy lifestyle," Heim said. It seemed a good bit of PR. But it backfired. More than a dozen doctors publicly resigned from the organization over the partnership.[10]

Applebaum's more subtle and enduring partnership was with the American College of Sports Medicine. Applebaum and ACSM president Robert Sallis had founded the nonprofit organization Exercise Is Medicine two years earlier. The nonprofit group aims to focus attention on the activity side of the obesity ledger, not the nutrition side. Writing about the initiative in 2008, Sallis quoted Hippocrates: "Eating alone will not keep a man well; he must also take exercise." The organization, he wrote, would prescribe the "exercise pill."[11]

Both the American College of Sports Medicine and Exercise Is Medicine itself now take pains to distance themselves from Coca-Cola. But Coca-Cola was more than just a founding partner of Exercise Is Medicine. Applebaum personally structured and focused its work on behalf of Coca-Cola at the critical moments of its inception.

In the fall of 2009, Applebaum was organizing an event at a nutrition conference in Bangkok. The event would be called "Exercise Is Medicine—A Global Initiative to Improve Public Health."[12] Trying to line up speakers for the event, she reached out to University of Colorado obesity researcher James Hill. "My POV—it's time the 'calories-out' side of the eqn was given more prominence at these nutrition/health mtgs," Applebaum wrote to Hill. Applebaum offered to introduce the Exercise Is Medicine program. She also asked University of South Carolina obesity expert Steven Blair for his help in organizing.

It was an auspicious beginning. Exercise Is Medicine would not only conquer the United States; it would soon have projects all over the world. And it was founded and designed by Coca-Cola, in partnership with the American College of Sports Medicine.

Applebaum, Blair, and Hill also had separate plans for big projects. Coca-Cola would provide millions of dollars to fund them. Dedicated to the concept of energy balance—that diet is simply an equation of calories in and calories out—the trio would soon be jetting to conferences, press events, and workshops on several continents. They were a mind-melding dream team, a trio of energy balance all-stars, but their hubris might have raised some concerns, at least in retrospect.

9

Alex Malaspina is an interesting man who parlayed a successful stint at Coca-Cola into an influential, thirty-year career. A native of Athens, Greece, Malaspina came to MIT to earn a BS and a PhD. He joined Coca-Cola in 1961, as manager of the quality control and development department. He rose through the ranks quickly.[1] Photos from the 1960s show Malaspina—slender, amiably handsome, with brown eyes and receding brown hair—wearing the narrow-lapelled suits of the time. Malaspina soon became a vice president of the Coca-Cola Company, in charge of scientific and regulatory affairs.

But in 1978, Malaspina ran into a problem. Caffeine, an essential ingredient in Coca-Cola, was getting a bad rap. A federal committee even recommended that the FDA revoke caffeine's status of Generally Recognized as Safe (GRAS, a regulatory status that means what it sounds like). Coffee producers feared sales might slip as consumers questioned caffeine, and ramped up their production of decaf. Coca-Cola also had a lot to lose.

All of the top-selling sodas in the United States are caffeinated—Coke, Diet Coke, Pepsi, Diet Pepsi, Mountain Dew, and Dr Pepper. When caffeine was being scrutinized in the late 1970s and early 1980s, Coca-Cola even faced competitive pressure from 7 Up, which was billed as "the uncola." It began running TV ads with the tagline, "Crisp and clean, and no caffeine." Over time, 7 Up lost the soda wars—the caffeinated sodas are still atop the heap. The caffeine in sodas reinforces the habit—it makes consumers more likely to buy the same product again. And although the thirty-five milligrams or so in a twelve-ounce Coke is a modest amount, it is psychoactive and generally makes people feel good.

In 1978, Malaspina saw the efforts to regulate caffeine as a significant threat to Coca-Cola. He came up with a novel solution. He decided to launch an organization designed to intensively study caffeine.

This was the genesis of the International Life Sciences Institute, better known as ILSI ("Ill-see"). In Malaspina's vision, it would be an industry-funded consortium, intended to align academics and government staffers with the interests of Coca-Cola and other food corporations. Malaspina also roped in other soda companies.

ILSI's First International Caffeine Workshop, in Hawaii in 1978, included representatives from Dr Pepper, Royal Crown, Pepsi, and the National Soft Drink Association (precursor to the American Beverage Association). Other corporations were well represented, including General Foods, Hershey, Nestlé, and Pfizer, whose pharmaceutical plants synthesized caffeine. But, as would be the steady theme over the years, Coca-Cola staffers outnumbered the rest of the corporate staffers at the ILSI meeting. Federal regulators from the FDA and other agencies attended, as did academics from Harvard, MIT, and other universities. And ILSI's international element was already well established: people came to Hawaii from England, France, Italy, Japan, Switzerland, and West Germany.[2]

"When I started ILSI, I worked very closely with the Pepsi Cola Company, which was a major competitor," said Malaspina in a 2015 video. "But at the technical level, there was a great deal of cooperation between the scientists. And then we were able to bring government scientists to our meetings, and we had a very good dialogue with the government agencies about what we were doing. So we established a very good relationship with the regulatory agencies in the U.S., in England, in Germany. So it was kind of a catalyst in providing scientific information with ingredients. And today, ILSI is very well respected around the world."

As Malaspina organized ILSI, the criticism of caffeine in sodas only grew. Michael Jacobson of the Center for Science in the Public Interest was among those beating the drum. But the critics were no match for ILSI.

ILSI's campaign against caffeine regulation was broad and deep. It held workshops, generated scientific publications, and even authored a book on caffeine science. Though it is hard to know exactly how ILSI's influence affected the FDA, the agency reconfirmed the safety of caffeine as added to sodas, leaving caffeine in the category of Generally Recognized as Safe.

ILSI had scored a major victory in its first effort to safeguard the future of the soda industry. And Jacobson had lost this round.

By 1981, ILSI was holding meetings as far away as Japan and working closely with a growing network of international researchers. It was considering food issues, like phosphorous and calcium, but also non-food matters, such as health risks for construction workers exposed to asphalt.

And increasingly, ILSI was interested in sugar. When the ILSI trustees met in March 1981, they discussed the threats posed to Coca-Cola and other soda companies by concerns about sugar. So it seemed appropriate that the meeting was chaired by former Coca-Cola staffer Malaspina, at the Atlanta headquarters of Coca-Cola.[3]

Dr Pepper executive William Massmann suggested to the board that ILSI become more engaged in sugar research. In his memo to the board proposing a "Sweeteners Technical Committee," Massmann showed that the industry was way ahead of the public in understanding that sugar consumption was very high and that health concerns were mounting. Massmann noted that consumption of sugar in the United States was already 100 pounds per capita, per year, and he said sugars were under assault.

"They are constantly challenged as being detrimental to health," Massmann wrote. Among the health concerns he pointed out were obesity, dental caries, hyperkinesis [hyperactivity], diabetes, hypertension, cardiovascular problems, and empty calories. Massmann added, "This has been mainly against sucrose, but corn sweeteners can be expected to get more attention because of their increased use." (High-fructose corn syrup was then just becoming popular; FDA would list it as Generally Recognized as Safe in 1983.)

Massmann then listed a number of reasons that ILSI would be a better home for the sugar research than the Sugar Association. It would have greater scientific credibility, Massmann said, because it is not as closely identified with the sugar manufacturers and users. And it would be better at spreading "scientific information through symposia, seminars, etc. sponsored by ILSI. . . . Public relations would be done by member companies and trade associations; e.g. NSDA, Confectioners Association, Chocolate Assoc., Ice Cream Manufacturers, The Sugar Association (Lobbying and PR)." Massmann also pointed out that ILSI already had a template for doing the work: its own caffeine committee.

In 1981, back when Ronald Reagan had just assumed the presidency, ILSI was already on a trajectory it would follow for the next forty years. It would push back against concerns about sugar, including obesity, cavities, type 2 diabetes, and cardiovascular disease.

Over the next few decades. Malaspina spent much of his time using ILSI to aggressively protect Coca-Cola and other soda companies from the growing body of research showing the health risks posed by sugar. Malaspina's strategy was consistent—let the soda companies fund ILSI, then have ILSI produce results favorable to the industry. The research was then published without Coca-Cola's name attached to it. It gave the patina of neutrality, the appearance of a science-based nonprofit organization. And as suggested at that 1981 meeting, trade associations could relay messages to the public, insulating Coca-Cola and other ILSI members from any public concerns.

Malaspina's work with ILSI cracks a window into the sprawling, interwoven ecosystem of industry front groups. These are the myriad nonprofit groups whose primary objective is to pave the way for their corporate funders to thrive, unfettered by regulation.

In the case of Coca-Cola, there are two types of nonprofit organizations to consider. The first are those that overtly state their purpose, more commonly known as trade associations. American Beverage, formerly known as the American Beverage Association, is an example of this type of organization. A trade group, the association makes no secret of its funders—primarily Coca-Cola, Pepsi, and Keurig Dr Pepper. And it makes no bones about its mission: advancing the corporate interests of those funders. The Sugar Association is another relevant trade group.

The more interesting nonprofit groups are less understood, and this is by design. These are organizations that cloak their funders, even if subtly. Their goals are the same as the trade groups'—to promote the interests of their corporate supporters—but their methods are different. These organizations like to cast themselves as independent third parties, nonprofits solely interested in making the world a better place and in advancing science. In reality, they are front groups for industry.

In *Dark Money*, Jane Mayer quotes an environmental lawyer describing the practice: "'You take corporate money and give it to a neutral-sounding think tank,' which 'hires people with pedigrees and academic degrees who put out credible-seeming studies. But they all coincide perfectly with the economic interests of their funders.'"[4]

Rick Berman, a DC lobbyist, was a pioneer in the field with his Center for Consumer Freedom. First funded by Philip Morris to fight restrictions on smoking, it branched out into food with funding from Coca-Cola.[5]

The word "science" in the name of these organizations is often a subtle tell. There may even be an informal rule to consider here—the more often, and more loudly, an organization shouts "science," the greater the likelihood that it is actually a front for corporate-funded pseudoscience. So you have Sense about Science, Real Clear Science, and the American Council on Science and Health. It's an interwoven, often overlapping, network of deceptively named groups purporting to promote science, but actually established with industry money to do industry's bidding.

A subset of these nonprofit organizations is the sophisticated and complicated network of front groups specific to the food industry, designed to counter the steady trickle of bad health news for Coca-Cola and other corporations. Many of these groups have intentionally opaque names, like the International Life Sciences Institute and the International Food Information Council (which, as we'll see, Malaspina considered a sister to ILSI).

To further stir this alphabet soup, each of these groups sometimes coordinates with the others. And to make it messier yet, they sometimes work together to create still other nonprofits to do their bidding. In some cases these are "astroturf" groups (industry-aligned efforts posing as grassroots movements) formed to fight soda taxes; in others, these are groups formed by the soda industry to emphasize physical activity over diet.

* * *

Malaspina scored a coup in 1998 when the United Nations Food and Agriculture Organization (FAO) commissioned a report on carbohydrates, funded and organized by ILSI. Some academics saw this as an inflection point in the battle over public opinions about sugar.

"The skewed panel report was a boon to the sugar industry, which issued a press release on it entitled: 'Experts see no harm in sugar—Good news for kids,'" Thomas McGarity and Wendy Wagner reported in *Bending Science*. "Several years later, the ILSI managed to situate itself as a consultant to the WHO; its role may explain why all statements regarding the adverse role of sugar in diets were eventually dropped from the first world wide Nutrition Plan of Action."[6]

Meanwhile, Malaspina was soliciting tens of thousands of dollars from Philip Morris and R. J. Reynolds to influence the World Health Organization on tobacco policy. "Findings indicate that ILSI was used by certain tobacco companies to thwart tobacco control policies," a 2001 WHO report stated. "Senior office bearers in ILSI were directly involved in these actions. . . . While it is appropriate for tobacco company–owned food subsidiaries to sponsor nutrition of food science research with groups like ILSI, it is of great concern when tobacco companies use these same groups to undermine tobacco control efforts."[7]

And by 2003, *The Guardian* reported on a confidential, independent report by Dr. Norbert Hirschhorn, a consultant to the World Health Organization, that found that ILSI had infiltrated the organization.[8] "One industry-led organisation, International Life Sciences Institute (ILSI), has positioned its experts and expertise across the whole spectrum of food and tobacco policies: at conferences, on FAO/WHO food policy committees and within WHO, and with monographs, journals and technical briefs," Hirschhorn wrote.

As Malaspina steered the ever-growing ILSI ship, he developed the financial underpinning for an enduring nonprofit. In 2001, he helped solicit $22 million to endow ILSI's research foundation. Malaspina said Coke executives were glad to contribute, because "they felt that by helping the world become healthier and safer, it would also be very good for the Coca-Cola company and its image."

Overall, Malaspina recalled ILSI's origins and mission fondly. "We were able to join together and decide that we were going to spend money to do good research to look at the long-term issues of saving the world, and making the world a better place to live in, and become a lot more generous," Malaspina said in the 2015 video. "I feel very strongly that scientists from industry have to cooperate with scientists from government and international agencies. Cooperation between scientists from all the sectors is really the goal of ILSI."[9]

Malaspina retired from ILSI in 2001. But he remained the gray eminence, the man behind the curtain, for another fifteen years, an era in which ILSI would cement its influence—and its infamy.

II

A BALANCING ACT, 2010–2015

10

For more than a decade, in a blocky building in Boston's Longwood Medical Area, a soft-spoken yet determined doctor has been chasing leads in a deadly mystery: What is making Americans gain so much weight and develop so many chronic diseases?

Dr. Frank Hu is the chair of the Harvard T. H. Chan School of Public Health's Department of Nutrition. He's also, in an interesting historical echo, the Fredrick J. Stare Professor of Nutrition and Epidemiology. Hu earned his medical degree at Tongji Medical University and worked in Beijing, Hong Kong, and the Netherlands before earning a PhD from the Chicago School of Public Health. By 2009, he was a tenured professor at the Harvard T. H. Chan School of Public Health and a professor of medicine at Harvard Medical School.[1]

An epidemiologist, Hu studies the distribution and causes of diseases, looking for broader patterns and risk factors. Hu is pleased that researchers have been learning more about soda's impacts on health, a focus of his studies. "It's been a kind of scientific journey for me," he told me during an interview in his office. "When we started the research on sugary beverages and health outcomes, we knew it was not a healthy product, but we didn't know the magnitude of the health risks associated with sugary beverages.

"And then in the past fifteen years, we began to look at various health outcomes, such as obesity, diabetes, cardiovascular disease, and so on and so forth," he continued. "And we have realized that the cumulative health effects of sugary beverages are so big, because it impacts not just one health outcome, but a spectrum of health outcomes, and also the intake is high in the population."

Until about the mid-1990s, soda's effects on health had not been very well quantified. However limited, there had been some intriguing research suggesting serious health risks. In 1990, a pair of scientists at the Monell Chemical Senses Center wanted to understand how artificial sweeteners affect food intake and body weight.[2] So they assigned one of three treatments to their subjects: drink no specific drinks, drink one liter daily of artificially sweetened soda, or drink one liter daily of sugar-sweetened soda. Like most sodas, they were sweetened with high-fructose corn syrup (HFCS). In the nine-week study, the three dozen subjects rotated through each treatment for three weeks. The findings regarding the sugar-sweetened beverages were especially interesting. The subjects gained weight.

"Judging by the increase in body weight when subjects drank HFCS-sweetened soda, most (if not all) of the energy provided by the HFCS was probably stored as fat," the Monell scientists wrote. "This is consistent with work showing that sugar given in a liquid vehicle produces greater obesity more consistently than does sugar given as a solid."

A turning point for soda research came in 2001. That's when David Ludwig, Steven Gortmaker, and Karen Peterson studied 548 schoolchildren in four communities in Massachusetts.[3] Following the subjects for nineteen months, the researchers tallied their diets, physical activity, and weight. They found that "the odds of becoming obese increased significantly for each additional daily serving of sugar-sweetened drink."

This was notable, but puzzling. They asked the question: "Why should consumption of sugar-sweetened drinks promote obesity any more than other categories of food?" And they posited an answer: "The results of our study are consistent with a plausible physiological mechanism, that consumption of sugar-sweetened drinks could lead to obesity because of imprecise and incomplete compensation for energy consumed in liquid form."

"Incomplete compensation" is simpler than it sounds. When people are overfed—when they eat more than they need—they tend to compensate for the extra food by eating less at subsequent meals. Ludwig's team wondered if this pattern was somehow different for sodas—if sodas do not decrease your appetite, as solid foods do. If so, the incomplete compensation meant the students may have been packing on the calories from soda on top of the calories they were getting from solid food.

In 2004, Dr. Hu and colleagues published a prospective analysis on sugar-sweetened beverages and the risk of developing type 2 diabetes, in the *Journal of the American Medical Association* (*JAMA*).[4] Prospective analyses are those that allow researchers to follow a similar group of subjects, over time, to see what behaviors might be linked to outcomes. At that time, the USDA Dietary Guidelines Advisory Committee was revising its guidelines. When Hu presented his findings to the committee, members were surprised to learn about the paucity of soda research.

Hu said that research into the effects of sugar on the human body has snowballed since then, and the results have been remarkably consistent. This growing body of evidence clarified the risks for soda drinkers. And the evidence showed that even people who drink what might be considered a moderate amount of soda are at risk of disease. "One can of soda a day is associated with about a 25 percent increased risk of developing type 2 diabetes," said Hu. "It's significantly associated with increased risk of weight gain and obesity in both children and adults, and associated with increased risk of cardiovascular disease, and also increased risk of fatty liver disease, gout, and some other conditions. So I think the scientific evidence is quite strong and convincing that even 'moderate consumption' is associated with a wide range of health risks."

For years, most Americans had sensed that sodas are not good for you. But the health risks had not been so well calculated, nor had the metabolic pathways been so precisely traced. "Now we have a much better understanding of the biological mechanisms through which different types of sugars affect our metabolic pathways," Hu said. "I think it is very important for people to appreciate the physiological or biological changes high amounts of sugary beverages can cause."

The sugar in sodas is typically blended in the form of high-fructose corn syrup. HFCS is very cheap and very sweet, and it has flooded food markets since the early 1980s. The corn syrup in sodas is typically 55 percent fructose and 45 percent glucose, but the ratio can vary. This is known as a disaccharide, or two-sugar molecule, like sucrose (aka table sugar), which is also composed of fructose and glucose.

It is much more instructive to consider these sugars individually, because the body quickly breaks them apart. Fructose and glucose are then metabolized in separate and distinct pathways. Some fructose will be converted to glucose, and some will be converted to triglycerides and stored as fat, often in the liver. This can lead to a condition known, appropriately, as fatty liver disease. As the liver stores more fat, the disease becomes more severe. Left unchecked, this process will eventually lead to fibrosis, which is scarring of the liver tissue.

"And that's a very serious condition," Hu said. "Because fibrosis is a precursor to cirrhosis. And, of course, [in] people who develop cirrhosis, that can lead to liver cancer and it can lead to liver failure. And now in the US there is increased death due to liver-related conditions, and to some degree that is because of the increasing obesity, and the increasing rates of fatty liver disease."

That's just the fructose. Meanwhile, glucose is hiking a separate trail through your body. The glucose in Coke and other sugary beverages causes blood sugar levels to rise quickly, requiring the pancreas to work overtime producing insulin.

"Insulin is the hormone that opens the door for your muscle cells and fat cells to utilize the glucose," said Hu. "That's why you have this kind of one-to-one response. Your blood sugar shoots up and your pancreas—your beta cells—produces insulin.

"It's like pumping your gas pedal: you have to push it hard to produce more insulin," said Hu. "In the short term, it's not a problem—especially for young and middle-aged people. If you put your foot on the gas pedal all the time, your engine will burn up at some point. That's what's happening to your beta cells.

"In the long run, your beta cells cannot keep up with the rising sugar levels," Hu continued. "That leads to insulin resistance. That means that even if you can pump out a lot of insulin, your body is not as responsive to the hormone as it should be. Once you have that stage, if the hyperglycemia continues, your beta cells will burn out and produce less insulin, eventually. That's why most type 2 diabetics, in the later stage, need to inject insulin, because their beta cells are mostly exhausted."

Some of the glucose will be converted to glycogen, which supplies needed energy stores for the body. Additionally, if there's excess glucose in the bloodstream, it can also go to the liver, just like fructose, and be converted to liver fat.

In all, the sugary beverages can lead to a variety of health problems that can occur independently. A person can have obesity without fatty liver disease. Or fatty liver disease without type 2 diabetes. Or type 2 diabetes without obesity. But most often, they come in a cluster known as metabolic syndrome. This is a condition that includes increased abdominal fat, high blood sugar, high blood pressure, and high triglyceride levels.

There is a common misperception that slender people don't have to worry about the health risks from sugary drinks. But you need not be heavy to be at risk. Hu said researchers have not yet figured out all of the biological mechanisms behind soda's health risks that are unrelated to obesity, but inflammation appears to be one.

Inflammation is the body's reaction to foreign, and possibly noxious, substances. Habitual soda drinking leads to chronic inflammation, which is a risk factor for many ailments, including cancer, diabetes, and heart disease. The inverse is also true: recent studies found that people who stop drinking soda show decreased markers for inflammation within just a week.

Hu said another problem is caused by one of the qualities that is unique to sodas and other sugar-sweetened beverages. They pack a large number of calories, but do not satisfy your appetite. This is the pattern that David Ludwig and his colleagues discussed in their 2001 paper. So most people don't choose between the calories in a Coke, say, and a burger; they consume both. (In a related trend, McDonald's has long been Coca-Cola's largest soda fountain customer.[5]) "The large amount of sugar and large amount of calories in those sodas can easily lead to positive energy balance and weight gain," said Hu. "For example, twenty ounces of soda, you would need to run almost an hour to burn all those calories."

Because the best research is relatively new, Hu said even doctors and nurses are a bit behind the curve. "There is certainly a gap between the science and the practice at this point. We need to educate health professionals. Not just the general public, but also health professionals, about the harmful effects of soda on health outcomes, and also about the biological mechanisms through which different types of sugars influence insulin resistance, diabetes, and cardiovascular disease."

Hu and others have also shown that soft drinks pose especially great risks to children and adolescents. Sugary drinks can lead to obesity and overweight among teens, setting metabolic trajectories they will carry into adulthood.

Hu makes the case that there is "a continuum of carbohydrate quality." On the healthful end of the continuum are minimally processed whole grains and legumes. Next come somewhat refined grains, with less protein and less fiber. Then there are highly processed foods, such as white flour. On the unhealthy side of the continuum are sugars. And holding up the extreme end of the unhealthy side of the continuum are liquid sugars.

Taken as a whole, Hu said sodas have something in common with trans fats. "Certain elements of the diet can be characterized as really bad," he said. "Sugary beverages are one of them."

It is worth noting that nutritional science is quite complex. Researchers still diverge on the exact mechanisms of obesity, and on the evolving science of nutrition. They know, for certain, that much of it is individualized, varying from person to person. A diet that is perfect for one person will seem awful to the next. And some researchers make the case that the root of all nutritional ills is in the brain or in the endocrine system, that hormones are the linchpins to a healthy diet.

All are right, to a degree, even if many overstate their cases, especially in the hyper-opinionated, social-media-amplified dietary wars.

But if diet is complicated in some ways, it is also simple in others. And the simple truth that Hu was positing is that sugar-sweetened beverages are uniquely unhealthful.

This should have been old news by now. Sugars, especially liquid sugars like those in sodas, have been proven to make you fat and sick. Although this truth is simple, many millions of Americans have not gotten the memo. This is because of a sophisticated, well-funded campaign of disinformation by Coca-Cola and its allies in the sugar industry.

Even as Hu and his colleagues were firming up the sugar science, Coke and its allies were ramping up their disinformation efforts.

11

When Rhona Applebaum signed off on the deal in October 2010, Coca-Cola committed $2.5 million to University of South Carolina researcher Steven Blair and his colleague Greg Hand. Along with advisors such as the University of Colorado's James Hill, they planned a large-scale obesity study.[1] Actually, they would be studying a specific aspect of obesity: energy balance. And the researchers had a specific aspect of energy balance that they wanted to study: the energy expenditure side.

Energy balance is a concept that Coca-Cola and its allies repeat ad infinitum. The idea is simple—balance calories in and calories out, and don't focus on the quality of the calories, or the type of food providing those calories. If you are in positive energy balance—taking in more calories than you are expending—then, all else being equal, you will likely gain weight. The catch is that all else is rarely equal.

The simplest energy balance argument posits that a calorie of food will be metabolized the same whether it comes from cashews, kale, or Coca-Cola. As Coke executive Katie Bayne said in 2012, "A calorie is a calorie. . . . We don't believe in empty calories."[2]

Therefore, people need not worry so much about what they are eating as ensuring that they stay active enough to burn those calories. But in the human body, 140 calories of almonds, for example, are not metabolized the same as the 140 calories of sugar in a twelve-ounce can of Coke. A calorie is not a calorie.

For one thing, the almonds include fat (the polyunsaturated kind), protein, fiber, and vitamins. Sucrose has none of these. But the bigger difference is in the body's immediate response to sucrose—blood sugar levels rise, the pancreas pumps insulin to compensate, and much of the sugar is quickly converted to fat. Additionally, sucrose does not satisfy the appetite for as long as almonds. Consume 140 calories of sugar in a can of Coke, and you are likely to be hungry again far sooner than if you consume those calories as almonds.

The term "energy balance" has been in circulation for a while. It was touted by the American Beverage Association and Pepsi in 2005, when they were announcing an age-graduated policy for selling sodas in schools. "PepsiCo and America On the Move developed a lesson plan called Balance First™ to help educate kids about energy balance," they said in a press release.[3]

The phrase became a mantra for the soda industry in general, and Coca-Cola in particular. In the fall of 2010, the University of North Carolina Gillings School of Global Public Health, touting its partnership with Coca-Cola, quoted Applebaum extensively. "Obesity is a serious and complex global health problem that requires the collective efforts of everyone—individuals, governments, academia, health professionals, communities and businesses—to work in partnership to develop workable solutions," said Applebaum. "Partnerships with institutions like UNC, efforts to educate and inform consumers on proper nutrition, energy balance and programs that support physical activity are some of the many ways we are developing workable solutions for obesity."[4]

The piece closed by noting Coke's support of Triple Play, a partnership with the Boys & Girls Clubs of America. "Globally," it concluded, "The Coca-Cola Company supports more than 100 physical activity and nutrition education programs in more than 150 countries."

These three pet projects of Applebaum's—collaborations with universities, the concept of energy balance, and the funding of physical activity programs—would soon come back to bite Coca-Cola in general, and Applebaum specifically.

12

"David Allison is a renowned scientist who runs an obesity research center at the University of Alabama at Birmingham," began the June 15, 2011, ABC News story "Is 'Big Food's' Big Money Influencing the Science of Nutrition?"[1] "He has a 108-page résumé and was honored at the White House," the story continued. "But even though study after study have shown soda to be a significant contributor to America's staggering obesity crisis, he says there is too little 'solid evidence.'" Allison had been awarded at least $2.5 million in research grants from private industry, including $299,000 from Coca-Cola in 2011.[2]

It was not Allison's first controversy. In 2008, he was the incoming president of the Obesity Society. But he overstepped even before he assumed the presidency. When he filed an affidavit, on behalf of the New York State Restaurant Association, opposing a New York City law requiring calories be listed on menus, he signed it as incoming president of the Obesity Society. This was a bridge too far for some of his colleagues, who expressed outrage at his actions. Allison resigned the post.[3]

But in 2011, Allison had his allies. Or one ally, anyway, who rushed to his defense with a *Forbes* article titled "ABC News Attacks Scientist Who Exposed Bias in Obesity Research."[4] The author was Trevor Butterworth.

Butterworth systematically dismantled the sugar science, in an effort to bolster Allison's credibility. He noted Allison's analyses that found the research into sugar-obesity links to be weak, especially when conducted by scientists like Kelly Brownell, who also advocated for regulation or taxes. Butterworth expressed particular outrage that Allison's character had been assassinated. "And so, the result is that thanks to ABC's totally misleading account of the evidence on sugared drinks and weight gain, Allison will almost certainly be removed from legitimate debate, tarred forever with the insinuation that he is merely a shill for industry," Butterworth wrote.

Butterworth's bio touted his bona fides: "Director, Sense About Science USA, which advocates for an evidence based approach to science and technology and for clinical trial transparency. Editor, STATS.org, a collaboration between the American Statistical Association and Sense About Science USA. Visiting Fellow, Cornell University." To boot, he'd written for the *New Yorker* online, the *Wall Street Journal*, and the *Harvard Business Review*, and boasted degrees from Trinity College Dublin, Georgetown, and Columbia. But Butterworth also had a long history of advocating for corporate interests through industry front groups.

STATS was a US nonprofit whose founder had also worked for the tobacco industry. Sense about Science was founded by a British business consultant who fought tobacco regulations. Writing for the *Intercept*, Liza Gross showed that most of the funding for these groups came from antiregulatory groups funded by the Koch, Scaife, and Searle families.[5]

Butterworth was best known for supporting the chemical industry, pushing back against critics of genetically modified organisms and the gender-disrupting chemical bisphenol A.

Butterworth's group was just one of many nonprofits carrying water for the food industry, but he would become closely associated with Coca-Cola. And his defense of Allison here gave a hint of why that would be.

Let's assume that Butterworth was onto something here, and that Allison was being maligned unfairly by ABC. Still, any reader, even one without a great deal of skepticism, might ask: Why do the researchers like Allison who are asking the tough questions about sugar research also happen to be those who receive millions of dollars of industry funding?

Butterworth and Allison had a handy answer. Those industry-funded researchers are free of "white-hat bias." Allison and his University of Alabama colleague Mark Cope had coined the term in a 2009 article for the *International Journal of Obesity*. They defined it as "bias leading to distortion of information in the service of what might be perceived to be righteous ends."[6]

It was a remarkably bold assertion—an industry-aligned writer defending an industry-funded researcher, using that researcher's own defensive term. Butterworth would become a useful Coca-Cola ally.

13

Rhona Applebaum was up early on June 1, 2012, ready for her turn on CNN. The segment covered a topic of great controversy at the moment—New York mayor Michael Bloomberg's proposal to limit serving sizes of soft drinks to sixteen ounces.

Bloomberg had announced the proposal two days earlier. "Obesity is a nationwide problem, and all over the United States, public health officials are wringing their hands saying, 'Oh, this is terrible,'" he told the *New York Times*.[1] "New York City is not about wringing your hands; it's about doing something. I think that's what the public wants the mayor to do."

The pushback was swift, with cries of "Nanny Bloomberg." But the measure had some high-profile support. Introducing the segment,[2] the CNN producers included a clip of former president Bill Clinton supporting Bloomberg's proposal.

"I think he's doing the right thing," Clinton said, in the earnest, compassionate tone Americans knew so well. "We've got this explosion of type 2 diabetes among young people, for the first time, type 2 diabetes showing up in nine-year-olds, and among the baby boomers who are retiring. And together these things are going to bankrupt us. It's a terrible human tragedy, and it's basically too much sugar going into the body; we can't process it all."

Responding on air to the Clinton clip, Applebaum sounded compassionate but quickly turned the discussion to exercise. "And it is a tragedy," she said. "But what's even a bigger tragedy, when we are talking about our children, and a travesty, is the fact that we've taking physical education and physical activity out of our schools.

"And we're not saying that the diet should not be addressed—absolutely, we want our public and our consumers to have a sensible, balanced diet," she said, "but they also have to have regular physical activity."

Then Applebaum squeezed in references to stakeholders with "good ideas and proven interventions"—the National Physical Activity Plan and the Academy of Nutrition and Dietetics. The former has received tens of thousands of dollars from Coca-Cola, the latter hundreds of thousands.[3]

14

Todd Putnam was a man that Coca-Cola definitely did not want to see on stage. But there he was, speaking at a June 2012 National Soda Summit in Washington, DC.[1]

"It took me ten years to figure out I have a large karmic debt to pay for the number of Cokes I sold across this country," the former Coca-Cola executive told the crowd.

The summit was the brainchild of Michael Jacobson, of the Center for Science in the Public Interest. He had been a persistent fly in Coca-Cola's ointment, and even coined the memorable term "liquid candy" to describe sodas. At DC's Hyatt Regency hotel, Jacobson had gathered luminaries of the anti-soda movement, including Philadelphia mayor Michael Nutter and US representative Rosa DeLauro, a consistent public health advocate from Connecticut.

But it was Putnam's talk that really stood out, because he knew the corporation's strategies from inside the building. In 1998, he had led a $75 million campaign using a Coca-Cola Card that offered discounts at movie theaters and theme parks popular with young people. "Targeting teens and young adults, it is running in 280 markets, with deals tailored to each local area," wrote Mickey H. Gramig, reporting on Putnam's promotion for the *Atlanta Journal-Constitution*. "For instance, among the thirty-two discounts offered in Atlanta is a deal for a free 'naked dog' or chili dog at the Varsity with the purchase of another hot dog and a thirty-two-ounce Coca-Cola."[2]

It was the kind of promotion that gave indigestion to soda critics, especially that 370 calories' worth of Coca-Cola and the overt push to market to teens.

At the summit, fourteen years later, Putnam was contrite. "For all the range and reach of Coke's marketing operation," wrote N. C. Aizenman, reporting for the *Washington Post*, "Putnam said he quickly learned it was built around one goal: per capita consumption. 'How can we drive more ounces into more bodies more often.' The term of art among company executives was one Putnam had never heard before: 'share of stomach.'"[3]

Something Putnam said to Aizenman put the longtime struggles over Coca-Cola's marketing to youth into context. Although Coca-Cola had long been emphatic that it did not market directly to children under twelve, Putnam said all bets were off later; "magically, when they would turn twelve, we'd suddenly attack them like a bunch of wolves."

Coca-Cola's efforts to sell sodas to children and teens were a perennial bone of contention, and skirmishes flared periodically between the soda industry and health advocates. In 1994, Senator Patrick Leahy, chairman of the Agriculture, Nutrition and Forestry Committee, introduced a bill to restrict the sale of soft drinks in schools. Coca-Cola pushed back hard and fast, organizing a letter-writing campaign from school principals, superintendents, and coaches. Some argued that schools earned much-needed money from the vending machine sales.

"I have fended off attacks from drug companies, petty crooks, price fixers, budget cutters and critics of all kinds," Senator Leahy said of the conflict. "I never thought I would see the day that I would have to defend our child-nutrition programs under heavy attack from the Coca-Cola Company, one of America's corporate giants, with worldwide profits of $2.1 billion last year."[4]

At a hearing about the bill, Leahy sparred with Drew Davis of the National Soft Drink Association. Leahy said that Davis was hoping kids would get hooked on sodas and become customers for life.[5] Davis replied, "We're suggesting you have no evidence that this consumption of soft drinks is in any way harmful."

Leahy then held up a can of Coke and read off the ingredients. "Is this anything more than just empty calories and a caffeine boost?" he said.

"We don't believe that there's any such thing as empty calories," Davis replied. "We're talking about teenaged children here, Senator. We've already established that we are not selling soft drinks in elementary and grade schools."

"Well, you're not selling cigarettes either to them," said Leahy.

At this, Davis appeared outraged. "Certainly you're not suggesting that the consumption of soft drinks is in any way related health-wise to the consumption of cigarettes," he said.

"No, but what I am suggesting is that you have the same profit motives that the cigarette companies do," said Leahy, "and not the good nutritional values for the children."

"We're suggesting that we provide a safe product that has a role in a diet, and to suggest otherwise based on personal nutritional beliefs is not the basis for legislating a change," Davis said. He then waved a letter and said, "I'm suggesting that there are scientists on all sides of this issue who would argue about the proper role of foods like soft drinks in an overall diet."

Coca-Cola won the round, with the bill requiring only a watered-down provision directed at soda sales in elementary schools. As the Associated Press reported, "Coca-Cola officials have refused throughout the controversy to respond to Leahy, referring all questions to the National Soft Drink Association."[6]

It would presage much. For decades, the National Soft Drink Association would run interference for Coca-Cola; it would challenge health concerns over soft drinks; it would take umbrage at comparisons to tobacco; and it would wave around scientific reports vouching for soft drinks' safety.

In 2003, the association's Richard Adamson issued one typical defense: "There is no association between sugar consumption and obesity. The opposite is true. People who have diets based on carbohydrates have a lower body mass index."[7]

The debates over sodas in schools continued for years. In 2005, Massachusetts attorney Richard Daynard, a veteran of tobacco lawsuits, was threatening to sue Coca-Cola over its use of caffeine to hook schoolchildren on sugary drinks.[8] He would have the support of Michael Jacobson's Center for Science in the Public Interest. It seemed this might finally be the big legal case many had discussed, a soda corollary to the tobacco suits that had been so influential. But nothing came of the threat.

That long, fraught history of soda sales to school kids informed Putnam's remarks at the Soda Summit. It was rare to have an insider spilling the beans on Coca-Cola. Putnam went on to play a central role in Michael Moss's bestselling book *Salt Sugar Fat*.

But even as the critics at the soda summit rallied, Coca-Cola was not taking the growing chorus of criticism lying down. Through its proxy, the American Beverage Association (ABA)—the new name for the National Soft Drink Association—it began working that summer to belittle health concerns. The ABA launched a website, LetsClearItUp.org, to push back against the emerging soda science.

"It seems every week (or day) a new study is released claiming a new absurdity about soda and other sugar-sweetened beverages," the ABA said. "Soft drinks may cause narcolepsy among snake charmers. . . . Sugar-sweetened beverages cause drowning if you drink more than 50 12 oz. cans per day. . . . Bat Boy claims soda aliens abducted his mother. . . . We made those headlines up, but you've seen enough crazy studies to know that it's time to clear things up. So that's what we're doing."[9]

It took aim at what it called a myth, that the obesity epidemic could be reversed by limiting soda consumption. "FACT: Sugar-sweetened beverages account for only 7% of calories in the average American's diet, according to government information," the ABA wrote.

That 7 percent number was a data point that most could agree on. The disagreement was over what those calories meant for health.

15

To open its annual conference, the Obesity Society offered up a keynote debate: "The Role of Sugar-Sweetened Beverages in the Obesity Epidemic: Plague Rat or Red Herring?" The September 2012 event pitted David Allison of the University of Alabama against Frank Hu of Harvard.

The differences weren't immediately apparent. Both researchers wore dark suits and stood at wood-paneled lecterns behind potted plants, on either side of the stage at a San Antonio conference center. Just twenty feet divided them, but their perspectives were worlds apart.

Allison, taking the "red herring" perspective, said he was unconvinced that decreasing soda consumption would reduce obesity. He cited a meta-analysis that showed that although sugar-sweetened beverages are linked to weight gain, reducing their consumption is not linked to weight loss. Meta-analyses are powerful tools—they essentially pool the findings of multiple studies, looking for a strong signal. But they are also controversial, because the further one gets from the original research, the easier it is to misrepresent the research—either passively, through sloppy analysis, or actively, through data manipulation. Still, they are standard tools of epidemiology, often cited by both sugar critics and sugar allies. Allison also found fault with the statistical analyses that Hu had conducted.

Allison is the doctor who had been criticized in the ABC News report for defending sugar-sweetened beverages while accepting $299,000 in research funding from Coca-Cola, and more from other food giants. He had consistently critiqued obesity science on two fronts. He argued that the data analyses in papers like Hu's were not rigorous. He also said that the actual data, often gathered in large public health surveys like the National Health and Nutrition Examination Survey (NHANES), was unreliable. To boot, Allison was the one who coined the memorable term "white-hat bias" to describe work by researchers like Hu.

Hu was on the "plague rat" side of the stage. In a reference to Allison's keen critiques of statistical analyses, Hu quipped that he'd rather debate an empty chair, as Clint Eastwood had at a recent political convention. Then Hu argued, as he long had, that reducing soda consumption would reduce obesity. And that the evidence had become ever stronger. Much of that evidence came from Hu's own research. In 2006, Hu and colleagues conducted a literature review for the *American Journal of Clinical Nutrition* and found that sugar-sweetened beverages (SSBs),[1] "particularly soda, provide little nutritional benefit, and increase weight gain and probably the risk of diabetes, fractures, and dental caries.

"The weight of epidemiologic and experimental evidence indicates that a greater consumption of SSBs is associated with weight gain and obesity," Hu and colleagues wrote. "Although more research is needed, sufficient evidence exists for public health strategies to discourage consumption of sugary drinks as part of a healthy lifestyle." Their analysis included fifteen cross-sectional and ten prospective studies, but only five experimental studies. More research was, indeed, needed.

In 2010, writing for the journal *Circulation*, Dr. Hu and colleagues noted that the science was getting stronger still.[2] With all of the concerns about obesity and associated problems, including a reduced quality of life and increased medical bills, they mentioned the importance of reducing the consumption of sugar-sweetened beverages. "SSBs are the greatest contributor to added sugar intake in the U.S. and are thought to promote weight gain in part due to incomplete compensation for liquid calories at subsequent meals."

Hu pointed out that sugary beverages may increase the risk of type 2 diabetes and cardiovascular disease, even independent of obesity. So skinny soda drinkers, too, are at risk of disease. To boot, sodas contribute to insulin resistance, high blood pressure, and the imbalance of fat circulating in the blood known as dyslipidemia. More specifically, sugar-sweetened beverages trigger a nearly instantaneous increase in triglycerides, and a slower increase in LDL cholesterol, the type associated with health risks.

"For these reasons and the fact that they have little nutritional value," Hu wrote, "intake of SSBs should be limited and replaced by healthy alternatives such as water."

Although the evidence had been mounting, Hu had long felt that soda science needed more randomized control studies evaluating soda's effects on humans, in a clinical setting. In an odd bit of timing, just such research was released the day after Hu debated Allison in San Antonio. That's when the *New England Journal of Medicine* published three papers on sugar-sweetened beverages and obesity.

This was another turning point in the obesity debate, not only because the papers showed links between soda and obesity, but also because two of the papers were randomized control studies. So the researchers were able to show more than an association; they showed causation. The studies provided further evidence that sugar-sweetened beverages put adults and children at risk for obesity. Conversely, they showed that reducing the drinks effectively reduces childhood obesity.

One study, "Sugar-Sweetened Beverages and Genetic Risk of Obesity," was from Hu's group.[3] Notably, researchers found that sugar-sweetened beverages actually amplified the risk of gaining excess weight. Put another way, the gene-environment interaction of genetic factors and sugar-sweetened beverage consumption together exaggerates the risk of excessive weight gain. The good news is that the inverse is also true: healthier beverage choices can mitigate the genetic predisposition to obesity.

The other two papers looked at the effects of reducing sugar-sweetened beverages on preventing childhood obesity. In all, Hu felt it marked a turning point for obesity research.

Due to a publication embargo, the papers were not released until after the debate. Allison told journalist Todd Neale that this put him in an awkward spot—he was debating without all of the evidence. And the papers changed his opinion, he told Neale, if only slightly.[4] "I think the *New England Journal* papers tip the needle a little bit," he said. "It's obviously not a 180-degree turnaround, but I think they lend some support to the idea that under some circumstances reducing sugar-sweetened beverage consumption can have a weight benefit for some people."

With its "some . . . some . . . some" construct, it was a remarkably muted statement. Still, it seemed a chink in Coca-Cola's armor.

Coca-Cola and Pepsi allowed the American Beverage Association to respond on the industry's behalf. The ABA remained unbowed. "We know, and science supports, that obesity is not uniquely caused by any single food or beverage," a statement from the ABA read. "Thus, studies and opinion pieces that focus solely on sugar-sweetened beverages, or any other single source of calories, do nothing meaningful to help address this serious issue. The fact remains: sugar-sweetened beverages are not driving obesity. By every measure, sugar-sweetened beverages play a small and declining role in the American diet."[5]

At the San Antonio conference, there were others who were on Allison's side, even on his team. James Hill was awarded the George A. Bray Founders Award from the society. Hill was the Coca-Cola ally and proponent of the concept of energy balance who was collaborating with Steven Blair on the large obesity study funded by the corporation. The director of the Anschutz Health and Wellness Center at the University of Colorado, Hill had spent years earning a reputation as an obesity expert, publishing widely on obesity and health.

In accepting the award, Hill argued, as he long had, the obesity is a complex blend of behavioral and environmental factors, and should not be targeted by singling out a single element of the diet, like sodas.[6] And reporting on the event, for an online publication called the *Awl*, was Trevor Butterworth, the industry-allied journalist.

16

With evidence mounting about the role of fructose in promoting disease, the National Institute of Diabetes and Digestive and Kidney Diseases (NIDDK) invited some of the top researchers in the field to Bethesda, Maryland, for a two-day workshop.

"Consumption of simple sugars (sucrose, glucose and fructose) currently is estimated at 20 percent of the U.S. diet, on average," the organizers said in announcing the November 2012 event. "This coincides with what has been described as an epidemic of obesity and its complications, such as fatty liver, heart disease and diabetes." The workshop aimed to guide future research by considering what questions should be answered about the effects of sugar on human health, and how.

Among those presenting were Kimber Stanhope of the University of California, Davis. Stanhope had become one of the nation's leading researchers on the effects of fructose on humans, but she had envisioned a different career. By her account, she was dragged kicking and screaming into the work.

Early in her career, Stanhope planned to study human insulin resistance through lab work on isolated fat cells. It's a lot easier than human research—you isolate the fat cells, keep them alive for a few days, and one week later you have great data. Fat cells are quiet and cooperative, and they never quit the study. Human research, by contrast, is very slow.

But one study changed the trajectory of her career. Stanhope was leading a team studying the effects of glucose- or fructose-sweetened drinks on obese or overweight people over ten weeks. She sent some of her data to her Japanese collaborators for analysis. When the numbers came back, she was amazed. Small, dense LDL cholesterol, the bad kind, and lipoproteins were both increased by fructose, while glucose had no effect.

When Stanhope saw the data, she said, "Oh wow, this is good data. Oh damn, I'm going to be studying sugar in humans for the rest of my life." That is exactly what happened. She could not walk away from the data, and that has been her career. That paper, published in 2009, was among the first to note the different metabolic effects of glucose- and fructose-sweetened beverages in humans.[1]

Stanhope's research had earned her a seat at the table at the workshop in Bethesda. Also attending the workshop, as one of the interested observers in the rows of chairs around the central table, was the erstwhile dentist and archive hunter Cristin Kearns.

Both Kearns and Stanhope were surprised to see another high-profile presenter at the workshop: John Sievenpiper of the University of Toronto.

Sievenpiper is a doctor whose name seems to bubble to the surface whenever the conversation turns to soda industry conflicts of interest. An MD and researcher affiliated with the University of Toronto and St. Michael's Hospital, he is an especially reliable voice in defense of sugar.

In a 2013 review for *Current Hypertension Reports*, Sievenpiper and colleagues had this to say: "The highest level of evidence from controlled feeding trials has shown a lack of cardiometabolic harm of fructose and SSBs under energy-matched conditions at moderate levels of intake. It is only when fructose-containing sugars or SSBs are consumed at high doses or supplement diets with excess energy that a consistent signal for harm is seen."[2]

In a 2013 editorial for the *American Journal of Clinical Nutrition*, Sievenpiper deflected blame from sugar-sweetened beverages: "Because of the small effect sizes and lack of demonstrated harm over other sources of excess energy in the diet, public health interventions that solely target SSBs are unlikely to be sufficient. A broader focus is needed. SSBs are one of many pathways to overconsumption. Other highly palatable foods such as refined grains, potato products, salty snack foods, and processed meats also contribute to overconsumption leading to weight gain and cardiometabolic complications."[3]

In a later paper for *Diabetes Care*, the journal of the American Diabetes Association, Sievenpiper and Richard Kahn argued against a paper by soda critics George Bray and Barry Popkin: "In the counterpoint narrative below, we argue that there is no clear or convincing evidence that any dietary or added sugar has a unique or detrimental impact relative to any other source of calories on the development of obesity or diabetes."[4]

Sievenpiper also wrote a letter to *Mayo Clinic Proceedings* critiquing a paper on fructose: "In the case of fructose, the totality of the highest-level evidence from the systematic reviews and meta-analyses of controlled trials and prospective cohort studies fails to implicate fructose as an independent driver of type 2 diabetes."[5]

Coca-Cola paid hundreds of thousands of dollars to support Sievenpiper's work while he was defending fructose as a healthy ingredient in soft drinks.[6] On top of this, he served as an expert witness for the Corn Refiners Association in a lawsuit over high-fructose corn syrup.[7] And he had received funding from Archer-Daniels-Midland, which produces high-fructose corn syrup, and the Calorie Control Council, a soda industry front group.

You get the idea. Although he disclosed his funding from Coca-Cola in some papers, Sievenpiper was often quoted in news stories as an academic. A *Scientific American* article titled "Is Sugar Really Toxic?" is one example: "In a series of meta-analyses examining dozens of human studies, John Sievenpiper of St. Michael's Hospital in Toronto and his colleagues found no harmful effects of typical fructose consumption on body weight, blood pressure, or uric acid production."[8]

And a story from the Canadian magazine *Macleans* quoted Sievenpiper like so: "Dr. John Sievenpiper, a scientist at St. Michael's Hospital's Li Ka Shing Knowledge Institute in Toronto, has published a series of papers concluding that excess calories from fructose aren't any worse from other sources. He believes science doesn't justify recommending a daily limit for sugar consumption: 'I don't care if it's five grams or 100 grams,' says Sievenpiper. 'If it's providing excess calories, it's a problem.'"[9]

Sievenpiper was also very active with the International Life Sciences Institute (ILSI), the industry front group founded by Coca-Cola's Alex Malaspina that works to influence food policy worldwide. Sievenpiper is a reliable voice in defense of soda. And he would be an increasingly important player in Coca-Cola's schemes.

Kearns, who was early in her research about the sugar industry's influence on health policy, was astonished when Sievenpiper got up at this important meeting and presented his systematic reviews to show that fructose isn't really harmful. "The guy from NIDDK was like, 'Wow, that's good!,'" Kearns said. "He just really was eating up what Sievenpiper was saying. . . . I couldn't believe that there was no critical thinking that this guy was clearly working with ILSI, and we might want to look at his systematic reviews a little more closely and not just take at face value what he's saying. Yeah, that was my introduction to how in bed everyone is."

17

Coca-Cola went on the offensive in early 2013. "Today, our Company launches an unprecedented campaign to help America beat one of the most serious issues of our day—obesity," a January Coca-Cola press release read.

The campaign involved a series of ads, "to educate people about the importance of making informed choices and balancing 'calories in' with 'calories out.' We're also telling people about all that we're doing to help them lead active, healthy lives—including putting calorie counts on the front of our packages, replacing full-calorie sparkling beverages in schools with more diet and light options, offering more than 180 low- and no-calorie choices and supporting vital physical activity programs like America is Your Park, Triple Play and many others."

It all sounded good. Coca-Cola's first ad, called Coming Together, looked innocuous. It was a slightly nostalgic, feel-good ad that mentioned low- and reduced-sugar options, calorie labeling, and its efforts to "voluntarily change what's offered in schools." And it also made this point: "All calories count. If you eat and drink more calories than you burn off, you'll gain weight. That goes for Coca-Cola, and everything else with calories."

Coke dropped another ad featuring a bright, catchy ukulele tune by the Swedish pop singer Ingrid Michaelson. The lyrics repeated a simple phrase, "I just want to be okay," again and again. In bold letters, over the video, the ad read, "Coca-Cola = 140 happy calories to spend on extra happy activities." It then suggested walking a dog, dancing, and laughing as ways to spend those calories.

The ads drew fire from critics like Michael Jacobson, of the Center for Science in the Public Interest, who called for Coke to stop advertising full-sugar drinks and fighting soda taxes.[1] When ABC News asked Coca-Cola for comment, it directed them to Russell Pate of the University of South Carolina.

Pate obligingly delivered a quotation focused on the calories-out side of the equation. "I believe strongly that we will have to increase the physical activity level of our population if we want to overcome the obesity epidemic," Pate said.[2] At the time, Pate was involved with University of South Carolina research that had received more than $1 million of funding from Coca-Cola. And he and his colleagues would soon take their ideas on energy balance to a wider audience.

18

Sitting on stage with Coca-Cola CEO Muhtar Kent at the annual shareowners meeting in Atlanta, in April 2013, Warren Buffett spoke of selling bottles of Coke around his Omaha neighborhood in his youth. His grandfather had a grocery store and gave him a deal on Coke. "He sold me at the rate of six bottles for a quarter, and I went around the neighborhood and sold them for a nickel each," Buffett told Kent, sitting next to a table with several bottles of Coca-Cola. "And I sold out every time. I had no inventory, I had no receivables, I had the best business I ever had."[1]

Warren Buffett had grown from those humble roots into one of the shrewdest, most successful investors of his era. He was also the single largest shareholder of Coca-Cola. Kent, a bald, robust Turkish American who had risen through the ranks after starting as a Coke-route truck driver, asked Buffet, "What excites you these days, in technology, innovation, new businesses?"

Buffett picked up a Coke bottle from the table, and said, "I like this one," with a laugh. The shareowners applauded. "I'm the type of guy who likes to bet on sure things, Muhtar, and since 1886 and Jacob's Pharmacy, you've just seen year after year after year, until now you have 1.8 billion eight-ounce servings a day around the world."

Buffett is the perfect cheerleader for Coca-Cola, where he has served on the board since 1988. Speaking of his company Berkshire Hathaway, he said, "We own four hundred million shares of Coca-Cola stock. As you know, we've never sold a share. And I wouldn't think of selling a share." An octogenarian who boasts of drinking Coke daily, Buffett appeared sharp, spry, and witty. "You're selling happiness," he said, "and having it an arm's length away is a big part of it."

Ever canny, Buffett's Berkshire Hathaway also happens to be the largest investor in DaVita, a for-profit chain of dialysis clinics that has been highly profitable as the epidemics of obesity and type 2 diabetes have led to widespread kidney failure. Berkshire Hathaway holds nearly 30 percent of DaVita's shares, worth $3 billion.[2] For chronic Coke consumers, Buffett gets you coming and going.

Buffet told Kent that he understands why some businesses fail. "The biggest thing that kills them is complacency," Buffet said. "And you want a restlessness, a feeling that somebody is always after you, but you're going to stay ahead of them, you always want to be on the move. And when you've got a great business like Coca-Cola—there aren't any like Coca-Cola—the danger would always be that you'd rest on your laurels, but I see none of that, obviously, at Coca-Cola."

Like any other business, there were people after Coca-Cola. But the company was working, doggedly, if not frantically, to stay ahead of them.

19

Rhona Applebaum stood at a lectern before a large auditorium, looking professional in a beige turtleneck and black blazer, with neatly styled auburn hair. Applebaum was there to convince a roomful of obesity experts gathered at a May 2013 conference in Vancouver that Coca-Cola was not the cause of the crisis, but part of the solution.

She introduced her employer as the world's largest beverage company—number one in sparkling beverages, juice, and ready-to-drink coffee. Coca-Cola products are sold in 207 countries, she said. And she said the corporate philosophy entails "doing well by doing good."

Applebaum then turned to the subject of her talk. "We cannot have a healthy and growing business unless the communities in which we operate are healthy," she said. "We know that unless our consumers, currently and in the future, are healthier, we are not going to be able to grow as a business." In a PowerPoint presentation, Applebaum reviewed the statistics the audience understood so well: obesity had doubled in thirty years in America; two out of three Americans were obese or overweight, more than in any other country. "We are still number one in obesity," Applebaum said. Pausing for emphasis, gesturing with her right hand, she added, slowly and emphatically, "That is unacceptable."

Then she laid out the corporate strategy. "At the end of the day, it's about calories in and calories out," she said. "Eat less, move more. I would be less than open and honest, which I want to be with you all," Applebaum added, "if I didn't say we can't overemphasize the importance of activity."

Applebaum talked about the value of good science, and explained how science can lead to false scares, like the idea commonly held in the 1980s that caffeinated coffee leads to a variety of health problems. Applebaum then segued into another scare wrought by faulty science, the fear that eating eggs leads to high cholesterol. "And if I can be so bold as to share personal experiences," she continued, "growing up on a farm, growing up on a poultry farm, on an egg farm, we lost the farm because of that."

Applebaum clicked on a slide showing that people are moving less, and another showing how much television kids are watching. Another slide, with more than twenty multicolored boxes with arrows arrayed among them, illustrated the complex factors influencing obesity.

Adamant, determined, and self-righteous, Applebaum was developing a head of steam. "We are very focused on evidence-based science," she said. "What do the data say? As a scientist, you can't be anything else, you shouldn't be anything else, but data-driven. Not based on what you believe, or what you think, or what's the right thing to do, but what do the data say? And informing with transparency, and marketing responsibly, absolutely essential. We do believe in choice. Absolutely we believe in choice. *I believe in choice in everything I do.* It's a *right* that I have as an American, that I also have as a citizen of the world, and all of you do also," she said.

Then she turned to the attributes of Coke. "And again, 127 years ago, we started off with one beverage that I personally am very proud of. It's safe, it hydrates, it's enjoyable." With that, a titter of laughter passed through the crowd. "You can laugh, thank you, you can laugh," Applebaum said, unfazed. "It's about the how, how much, and how often. We're not expecting all of your hydration needs to come from Coca-Cola. Lord knows, that's not balance, variety, and moderation."

Applebaum touted the company's 3,500 products, of which she said a quarter were low- and no-calorie. And she said Coca-Cola would like to see more and better health research. "There's a lot of questions we have," Applebaum said. "We wish there were government agencies and others who would take our questions and do the research. They don't. So we also support research. Hands-off, conflict of interest, independent advisory councils, six degrees of separation, if not six thousand degrees of separation. We want to advance and utilize the science," she said. "That is truth."

Regarding research collaboration, Applebaum said the corporation was utterly open and honest. She heard from people that industry corrupts, she went on, and didn't understand that. As a signal of her openness and honesty, she gave out her email address and phone number to anyone who wanted to discuss it. "Everyone that we support, we are very transparent right up front," she said, "if they take money from The Coca-Cola Company to answer a question."

Not transparent enough, it turned out, and with no degrees of separation. Applebaum would soon become notorious for developing an audacious scheme to dupe Americans about the health risks of Coke. In two years, she would be out of a job.

20

Georgia governor Nathan Deal, Atlanta mayor Kasim Reed, and Coca-Cola CEO Muhtar Kent were seated before a backdrop emblazoned with the Coca-Cola logo for a May 2013 press conference at World of Coca-Cola (the Atlanta tourist attraction with the Vault of the Secret Formula).

Coca-Cola had decided to donate $3.8 million to fight obesity in Georgia. One million of that was earmarked for the program known as Georgia Shape, a pet project of the governor's. In announcing the gift, Governor Deal said, "We are encouraged that, as a part of this effort, we are going to make sure that in our elementary schools, they set aside thirty more minutes for physical activity."

Kent added, "Together, we can . . . build a healthier future for people across our state and around the world."[1] Taking nothing for granted, Coca-Cola even placed two of its staffers on Georgia Shape's advisory council—Rhona Applebaum and Clyde Tuggle.

The next morning, Brenda Fitzgerald, commissioner of Georgia's Department of Public Health, appeared on a local TV news show to tout the effort. She was shown over a crawl reading, "COCA-COLA PLEDGES $3.8M TO HELP FIGHT OBESITY IN GA."

Fitzgerald said the program would focus on increasing activity in schools, and it also had a nutrition component. "We're going to concentrate on what you should eat," she said. "And the important thing is you need to eat five servings of fruits and vegetables a day." The message was clear: Fitzgerald was focusing on items that belong on a menu, not items that should be off the menu.

Fitzgerald was a strong presence in Georgia. She had practiced medicine for thirty years, worked as an advisor to House Speaker Newt Gingrich, and served as an officer in the US Air Force. She was a graduate of Emory School of Medicine and an adjunct professor at Emory's Rollins School of Public Health.[2] She had twice run for a congressional seat and had many powerful allies, Coca-Cola among them. Coca-Cola even posted a column by Fitzgerald on its website, titled "Solving Childhood Obesity Requires Movement." The column did not include the words *diet* or *sugar*.

Another example of the close ties between Fitzgerald and Coca-Cola would come in February 2015, when the International Life Sciences Institute announced its new president. It was a scientist who had been involved with the organization for decades, who knew her way around the world of corporate nutrition: Coca-Cola's own Rhona Applebaum. When news of the appointment got to Georgia, Fitzgerald sent the simplest note to Applebaum, copied to others at Georgia Shape and Coca-Cola: "Yea team."[3]

Fitzgerald would soon be bound for higher office, if fleetingly.

21

Later in May 2013, Coca-Cola trumpeted its success in reducing the calories Americans consume. "Yesterday, America's top food and beverage manufacturers announced an important milestone: more than 1.5 trillion calories have been removed from the U.S. marketplace," the Coca-Cola blog post read. "This achievement is the result of efforts made by the Healthy Weight Commitment Foundation (HWCF), a coalition of 16 food and beverage corporate partners, including The Coca-Cola Company, and over 230 organizations, who are working together to help reduce obesity, especially childhood obesity."

The post ran beneath a photo of former Department of Agriculture secretary Dan Glickman, Lisa Gable of the Healthy Weight Commitment Foundation, and author Hank Cardello, at an event sponsored by the Obesity Solutions Initiative at the Hudson Institute.[1]

The whole announcement is worth dissecting for its overwhelming deception. For starters, Coca-Cola could remove far more calories in a heartbeat by removing full-sugar beverages from the market or by reducing its advertising of those products. But even as it was taking credit for removing calories, it continued to give its flagship product—full-sugar Coke—top-shelf treatment and millions of dollars' worth of advertising worldwide. Not only was it aggressively promoting these calorie-dense beverages; it continued to introduce new, full-sugar blends.

That's to be expected. Coca-Cola is in the business of selling sugar water. If it actually tried to reduce sales, it would be violating its obligations to its shareholders. What is unexpected is for Coca-Cola to concurrently take credit for reducing calories.

And while the photo appears to be three independent experts jovially discussing the problem of obesity, the whole event was paid for by Coke, Pepsi, and other food corporations. Coke alone has given hundreds of thousands of dollars to the Hudson Institute, and $5 million to the Healthy Weight Commitment Foundation.

The foundation was so pleased with its progress that it bought a full-page ad in the *Washington Post*.

22

As some Americans became more concerned about sugar, they began switching to diet sodas. And then the sweeteners in diet sodas started getting more scrutiny, which made the soda companies anxious.

Let's say you were a bit paranoid about corporate influence. What might you imagine a powerful industry would do to counter a bit of bad news? Consider this very comprehensive action plan developed by the Calorie Control Council in September 2013. It was in response not to anything about sugar but to a segment that Dr. Oz would be running about diet sodas. Still, it illustrates the sophisticated playbook of Coca-Cola's front groups.

"The aforementioned multimedia press release was developed, which includes an infographic to illustrate actual low-calorie sweetener consumption levels compared to the incorrect figure Dr. Oz presented as well as a digital video featuring dietitian Robyn Flipse's perspective on the issue," wrote Theresa Hedrick, a nutrition and scientific affairs specialist with the Calorie Control Council, in an email. "Council staff has also reached out to the show's producers to request a correction of the overestimation of the average yearly consumption of low-calorie sweeteners. Additionally, Council staff alerted Dr. Fernstrom and Robyn Flipse of the segment; both are prepared to take media calls if necessary. Council staff is also available to take media calls, if necessary."[1] Hedrick was just getting started.

"The press release will be issued on the wire the day the show airs and will be posted on the Council's website as well. Digital Marketing, including Google advertisements, will drive web traffic to the Council's website. Those ads will run for 7–10 days. Council staff will also contact key opinion leaders and key reporter contacts after the segment is aired to alert them of the Council's position. Further, Council staff will work with Working Group social media advocates to engage social media outlets as appropriate. In addition to the Council's normal media monitoring, Council staff as well as Robyn Flipse will monitor the comments of healthcare professionals on dietitian listservs. Finally, the Council is also discussing the possibility of meeting with Dr. Oz and/or Purdue University."

At the bottom of the email was a note: "The Calorie Control Council is managed by the Kellen Company, an employee-owned association management company providing association and meetings management, public relations, government affairs, web site development, and graphic design services."

The Kellen Company is doing a brisk business in running interference for Coke and other corporations. Coca-Cola alone funded the Calorie Control Council with more than $2.5 million between 2010 and 2020.[2] Kellen has offices in Atlanta (of course) as well as Chicago, New York, Washington, Brussels, and Beijing.

23

Standing at the podium at the National Press Club on October 29, 2013, flanked by a large American flag and an even larger video screen, Jim Hill looked professorial with his blue blazer, red tie, neatly trimmed gray goatee, and stylish glasses.[1]

Hill, the director of the Anschutz Health and Wellness Center at the University of Colorado, had one message: people don't really understand obesity, and want to blame it all on food. "Food restriction doesn't work," Hill said. "Food is critical. But unless we increase exercise in the population, we have no hope of reducing high rates of obesity."

Hill was speaking at an event with a remarkably dull title: "The Effectiveness of Inexpensive Nonmedical Interventions in Improving Obesity and Diabetes Outcomes." Hill said Americans' focus on food overlooks a more important factor in the obesity epidemic: it's hard to eat little enough to stay slender if you are not at least somewhat physically active.

"I hear this all the time: 'Eat less, exercise more,'" Hill said, wrapping up his presentation. "*This is the wrong message.* . . . We have to change this to 'Move more, and eat smarter.'" He was clear about this—Americans should think less about what they eat, and more about how much they move.

It was a strong message echoed by other speakers at the National Press Club that day. Carl Lavie, a telegenic Louisiana cardiologist, talked about the importance of physical activity in preventing obesity and diabetes. (Lavie had also recently written *The Obesity Paradox*, a book asserting that heavier people are often healthier than those who are skinny.) "There's really been a lot of publicity that what's causing diabetes is sugary beverages, sugar in the diet, fast foods," Lavie said. "Blaming it on Pepsi-Cola,

Coca-Cola, McDonald's, and Taco Bell. But really there's tremendous evidence that the cause of obesity is the marked decline in physical activity that has occurred in the last five decades." The men were there at the National Press Club at the request of Coca-Cola's Rhona Applebaum, who had funded their research into energy balance and hired two public relations firms to coordinate the press conference.

John Sievenpiper, of the University of Toronto and St. Michael's Hospital, said the whole issue of obesity had been high on opinion and low on data. "We have lots of examples in recent history of wanting to vilify specific nutrients, and I think it's just given way to just another nutrient to vilify, and so on," Sievenpiper said. "And I think we have to stop that, and look at the whole diet, and we also have to look at the physical activity, or the energy state, if you like, of the individual, and how this debate relates to that." Sievenpiper said his research found no links between fructose-containing sugars and diabetes, hypertension, or obesity. He did concede that total-fructose-containing sugars from sugar-sweetened beverages were an exception, but only at "extreme intakes." (His slides bore the label of the Calorie Control Council, one of several industry-funded front groups organized by the Kellen Company.) Steven Blair, the University of South Carolina professor of exercise science who quarterbacked the event, emphasized the same points.

The event was organized by Touch Medical Media, which published peer-reviewed medical journals including *US Endocrinology* and *European Endocrinology*. In recent months, both journals had published papers on energy balance and the exercise-is-medicine concept by some of the researchers who were speaking at the event.

The whole event was organized and paid for Coca-Cola. Coca-Cola's Rhona Applebaum had gotten the ball rolling the prior month, when she wrote to Hill, Lavie, and Sievenpiper with a specific request. She said she had hired a medical communications company to spread the message of the three academics.[2] "With Touch Medical Media, we have been discussing best ways to further disseminate/amplify the excellent reviews you have done and the information contained there in," Applebaum wrote. "One of the best ways is via a Press Conference. I explained to TMM I would first clear the concept with you before they contacted you directly. Always good to make it as easy as possible for journalists to get solid information, and to ensure against misunderstandings, have them in the same room as experts." Applebaum proposed the two-hour press conference at the National Press Club in Washington, DC, in late October. Just to hedge her bets, Applebaum was also bringing on communicator Nancy Glick, from MSL, a DC powerhouse PR firm.

It seemed a long shot that academic obesity researchers would fly to DC at the request of Coca-Cola, in order have their industry-solicited research amplified by public relations firms hired by the soda company. But the researchers showed no hesitation.

Sievenpiper responded especially quickly, within a few hours. "Rhona: I am available . . . J."

At this event, the soda funding was disclosed. "I'd like to acknowledge the Coca-Cola Company, who have provided an unrestricted educational grant to support this activity. They've supported the publication of the articles, and also this activity here today," Touch staffer Genevieve Robson said. "The grant is unrestricted, which means that the opinions of the doctors that you'll hear today are entirely their own."

One way of looking at the event is as a straightforward press conference to discuss recent peer-reviewed research. The more accurate perspective was that Coca-Cola had orchestrated the whole thing—it paid to publish the papers, it paid the researchers to go to the event, and it paid Touch to coordinate the press conference. It was a good investment, because it also served as a dry run for a much bigger (and less transparent) Coca-Cola project coming down the line.

24

In May 2014, Matt Raymond perceived a threat from a film that would soon be released. A DC veteran who knew his way around Capitol Hill, Raymond had worked for the USDA, UNICEF, and the Library of Congress. Now he had landed a job with the International Food Information Council (IFIC), an industry front group.

In an email to his board, staff, and "media dialogue group," he warned about the film *Fed Up*, which was due to open in theaters in just a few days. Co-produced and narrated by celebrity journalist Katie Couric, the film pulled no punches in its appraisal of the modern American diet, especially the role of added sugars. Raymond wanted to get ahead of the public relations fiasco it could create for Coca-Cola and the other corporations funding the IFIC.

The IFIC aggressively protects the processed food corporations that fund it. For example, in February 2013, a week before the release of Michael Moss's book, *Salt Sugar Fat*, an exposé on the processed foods industry, the council was closely monitoring the press coverage and the author's scheduled appearances. It had also developed a campaign to counter the book's messages[1] by developing talking points and increasing its engagement in digital media.

The front group typically keeps many irons in the fire. The same week it was developing its campaign for the Moss book, it was soliciting help to counter a soon-to-be-released paper by Dr. Robert Lustig and colleagues. The conclusion of Lustig's paper was damning for Coca-Cola and other soda companies: "Duration and degree of sugar exposure correlated significantly with diabetes prevalence in a dose-dependent manner, while declines in sugar exposure correlated with significant subsequent declines in diabetes rates independently of other socioeconomic, dietary and obesity prevalence changes."[2]

The IFIC's Kris Sollid knew just the guy to counter Lustig's science: Jim Hill, Coke's ally in Colorado. "We would be delighted to have the benefit of your analysis and given the likelihood of our receiving media inquiries once the paper is released," Sollid wrote to Hill, "knowing your level of willingness to be contacted for expert perspective on this issue."

Now, to counter the publicity around Couric's documentary, Raymond was working hard to get his sources into the media. His team had talked with a reporter for *USA Today* and given some quotes.

More ominously, another national reporter was starting to dig into a bigger theme. "*New York Times* reporter Anahad O'Connor has been working on a story focusing on the notion that 'a calorie is not a calorie' and the issue of whether sugar consumption uniquely contributes to obesity," Raymond wrote. Fortunately, Raymond had just the source in mind for O'Connor: "In addition with our directly providing comments," Raymond wrote, "we successfully connected the reporter with Dr. John Sievenpiper, our noted expert in the field of sugars."

Hill and Sievenpiper, IFIC's favored sources, were also the men who'd spoken at the Coke-funded event at the National Press Club a few months earlier. Their views on energy balance—emphasizing physical activity over diet—and their reluctance to vilify sugar were making them quite valuable to Coca-Cola, more so with each passing month.

25

It seemed a great opportunity to more than a dozen journalists from CNN, NPR, and regional news outlets across the country—a four-day seminar in a Denver suburb in June 2014 to learn about obesity and obesity science.[1]

The Obesity Issues 2014 event was presented by the National Press Foundation in collaboration with the Anschutz Health and Wellness Center, a well-funded branch of the University of Colorado Denver. Jim Hill organized the training. Attendees heard from experts about a range of issues. Hill, who was also the director of the Colorado Nutrition Obesity Research Center, delivered the keynote: "Obesity, the Big Picture." His colleague John Peters's talk asked, "Why Are We Fat?"

At first glance, the gathering appeared legit. It also seemed healthy. Attendees were able to sit on inflatable ball chairs or at standing desks. They had stretch breaks led by professionals, and they enjoyed healthy meals. They convened for a "journalists-only" dinner to talk shop.

But scratch the surface only slightly, and things looked amiss. The only talk about sugar taxes was delivered by Christopher Snowdon of the Institute of Economic Affairs. Snowdon is a free-marketeer and a critic of soda taxes. He once wrote that such taxes have no effect on consumer behavior: "As a consequence, the effect on their calorie consumption is negligible and the effect on their waistline is non-existent."[2]

There was also a guest speaking on "food for thought in evaluating research," and he, too, was a critic of soda taxes.[3] This was Trevor Butterworth, who had taken to the pages of *Forbes* to defend Coke-funded scientist David Allison. Butterworth had become a trusted, consistent ally of Coca-Cola. (He'd written a takedown of sugar research for the *Harvard Business Review* a few months earlier, which Rhona Applebaum had forwarded to her colleagues with the simplest description of Butterworth: "Our friend."[4])

Hill gave a talk titled "The Big Debate, Food or Physical Activity?"[5] He highlighted the matter of energy balance, but took pains not to implicate sugar. "Yes, sugar is a reasonable target to reduce body weight, but I would argue that fat reduction is also a way of doing it," Hill said. "And it's really a matter of calorie reduction. I don't think there's anything magical about sugar. I get sort of upset when I see all of this stuff attributed to sugar."

Another presentation at the journalism symposium was about "industry initiative and opportunity." It featured L. Celeste Bottorff, Coca-Cola's vice president of global health and well-being, and Steve Hilton, vice president of global government and public affairs for McDonald's.

Many of the journalists seemed to enjoy the program, and some attendees thought it was the greatest thing since sliced bread. "You had all the rock stars of the obesity topic—the quality of the speakers you chose really was incredible," a CNN journalist wrote in an evaluation of the event. "Never have I been to such a helpful fellowship. I especially loved the locals—Dr. Peters and Dr. Hill are truly one of a kind. I love that they are clearly legit scientists, but Dr. Hill especially has such a realistic understanding of what it might take to end this epidemic."

The center rigorously tracked the articles produced after the seminar: "Over 10 months since the program, 21 articles have been published by fellows, and reposted in 99 venues," the program recap noted. "As of April 2, 2015, speaker slides and audio recordings had been accessed 663 times."

On the cover of its final report on the conference, the organizers made this bold and deceptive claim: "Funding for this program was provided by the University of Colorado Foundation and the NPF [National Press Foundation] Training Fund."

The truth was that the journalism conference was bought and paid for by Coca-Cola. Not by the University of Colorado, or the National Press Foundation, which only acted as fronts for the soda money. Coca-Cola footed the $37,500 bill. In essence, the corporation purchased media coverage and media influence by laundering its money through two nonprofits—the University of Colorado and the National Press Foundation. It was a corporate smokescreen, the antithesis of transparency.

The 2014 workshop was actually the second journalism workshop Hill had fronted for Coca-Cola. The corporation had funded a similar 2012 conference with $45,000. After that event, Hill wrote to Coca-Cola's Rhona Applebaum: "I have been remiss in updating you about the journalists conference. We believe it was a 'home run.' The journalists told us this was an amazing event and they generated a lot of stories."

Overtly influencing mainstream journalists was a long-term strategy for Coca-Cola. Even earlier, in 2011, Coca-Cola's Arti Arora and Applebaum discussed with Hill the "establishment of The National Center of Health and Science Writing for Journalists."[6]

After the Coca-Cola funding of the 2014 Denver conference became clear, David Olinger reported on the event for the *Denver Post*.[7] Kristin Jones, who attended the conference while working as a journalist for Rocky Mountain PBS, said she felt duped. "What I thought I was getting was a presentation of the science of obesity," Jones told Olinger. "I wouldn't have gone through a three-day conference on the science of obesity if I knew it was partly sponsored by Coca-Cola."

26

By June 2014, Coca-Cola was formalizing a campaign to emphasize motion over diet. But Alex Malaspina was becoming anxious, because First Lady Michelle Obama had launched her own program, independent of Coca-Cola. Malaspina, the former Coca-Cola executive who had founded the International Life Sciences Institute, worried that Obama would steal Coke's fire.

"I have an idea," Malaspina wrote to Jim Hill and his colleague John Peters. "Convince Mrs. Obama that your program was first and she must change her name to yours. . . . Also, yours is a much better name, more catching and much more attractive. In return, she must recognize your new program and make it a subsidiary to 'America on the Move,' kind of the supporting scientific program, which will provide her with the scientific facts to support the main program, 'America On The Move.'"[1]

By mid-June, Malaspina's ideas were becoming grandiose. He asked Peters to send along the latest version of his plan. Malaspina was playing the role of a connector here, still working the tripartite scheme he based ILSI on: the overlap of industry, academics, and regulators. Now he wanted to connect the University of Colorado obesity experts with Coca-Cola executives Clyde Tuggle and Ed Hays, and Coca-Cola board member Howard Buffett (son of Warren Buffett). He also wanted to connect them with FDA deputy commissioner Michael Taylor, an old friend, and even, if he could swing it, with Michelle Obama.

"Is it OK to show Clyde?" Malaspina asked. "Can Clyde show it to H. Buffett, if this could be proper, as HB is a Director of the Company. Also is it OK to send to Mike Taylor and ask him to meet with Jim when Jim visit[s] DC? Mike might be able to arrange for Jim to meet Mrs. O, as I had explained to Jim."[2]

Malaspina made it clear that Hill and Peters were key players in forming Coca-Cola's response to concerns about obesity and suggested its executives might "pay your Center a visit and have a thorough discussion of what the Company's strategy should be on the obesity issue."

Malaspina wanted to take these ideas to DC in a deluxe ride—the Coca-Cola corporate jet.

"What do you think of the idea to take the Company plane for the visit," Malaspina wrote. "If we can swing it and include HB, are you sure you can make it really interesting to him. Maybe you need more time for such a visit. Clyde and Ed may want to come now and I may be join them."[3]

Increasingly, it was becoming clear that Coca-Cola was worried about obesity, and that Hill and Peters, and the rest of Rhona Applebaum's energy balance team, were going to be at the forefront of the company's strategy to assuage public concerns over obesity, with an assist from ILSI. The academic/corporate lines were getting blurry, and they would soon be erased altogether.

* * *

A few months later, in September, the stage was grand and glittering at the Clinton Global Initiative in New York, where the American Beverage Association made a strong claim: it would reduce calories by 20 percent in ten years.[4]

Former president Bill Clinton read his notes from the dais. "Today we announce a profoundly important commitment to combat the obesity epidemic, by cutting calories in America's soft drinks, outside of schools, and beyond children," Clinton said. "This is really important," he went on, gesturing with his index finger. "This strategy can sustainably lower the aggregate weight of the country in a way that will dramatically improve health outcomes, reduce the risk of obesity, and diabetes and its attendant consequences, and in particular cases can help us to reverse type 2 diabetes, which is profoundly important."

Standing a few yards away on stage, smiling, was Susan Neely of the American Beverage Association. Never mind that Clinton was suggesting what the ABA had long contested—a link between sodas and obesity and type 2 diabetes. The important thing was that Clinton was applauding the soda industry.

The ABA was making a pledge to reduce the calories Americans consume in soft drinks by 20 percent in ten years. It planned to do so by making more low-calorie drinks available, selling smaller servings, and educating consumers. It was a lot of hype, industry observers noted. NYU's Marion Nestle told the *New York Times* that even as the association made this pledge, "They are totally dug in, fighting soda tax initiatives in places like Berkeley and San Francisco that have exactly the same goal."[5]

The announcement came during a busy few months for the ABA. In June, it had earned a decisive win in court. After the ABA fought tooth and nail against New York City's limits on the sales of jumbo sodas, the judges of the New York State Court of Appeals killed the proposal that June in a 4–2 decision. "In other words, the soda ban is dead," the American Beverage Association had proclaimed in a press release. "What people eat, drink and feed their family is their choice and not the government's."[6]

Also in June, Neely had announced another initiative, to remove sodas from schools, also with the support of Bill Clinton. "Working with the first lady and the Partnership for a Healthier America, President Bill Clinton, and his Alliance for a Healthier Generation, the U.S. Conference of Mayors and others, we have voluntarily removed full-calorie soft drinks from schools nationwide," Neely said, "placed calorie labels on all of our packaging as well as on vending machines, supported community programs that promote balanced diets and physical activity and much more."[7]

The word "voluntarily" was a bit jarring in this context, because health advocates had been fighting to have sodas removed from schools for more than sixty years, and the industry had fiercely resisted the efforts.

Neely also pointed to something that the industry considered a conundrum: that while soda consumption was declining, obesity rates and incidences of diabetes continued to rise. "The numbers just don't add up to support the claim that soft drinks are a unique driver of obesity and diabetes," Neely said.

In all, it was a big, high-profile campaign to ease consumers' worries about obesity. And if Bill Clinton had to take Coca-Cola's side in this fight, it was a small price to pay.

Coca-Cola had donated more than $5 million to the Clinton Foundation and the Clinton Global Initiative.

* * *

A month later, Muhtar Kent was doing a bit of media outreach. It's not normally the sort of thing he fooled around with. He had people who did that. Entire departments that did that, in offices all over the world.

As the CEO of the Coca-Cola Company, including salary and stock options, Kent was making about $69,000 a day, every day, year-round, and his time was best spent elsewhere.[8] But on October 18, Kent was reaching out to Charlie Rose, the host of *CBS This Morning.*

Kent knew Rose. He'd been a guest on *The Charlie Rose Show* in 2009. And now Kent thought he had the perfect guest for Rose to interview on the morning show: Jim Hill.

It seemed odd that someone of Kent's stature—the CEO of a $40 billion corporation—would deign to do media outreach on his own, especially on behalf of a Colorado obesity researcher. But the effort underscored the importance to Coca-Cola of managing the obesity message.

For all of its attributes, Coca-Cola was performing lackadaisically. Americans' love for soft drinks had peaked in the late 1990s and declined since. More and more research was showing that sugar-sweetened beverages like Coke are not just unhealthful but actually worse than other items in the American diet, in a category of their own. As some American consumers were catching on to the health risks, sales were lagging.

One indicator of Coca-Cola's slowing growth was Kent's declining salary. He'd been making $84,000 daily two years earlier. People were starting to compare sodas to cigarettes, Coke to Marlboro. True, the cigarette companies had shown that corporations can remain viable, and profitable, long after being declared public health enemy number one, but tobacco is now permanently linked with death in the public mind. Kent wanted Coca-Cola to be associated with fun.

That's why Kent wanted to get Hill on national TV, to pitch the notion that all it takes to mitigate the health impacts of sugary sodas is an increase in physical activity. Hill's ideas about energy balance were music to Kent's ears.

Kent knew that one of his vice presidents was in contact with Hill, so he asked Rhona Applebaum to send along Hill's CV, so he could forward it to Rose.[9]

Despite Kent's efforts, Hill did not get an appearance on *CBS This Morning*. But Applebaum and Hill were busy hatching another plan to promote their ideas about emphasizing activity over diet.

* * *

The University of South Carolina (USC) had some big news in late 2014. After years of preparation, several obesity experts were launching a new network. "USC PRC Affiliate and Professor of Exercise Science Dr. Steve Blair collaborated with Dr. James Hill of the Anschutz Health and Wellness Center at the University of Colorado Denver to launch the Global Energy Balance Network (GEBN) on December 5: http://gebn.org/," a USC press release read. "Though separately known for their expertise in energy balance, Blair and Hill recognized the need for a network of experts within the field."

The network would use conferences and research to improve the understanding of energy balance and use its website to provide a directory of experts and a library of resources, including videos. "With current lifestyle behaviors (e.g., physical inactivity) serving as causal factors in chronic diseases, such as cardiovascular disease and diabetes, researchers are turning to energy balance to provide sustainable solutions," the release continued. "'There is a disconnect among energy balance scholars and practitioners, which has led to inconsistent and inaccurate information within the media and the public regarding the science of energy balance,' said Dr. Blair, co-founder of GEBN." The $1.5 million campaign was specifically designed to shift the focus from what you eat to how you move. The Global Energy Balance Network was pitching the notion that a calorie is a calorie.

Over the next few months, the group began posting slick videos emphasizing its message—obesity is more about how you move than what you eat. The videos detailed the credentials of experts like Hill and Blair, and showed them sitting in labs, talking in measured, reassuring tones, always about science, always about getting the science right.

In one video, Blair put the message this way: "Most of the focus, in the popular media, in the scientific press, is 'Aww, they're eating too much, eating too much, eating too much. Blaming fast foods, blaming sugary drinks, and so on, and there's really virtually no compelling evidence that that in fact is the cause. Those of us interested in science, public health, medicine, we have to learn how to get the *right* information out there."[10] Blair's message would reach more Americans than he might have expected, and for different reasons.

27

Every five years, a select group of nutrition experts convenes under the auspices of the US Department of Agriculture and U.S. Department of Health and Human Services to update the Dietary Guidelines for Americans. When the Dietary Guidelines Advisory Committee released its report in early 2015, the guidelines were not very dramatic but did cause a stir. Frank Hu, the Harvard epidemiologist and obesity expert, was among the group of experts who had been meeting for months to hash them out.

Among their recommendations: Choose a healthy lifelong eating pattern to reduce the risk of chronic disease. Eat a variety of nutrient-dense foods. Support healthy eating patterns for all, in a variety of settings—home, work, school—and other common-sense measures.

More specifically, the committee advised limiting saturated fats, trans fats, and salt. The report got a lot of attention for noting that dietary cholesterol—as in eating eggs—is not directly tied to blood cholesterol. So eating an egg is fine. But red meat aficionados were unhappy about the suggested limits on saturated fats.

The committee also suggested caution with sugar. It recommended that people consume no more than 10 percent of their calories from added sugar. That might sound reasonable, but more than 60 percent of the population exceeded that level of consumption. And it was a significant change from the existing guidelines that recommended a limit of 25 percent. Researchers like Kimber Stanhope, of UC Davis, had been arguing this was too high, that consuming a quarter of your calories through added sugars posed significant metabolic risks.

For reducing the consumption of added sugar, the committee made clear where the fruit was hanging low. Fully 47 percent of all added sugars were coming from sugar-sweetened beverages.

Among the actions the committee promoted: require front-of-package labels listing calories; discourage the purchase of sugar-sweetened beverages with WIC and SNAP funds; and earmark tax revenues from sodas for obesity prevention programs. "Strategies include choosing beverages with no added sugar, such as water, in place of sugar-sweetened beverages," the committee wrote, "drinking those beverages less often, and selecting beverages low in added sugars."

Overall, it seemed a relatively modest proposal. But not to Coca-Cola.

* * *

With the release of the recommended dietary guidelines, journalists were curious. And the International Food Information Council was glad to help out. The council occupies an interesting niche in the ecosystem of Coca-Cola front groups. Alex Malaspina, the former Coca-Cola executive who founded the International Life Sciences Institute, once defined the nonprofit's role. "IFIC is a kind of sister entity to ILSI," he wrote. "ILSI generates the scientific facts and IFIC communicates them to the media and public."[1] Between 2010 and 2020, Coca-Cola funded it with more than $3 million.[2]

The council hosted a conference call, and more than forty journalists dialed in. They included top dogs in health reporting, from the Associated Press, Politico, and WBEZ-Chicago, among others.

In an hour-long presentation, the IFIC presented former panelists from the guidelines committee. And it released a new infographic about the guidelines. Among the topics discussed was added sugars. In notes from the presentation, IFIC's Marianne Smith Edge wrote, "Added sugar recommendation was based on insufficient evidence to change from a limit of 25% to 10% of calorie intake. Evidence about restricting SSB and Added Sugar should be held to the same rigor of evidence as other recommendations."

A journalist quickly filed a story for Politico Pro. The lede read: "Members of the 2015 Dietary Guidelines Advisory Committee aren't just catching grief from the meat and soda industries for their report. On Friday, members of two former dietary advisory panels piled on as well." The event effectively cast doubt on the committee's recommendations through articles in the mainstream media.

By any metric, it was a successful event, and the IFIC staffers carefully quantified it. They tallied a total of 393,500 impressions from that day's work alone, and quickly sent a memo[3] on the event to Malaspina. Malaspina, in turn, forwarded the note to several people. His note was brief: "Dear Ed and Clyde, IFIC is coming through for industry. I am looking forward to visiting them on March 4. Warmest regards, Alex." All three recipients—Ed Hays, Clyde Tuggle, and Hope Laman—were Coca-Cola staffers.

It was a good example of how Coca-Cola gets its message out through front groups like IFIC. In this way, forty journalists got Coke's perspective on the new dietary guidelines, but with the perception that they were hearing from an independent nonprofit.

Put another way, forty journalists would not have called in to hear a soda company's views on the dietary guidelines. But the effect was the same. The journalists got Coca-Cola's message through the front group that served as its proxy. And all of the industry players—IFIC, ILSI, and Coca-Cola—were tickled by their surreptitious success.

28

By March 2015, the Global Energy Balance Network website was looking more sophisticated with each passing day. The home screen displayed photos of a diverse group of Americans: Asian Americans on bikes, elderly white people jogging, a Black woman buying vegetables in a store. Text scrolling over the photos read, "Be the voice of science in ending obesity" and "Healthier living through the science of energy balance."

The team was populating its news page with various items. One directed people curious about energy balance to a webinar by the European Food Information Council (the overseas sibling of the International Food Information Council). Another headline read: "Processed food not always a bad thing."

And remember David Allison, the Coca-Cola-funded researcher who coined the term "white-hat bias"? The network boasted about his research getting some ink. "If humans are 'notoriously bad' at remembering what they eat, why does nutrition research rely largely on self-reported data? NPR's *The Salt* considers this dilemma in a recent article, citing GEBN member David Allison's new paper on energy balance measurement." The network was starting to look like a success. Visitors to its webpage would not realize that Coca-Cola conceived of, designed, and funded the entire project. But Americans would learn that soon enough.

* * *

After its launch in December, Rhona Applebaum was trying to move the Global Energy Balance Network to the next level. In late March, she circulated a "phase two launch plan."[1] Applebaum touted the group's executive committee, "with leaders from North America, Latin America and the Caribbean, Europe, Africa Asia and Oceania." More than 120 scientists and experts supported the group, she noted, and it was working to build awareness.

Since its inception, the plan was to use corporate front groups and other proxies and allies to promote the network. "We will look to establish partnerships with global organizations including, but not limited to, the American Society for Nutrition, ACSM [American College of Sports Medicine], ECSS [European College of Sport Science], The Obesity Society, ILSI, IFIC, IFT [Institute of Food Technologists] and others that would be sympathetic and supportive of our initiative and would highlight our message," Applebaum wrote in 2014.[2]

Now she was more directly targeting health and science journalists to get the message across. Working with food consultants FoodMinds, Applebaum was leaving nothing to chance. Not only would the network pitch to food and science beat reporters and bloggers; it would specifically target a handful of "news-driving reporters." Those included Nanci Hellmich of *USA Today*, Tara Parker-Pope of the *New York Times*, Allison Aubrey of NPR, and Annie Gasparro of the *Wall Street Journal*. To boot, Applebaum was already planning a "Think-Do Tank" summit for the summer of 2016.

Leaving little to chance, it appeared that the network had a clear flight path and was ready for takeoff.

29

Just as Coke's Global Balance Energy Network was gathering steam, more bad news for the soda industry was trickling in.

Among industry observers, *Beverage Digest*'s annual report is eagerly awaited. It's one of the few metrics for accurately tracking soda sales. In its March 2015 report, the digest had more bad news for soda sellers. Carbonated soft drinks—CSDs in the industry jargon—had fallen again in 2014. "Per capita consumption in the U.S. fell to about 674 eight-ounce servings per person per year," the digest reported. "That compares to a per cap of 675 for 2013. The declining per caps are a function of volume falling and the U.S. population modestly increasing." *Beverage Digest* noted that the decline had been steady, from 728 servings in 2010 to 714 in 2011 and 701 in 2012. "The level of per capita consumption in 2014 is the lowest since about 1986," the digest noted.

The number included sugary sodas, diet sodas, and energy drinks. Oddly, some of the largest declines were in diet sodas. Notably, Coca-Cola claimed 42 percent of the carbonated soft drink market; Pepsi just 27 percent. One legacy brand at least held its own. Coca-Cola grew by 0.1 percent, and claimed fully 18 percent of the soft drink market, twice as much as Pepsi, its closest rival.

30

The National Academy of Medicine is an august body, near the mall in Washington, DC, adorned with a fine, oversized bronze sculpture of Albert Einstein. Along with its sister organizations, the National Academy of Engineering and the National Academy of Sciences, it is often called upon by congressional leaders to investigate matters of national interest.

Because of its name and its close relationship to the government, it would be easy to mistake it for a federal entity when it is, actually, a nonprofit organization. Regardless, it is an honor to be a member of the select group (disclosure: the author's father was one).

On an April day in 2015, a member of the academy (a PhD, not an MD) was addressing the group as the keynote of a two-day conference. The title of the talk: "Does Physical Activity Have a Role in Reducing Obesity?" "This is a very complex system, because the components are interrelated; you change any one thing, everything changes," the speaker said. "I'll also point out this box called active regulation. There's a whole physiological system, from the brain on down, to regulate body weight. And we know that there are a lot of things that affect this. It's affected by inherited factors, it's affected by environmental factors. So what I want to consider this morning is what do we know about physical activity? How does physical activity, adding or subtracting it to the system, work? What science do we know, what science do we not know?" The speaker was none other than Jim Hill, the Colorado obesity expert, speaking from a rather prestigious stump.

Hill ran through an overview of how sedentary people react to adding exercise. "What I want to point out is [that a] vast number of people lose weight." On the other hand, he said that "decreased physical activity likely is an important risk factor for weight gain."

Hill went on to joke about how housewives are burning fewer calories than they did in the 1950s. This referred to a paper by Edward Archer, who worked under Hill's colleague Steven Blair at the University of South Carolina.[1] The paper had gotten a lot of press; its Coca-Cola funding had gotten comparatively little. "I think men doing housework is the cause of obesity," Hill said, to laughter from the audience. "And I think we've got a solution to this." Hill continued, "But the concept is, we are continuing to get physical activity out of our lives. I believe that it was probably post–World War II where most of the decrease in physical activity happened, and that affected the active regulation, but it's still going down. And if you look around the rest of the world, China, for example, is experiencing this very, very quickly. Everything we know about the science of energy balance suggests that this trend is a risk factor for weight gain."

Hill went on to discuss studies showing how increased physical activity affects weight gain. Then, twenty-six minutes into a half-hour talk, he subtly shifted into nutrients. He showed a slide with a team of Tour de France cyclists, and noted that their diets included a massive energy intake of 6,000–9,000 calories a day.

The slide read:

—carbohydrates: 75–80%
—About 1,000 grams a day of CHO
—400 grams simple sugars!
—4,000 kcal/day of CHO
—kcal/day Simple Sugars!
—13–14g/kg/day!!

"They were eating a thousand grams a day of simple carbohydrate, four hundred grams of simple sugar. Now, I'm not saying you should do this," Hill said, "but if you're at the level where you are burning calories like that, the recommendation for sugar intake may be a little bit different. If we're going to take on sugar or fat, or some of those other nutrients, I think we have one hand tied behind our back if you just look at the intake side, you've got to look at the oxidization side as well."

In conclusion to the keynote speech, Hill said, "We cannot reverse the obesity epidemic without increasing physical activity in the population. Thank you very much." The audience applauded.

It was a solid talk, by a thoughtful, accomplished, and charismatic speaker. A man so esteemed by his peers that he'd not only become a member of the National Academy of Medicine but was the keynote speaker at a two-day conference there. But the most fascinating element of Hill's talk was what he did not mention. Hill said nothing about the million dollars Coca-Cola gave the University of Colorado in 2014 to support his work, nor the $550,000 it had funneled directly to him since 2010.[2] He did not mention that he was, that very month, corresponding extensively with Rhona Applebaum about Coca-Cola's secret campaign to emphasize movement over diet.

* * *

Two days later and 200 miles away, Dr. Frank Hu spoke at another august organization, the New York Academy of Sciences. His talk sounded complex: "A Systems Epidemiology Approach to Understanding Nutrition and Obesity and Diabetes." Like Hill, Hu stood at a lectern, dressed in sport coat, blue button-down shirt, and tie. But the similarities ended right there.

Hu began by discussing "black box epidemiology." In essence, this is the model of looking at the human body as a mystery. Known exposures—diet, smoking, exercise—go in on one side of the box, and outcomes—diabetes, cardiovascular disease, cancer—come out on the other. "But in most situations, we really don't understand the biological mechanisms underlying those relationships," Hu said. "For example, we know that exercise is good for preventing diabetes and heart disease, and certain dietary factors such as higher amounts of fruits and vegetables are beneficial for reducing risk of cardiovascular disease, but we really don't know what are the metabolic processes or the metabolic pathways underlying those relationships."

Hu said there had been, over a decade, a paradigm shift from black box epidemiology to systems epidemiology. This approach includes gathering detailed data on diet, sleep, stress, and other factors, in order to better understand metabolic pathways that might lead to risk for disease.

He went on to deliver a fairly wonky talk that hit upon the interactions between metabolism and genetics, including the odd, inverse relationship between coffee drinking and the risk for type 2 diabetes. And he discussed the relationship between coffee and inflammation. (More coffee, even decaf, equals less inflammation.) One of Hu's papers showed that people with a genetic variant that predisposes them to slow caffeine metabolism consume less coffee than others.

It was easy for a layperson to get lost in the jargon. When Hu referred to that caffeine study as a GWAS (pronounced "gee-wahs"), he meant it is a genome-wide association study. And when he talked about "omics," he referred to the fast-growing biological studies of topics ending in that suffix. Genomics is, of course, the study of genetics in biology. Metabolomics was defined by Hu as "the systematic study of small-molecule metabolites in a biological sample under a given set of conditions."

Hu discussed the intake of BCAAs, which his research showed to be associated with a risk for type 2 diabetes. These branched-chain amino acids, such as leucine, isoleucine, and valine, are typically found in eggs, meat, and dairy products.

He talked about the benefits of plant-based foods in decreasing the risk of cardiovascular disease, which may be due to the polyphenols in beverages and foods such as coffee, red wine, tea, beans, blueberries, and citrus fruits.

Not only was the talk peppered with jargon; it was also academically rigorous. Hu mentioned one GWAS study published in *Nature* that found nearly 100 loci—specific genetic locations on chromosomes—associated with body mass index. But all of those loci combined explain less than 3 percent of BMI variation. This is where Hu pivoted to sodas. "It means that the population variation in BMI/obesity is largely influenced by environmental factors or perhaps gene/environment interactions," Hu said. Environmental factors include diet.

After the talk, Hu took questions. A Rutgers researcher asked if the recent decrease in sugar-sweetened beverages should result in a reduction in obesity. It's a question that the soda industry and its allies have asked extensively. The American Beverage Association's Susan Neely had often repeated it. Dr. Hu gave the sort of nuanced response often missing in the polarized conversations over the topic: "Obesity, of course, is a very complex phenotype; it's influenced by a lot of factors. And obesity has been increasing in the past several decades in both children and adults, and then has plateaued, in the past several recent years." Hu gestured with his left hand to show a horizontal line. "In some age groups, among children, the prevalence of childhood obesity has been decreasing." He gestured to a dropping line. "So what's the role of SSBs in the overall obesity trend? I think the decreasing consumption of SSBs should have some beneficial effects on the obesity trends. But, of course, the small reduction in sugar consumption is not going to completely reverse the obesity trend. It may help to stabilize the trend. Maybe in some age groups, it may help reduce the trend to some degree. But based on this kind of time-series data, it's hard to draw this kind of cause-effect relationship."

Hu left his audience with food for thought. Obesity is complex, he said, but the biggest contributors to obesity are simple. They are environmental factors, like diet and activity. And among those environmental factors, sugar-sweetened beverages played an outsized role.

31

In late May, the San Diego Convention Center was bustling with health and fitness experts. The occasion was the annual meeting of the American College of Sports Medicine, the world's largest sports medicine and exercise science organization.

Jim Hill, the University of Colorado obesity expert, delivered the keynote speech. He used the opportunity to introduce the Global Energy Balance Network. His white hair neat, glasses stylish but unobtrusive, sporting a yellow power tie and a blue blazer, Hill spoke from a lectern bearing a plaque reading, "World Congress on Exercise Is Medicine." Hill made the same points that he had made at the National Press Club event, a year and a half earlier.

The gist of his talk, again, was that the calories-out side of the equation deserves more attention. But he'd refined some of his talking points. To emphasize the role of tech-induced inactivity, he said, "I oftentimes say that Bill Gates is responsible for as much obesity as Ronald McDonald."

The ACSM had long and deep ties to soda. Two of its past presidents, Russell Pate and Steven Blair, were involved with the large Coca-Cola–funded study at the University of South Carolina, and had spoken forcefully on the corporation's behalf.

The San Diego conference was purportedly a health event, but the soda industry had its fingerprints all over it. It was not just soda's longtime role in funding the American College of Sports Medicine; the conference program also noted that Coca-Cola was a founding partner of Exercise Is Medicine.[1]

The event was the confluence of several streams of Coca-Cola funding, but hardly anyone knew it at the time. One person who understood this,

Greg Glassman, founder of the CrossFit fitness empire, was in the audience, seething at the soda links.

* * *

A couple of months after watching Jim Hill's talk in San Diego, CrossFit's Greg Glassman sounded off about the Global Energy Balance Network (GEBN) with a typically profane tweet: "@CocaCola's @gebnetwk trolls for 'scientists' to make a case for hiding metabolic syndrome w/ exercise. Watch @ACSMNews suck the soda tit!" Then he added this to the tweet: "@EIMNews is the lobbying arm of a deadly idea, @gebnetwk. Such @ CocaCola projects aim to silence all who warn about sugar. #CrossFit."

A self-made millionaire, opinionated and unfiltered, Glassman had become a prominent soda industry critic. Partly it was his anti-sugar, low-carb, dietary stance. And partly it was a longtime feud with the ACSM and the National Strength and Conditioning Association, another mainstream fitness group. Glassman felt both had been working to stymie his fast-growing fitness company, and were aligned with and funded by Coke and Pepsi.[2]

In his tweet, CrossFit was taking on not just Coca-Cola but also the ACSM and Exercise Is Medicine (EIM), its partnership with Coke. It wasn't a big deal, really. It was retweeted just fourteen times. But the tweets were the first public shots across the bow of Coca-Cola's Global Energy Balance Network.

Meanwhile, Glassman and his CrossFit team were taking their soda critiques directly to their network of fitness aficionados. In mid-July, at the District CrossFit gym in DC, several dozen athletes watched from folding chairs as Glassman worked a whiteboard like a professor.[3] The subject was arcane: a bill passed by the District of Columbia to require the licensing of personal trainers.

The whiteboard soon became cluttered. The top line read "District licensure bill." Below that was a confusing array of shorthand and acronyms. There was NSCA [National Strength and Conditioning Association] and ACSM [American College of Sports Medicine], Glassman's longtime foes. Beneath that, GEBN/EIM [Global Energy Balance Network/Exercise is Medicine]. At the very bottom of the whiteboard, Glassman had written: "Diabetes (I know the difference, Nick)."

The latter referred to another Twitter dustup from that summer. In a very in-your-face move, he had tweeted an image of a Coke bottle. But instead of the corporate phrase "Open Happiness," the image read "Open Diabetes." If that was not confrontational enough, he wrote, "Make sure you pour some out for your dead homies."

The tweet caused a brief firestorm. Especially when representatives of the type 1 diabetes community criticized Glassman for not being specific about referring to type 2 diabetes, the kind that is associated with the consumption of sugar-sweetened beverages. The pop star Nick Jonas was among them. "This is not cool," Jonas tweeted. "Please know and understand the difference between type one and type [two] diabetes before making ignorant comments. Sensitivity to all diseases, and proper education on the cause and day to day battle is important."

A *Good Morning America* producer contacted CrossFit with this request: "We're doing a story tomorrow on recent Twitter interactions between CrossFit and singer Nick Jonas on the issue of diabetes, including his response to your tweet. . . . We'd like to obtain a comment from CrossFit that we can use in our story commenting on the Twitter interaction for a piece that's airing on the show tomorrow."

Glassman replied directly to the producer:

> Hi, Matt,
>
> Fuck Nick Jonas.
>
> This is about the scourge of Type 2 Diabetes and its underlying causes. His sponsor, Coca-Cola, is a significant contributor to the diabetes epidemic both with product and "marketing" spend.
>
> Greg Glassman CEO
> CrossFit Inc.

The ABC report used the latter half of the statement, but referred to the rest of it rather delicately: "The rest of Glassman's statement was so aggressive," ABC reported, "it was not suitable for print." In response, Jonas and Coca-Cola denied any relationship. And a Coca-Cola spokesperson touted its efforts to improve health, through the Clinton-affiliated Alliance for a Healthier Generation.

At District CrossFit, you definitely needed the whiteboard to follow along, but the nut of Glassman's talk was simple: a cabal of mainstream fitness groups were out to destroy CrossFit. "They want oversight," he told the CrossFitters. "They want to control you, license you, regulate you." To an outsider, it might have seemed altogether paranoid. What might any of these organizations and food corporations want to do with CrossFit? An organized effort by a government agency to take over the business of fitness?

Glassman walked through the items, one by one.[4] "Exercise is Medicine, that's another soda thing," he said. "Guess what its first aim is—so you wonder, does soda want to get you?—guess what its number-one stated goal is. The licensure of trainers. Now why does soda give a fuck about whether trainers are licensed or not? I'll tell you why. Because they want to separate them. And they want to legally separate them. They want to get the ones that, like, 'It's all exercise,' and won't talk about the soda. And then get the ones like you that are going to say 'It's the sugar.' They want to make what you do illegal. It will be. See, this is Coke and Pepsi again," he said, tapping the whiteboard. "You have to understand that when exercise is medicine, what happens in here will then be medical malpractice."

As Glassman wrote on the whiteboard, he occasionally checked facts with Russ Greene, sitting off to his side, likely the only person in the room who understood the whole diagram. A CrossFit employee, Greene had been blogging prodigiously about the soda industry's influence on the mainstream fitness organizations that were CrossFit's competitors.[5] He took to the task with the aggressiveness of a pit bull and the rigor of an investigative journalist.

Glassman developed momentum, striding back and forth in his favorite camo Henry's Coffee ball cap, worn backward, and a pair of faded jeans. "You feel it? Put your hand up and show me if you're hearing what I'm saying," Glassman said, holding his hand high, revealing the sweat ring on his turquoise tee shirt. "Is anyone pissed? Alright, you oughta be. I mean what they want—whatever you used to do, they want you to go back to doing that."

Walking back to the whiteboard, he tapped the letters ACSM. "And they are perfectly willing to require that you employ some asshole from this organization and pay her to stand over there in the corner and watch you and report, 'He's talking that anti-sugar stuff again. Unh, unh, unh, Global Energy Balance Network, you know that he's just not exercising enough,'" Glassman said.

Taken as a whole, it shaped the outlines of a crazy plot. And Glassman's conspiracy theories and shoot-from-the-hip tweets would, in five years, contribute to his downfall. But the scheme Glassman was detailing—Coca-Cola's orchestration of the Global Energy Balance Network—would soon be validated by the mainstream media.

32

In early August, John Peters, a University of Colorado colleague of James Hill, was getting nervous. The *New York Times* was planning to publish a story on the Global Energy Balance Network. Peters emailed his friend Alex Malaspina, the former Coca-Cola executive who founded ILSI:

> This note is to alert you to a New York Times article that will be appearing either this week or next discussing GEBN and its connection to Coca Cola. The author, a reporter named Anahad O'Connor, has been talking to the Canadian blogger, Yoni Freedhoff, a well-known critic of industry and of anyone who associates with industry and has put together a story that we think will try to make the case that GEBN is nothing more than a defensive front for Coke. Both Jim Hill and Steve Blair have talked to the reporter and told him who we are and what we do . . . but, as you know in this day and age that will likely have little impact on what the story says. We won't really know what we may have to deal with until the story appears and we will share it once it is published. Anyway, we just wanted to keep you in the loop so there are no surprises if this story gets picked up and widely disseminated.[1]

Malaspina urged Peters to let the Coca-Cola executives Ed Hays and Clyde Tuggle know about the story. And Peters replied cryptically, "They are aware."

Malaspina was busy that same day, trying to help Coca-Cola on another front. He wrote an email to his old friend Mike Taylor, the deputy commissioner at the FDA, requesting he convene an "FDA Roundtable on Pseudo Science."[2] In a familiar tone, Malaspina said such an event "would be so important in FDA bringing good science to the table and as a result help people make the proper choices in such critical health issues." Malaspina attached a memo prepared by Kirsten Witt, one of Coca-Cola's senior public relations staffers.

Witt's memo referenced worries about vaccines and scares about consumer products driven by celebrities like the Food Babe and Dr. Oz. Witt said such scares "have created a window of opportunity to drive an important message about the pervasiveness of pseudo-science and the unintended consequences it creates among consumers who now fear perfectly safe and beneficial products." Witt proposed this strategy: "To help propel this conversation further we recommend FDA chair roundtable discussions on the topic of junk science and the erosion of consumer confidence with the goal being to introduce the issue, provoke conversation and a desire for solutions among thought leaders, as well as subsequent media coverage and social conversation."

Witt suggested that such a roundtable on pseudoscience include experts on health care, food policy, and nutrition science, as well as academics and journalists. The takeaway? "Ultimately these discussions will help establish the chorus of voices needed to restore balance to the conversation and improve consumer confidence," said Witt.

Like the journalism conferences that Coca-Cola organized through James Hill and the University of Colorado, Witt's proposal underscored something important to the corporation. Although it is a past master at taking its message directly to the consumer through terrific advertising, it is also extremely interested in channeling its messages through mainstream journalists.

There is no indication that Taylor took the bait. Witt and her team would have far bigger fish to fry in just a few days, when they would not be lecturing others about journalist integrity but defending themselves against accusations of pseudoscience. Still, the whole Global Energy Balance Network team was hoping for the best, as the *New York Times* exposé was imminent.

"Perhaps it will be a busy news day and this non-story won't get much attention," Peters wrote Malaspina; "we'll see."

33

The *New York Times* headline on August 10 was dramatic: "Coca-Cola Funds Effort to Alter Obesity Battle." And the front-page scoop by Anahad O'Connor was powerful: "The beverage giant has teamed up with influential scientists who are advancing this message in medical journals, at conferences and through social media," wrote O'Connor. "To help the scientists get the word out, Coke has provided financial and logistical support to a new nonprofit organization called the Global Energy Balance Network, which promotes the argument that weight-conscious Americans are overly fixated on how much they eat and drink while not paying enough attention to exercise."[1] O'Connor reported that the Global Energy Balance Network was rooted in $1.5 million of undisclosed funding from Coca-Cola.

O'Connor had been tipped off to the network's Coca-Cola funding by the Canadian doctor Yoni Freedhoff, an expert on obesity. The Coca-Cola team had been worried about the story since O'Connor requested an interview in May. To Coca-Cola's dismay, the story was not overlooked on a "busy news day," as John Peters had hoped. Instead, the fallout from O'Connor's piece was swift and powerful.

Longtime soda critic Michael Jacobson wrote a letter to the editor calling the Global Energy Balance Network "scientific nonsense." It was co-signed by Walter Willett of the Harvard T. H. Chan School of Public Health, along with thirty-four other researchers, academics, and advocates.

The *New York Times* followed up with an editorial. It noted that the network, which promised to deliver unbiased science, would likely not. It cited an analysis in *PLOS Medicine* that found that "studies financed by Coca-Cola, PepsiCo, the American Beverage Association and the sugar industry were five times more likely to find no link between sugary drinks and weight gain than studies reporting no industry sponsorship or financial conflicts of interest."[2] Within just a few days, Coca-Cola had gone from being a corporation that hoped to host a journalistic roundtable on pseudoscience to being the exemplar of the practice.

Coca-Cola CEO Muhtar Kent was aware of the network's efforts. After all, only a year earlier he had been working with Rhona Applebaum to get Jim Hill a slot on Charlie Rose's CBS show. But Kent did not defend the program. Instead, he penned a very public apology in the *Wall Street Journal*, promising, "We'll do better." He wrote, "I am disappointed that some actions we have taken to fund scientific research and health and well-being programs have served only to create more confusion and mistrust. I know our company can do a better job engaging both the public-health and scientific communities—and we will."[3]

Coca-Cola soon launched a transparency website, in an effort to disclose its health research and partnerships. It listed a total of $119 million doled out, over five years. The usual suspects were prominent. The University of Toronto soda ally John Sievenpiper alone was credited with receiving $273,000.[4]

The list would be an embarrassment for many in the health sciences, including the American College of Sports Medicine. This is the nonprofit that collaborated with Coke to found Exercise Is Medicine. The ACSM preemptively notified its members: "It has come to our attention that, in response to recent news, The Coca-Cola Company will soon publicly disclose the health and well-being partnerships it has recently funded."

Coca-Cola had funded ACSM with $865,000. And Steven Blair—the University of South Carolina cofounder of the Global Energy Balance Network—had been awarded more than $4 million in funding.

The exposé took many by surprise, but not the CrossFit blogger Russ Greene. He noted that Blair had also once served as the president of ACSM and was on the advisory board of Exercise Is Medicine. "So if we add Blair's total to the previous number," Greene wrote in a blog post, "Coca-Cola has paid ACSM and its officials at least $6,342,000 in the past five years." And, presciently, Greene noted that Coca-Cola had omitted a significant amount of funding from the list.

For more than a year, Greene had been writing about soda-funded corruption of the health sciences. At first it had seemed an improbable bit of collusion. But with the exposé of the network, it began to look as though he had not overstated the degree of the problem, and may even have underestimated it.

* * *

Even as Americans were absorbing the news about Coca-Cola's $119 million campaign of obfuscation, more mainstream health organizations were raising concerns about sodas. In September, it was the American College of Cardiology's turn.

The organization issued a statement reading, "There is compelling evidence that drinking too many sugar-sweetened beverages, which contain added sugars in the form of high-fructose corn syrup or table sugar (sucrose), can lead to excess weight gain and a greater risk of developing type 2 diabetes and cardiovascular disease."

The statement referred to a new paper by Frank Hu and his Harvard colleague Vasanti Malik.[5] Published in the *Journal of the American College of Cardiology*, the paper reviewed the scientific literature about sugar-sweetened beverages and health. Hu and Malik considered the available evidence and paid particularly close attention to the metabolism of fructose. They found the evidence was stacking up: "On the basis of available evidence from high-quality observational studies and experimental trials of risk markers, we conclude that consumption of SSBs causes excess weight gain and is associated with increased risk of type 2 diabetes and CVD [cardiovascular disease]; thus, these beverages are unique dietary contributors to obesity and related chronic diseases."

That phrase was notable: "*these beverages are unique dietary contributors.*" This was something that had become increasingly clear to Hu over more than ten years of research in the area. Some dietary items are particularly pernicious. Trans fats are one. Sugar-sweetened beverages are another. "Although reducing consumption of SSBs or added sugar alone is unlikely to solve the obesity epidemic entirely," Hu and Malik concluded, "limiting intake is one simple change that will have a measurable effect on weight control and prevention of cardiometabolic diseases."

34

Following the *New York Times* exposé, the Coca-Cola's Global Energy Balance Network unraveled strand by strand. Coca-Cola had originally claimed that it did not control the group's research and publications. But Associated Press reporter Candice Choi uncovered more emails, making it clear that Coca-Cola designed and controlled every aspect of the group and even exerted influence over the research.

CEO Muhtar Kent, who had already apologized in the *Wall Street Journal*, expressed more contrition still. Kent told Choi, "It has become clear to us that there was not a sufficient level of transparency with regard to the company's involvement with the Global Energy Balance Network. . . . Clearly we have more work to do to reflect the values of this great company in all that we do."[1]

The network disbanded. The University of Colorado returned $1 million in research funds to Coca-Cola. Organizations like the Academy of Nutrition and Dietetics and the American Academy of Pediatrics stopped accepting Coca-Cola's money. The University of South Carolina, on the other hand, opted to keep $500,000 of Coca-Cola money.

In addition, the emails showed that Coca-Cola's millions had bought undying loyalty, even from obesity experts. In a note to Coke, Jim Hill had written, "It is not fair that Coca-Cola is signaled out as the #1 villain in the obesity world, but that is the situation and makes this your issue whether you like it or not. I want to help your company avoid the image of being a problem in peoples' lives and back to being a company that brings important and fun things to them."

US Right to Know, a nonprofit that did yeoman's work in finding documents through Freedom of Information Act (FOIA) requests, pointed out how effectively Rhona Applebaum's network had used journalists. The organization listed thirty articles that quoted Blair and Hill after they received funds from Coca-Cola, but without citing the relationship. Some were by known Coca-Cola allies such as Trevor Butterworth, but others were by mainstream journalists with some of the nation's largest media outlets: the *Boston Globe*, the *Los Angeles Times*, NPR, the *New York Times*, and the *Washington Post*.

Another consequence of the *Times* exposé is that Applebaum became the public face of pseudoscience. She soon tendered her resignation to Coca-Cola, the inglorious end to a once-impressive career.

But even in the nadir of her career, one organization heaped praise on Applebaum. And it was an organization that earnestly promoted solid science and proudly claimed to fight conflicts of interest: the International Life Sciences Institute. "Dr. Applebaum has been involved with ILSI for over three decades," its December newsletter read. "As ILSI President, she has been especially focused on encouraging and helping ILSI improve its public outreach program. Please join us in thanking Dr. Applebaum for volunteering her time and energy to the organization. We greatly appreciate her commitment." The reason ILSI led its December newsletter with "A Special Thank You to Rhona Applebaum" was because she was stepping away from that organization, too. She relinquished her post as president after less than a year, and resigned from the board of directors.

* * *

In the months after the Global Energy Balance Network was exposed as a Coca-Cola front group, the consequences continued to mount.

Jim Hill left his post as executive director of the University of Colorado's Anschutz Health and Wellness Center amid a steady stream of news about his links to Coca-Cola. "A University of Colorado professor who launched a global campaign to fight obesity accepted $550,000 from the Coca-Cola Co., travels the world at company expense on speaking engagements and solicited a job at the soft drink giant for his son," the *Denver Post* reported in late December.[2]

In March 2016, Coca-Cola released a six-month update to its transparency website. In its initial transparency disclosure in September, it said it had spent $119 million on research, health experts, and health programs from 2010 to 2015. Now it said the number was substantially higher: $133 million. The corporation had omitted fully $14 million from the first tally.

At its headquarters in Atlanta, Coca-Cola closely monitors media notices from all over the world. At this moment, Coca-Cola was primarily worried about the public perception of the transparency update. "As follow up to our earlier inform, the six-month update to the U.S. transparency site continues to generate minimal traction in mainstream and social media. A full coverage report is attached," Kirsten Witt Webb wrote to her colleagues.[3] "As of this afternoon, only the Associated Press (Candice Choi), FORTUNE and Consumerist had filed reports. FORTUNE did not contact us but based its piece on the AP story and also pulled a Sandy Douglas quote from our transparency site. Food Dive updated a prior story. *New York Times* reporter Anahad O'Connor told us he does not plan to write."

Webb's assessment was accurate. While Coca-Cola's initial announcement on transparency generated a lot of ink in mainstream media, which was then tweeted and shared on Facebook, the six-month follow-up was quiet indeed.

Webb paid close attention to social media. "Both Anahad and Candice tweeted; however, neither tweet gained much traction (3 and 5 re-tweets, respectively)," she wrote. "Due to coincidental timing of reports about Dr. Jim Hill stepping down from the University of Colorado's wellness center, there was related coverage by AP [Associated Press], Denver Post, and The Chronicle of Higher Education. Also, the Denver Post Editorial Board re-posted an op-ed from December 31. Coverage is neutral and factual. No third-party critics are quoted. Together, the transparency update and the University of Colorado stories generated a relatively low-volume ~650 total shares in social media (~450 for transparency, and ~200 for Dr. Hill)."

And in better news for the corporation, public interest in the story seemed to be waning. "By comparison," Webb wrote, "our September 22,

2015 transparency site launch generated about 2,000 social media shares and 200 mainstream media stories."

Coca-Cola was effectively moving beyond the story. It had tossed a few people under the bus in the process—notably, Rhona Applebaum and Jim Hill. Alex Malaspina got off unscathed, though. That was because he had no post to resign. He had been a minister without portfolio, a convenient connector for Coca-Cola and for ILSI. A link, per his long-term vision, between Coca-Cola, academic researchers, and federal regulators at the CDC and FDA.

III

ASTROTURF AND TAXES

35

Throughout the fall of 2014, on street corners in San Francisco, the citizens rose up to protest. Black, brown, Asian, and white, bearing placards in three languages, they responded vigorously as an organizer shouted into a megaphone: "What do we want?" "An affordable city!" "When do we want it?" "Now!"[1]

The target of the protests was a proposed soda tax. The protesters were earnest. They were concerned. They hoped the City of San Francisco would not shift greater tax burdens onto their shoulders. They called themselves the Coalition for an Affordable City, and they marched, waved signs, and shouted.

The coalition was pure astroturf, funded by $9 million from the American Beverage Association. ABC's *Nightline* produced an exposé that aired just before Election Day. The reporters found ads on Craigslist offering $13 per hour to join the protests. They found that at least one business listed as supporting the protest, Joe's Cable Car Burger Joint, had been boarded up for months.

The soda industry already had some practice in these matters. When New York State governor David Paterson had proposed a soda tax in 2009, the industry hired the public relations firm Goddard Claussen. The firm formed New Yorkers against Unfair Taxes, another front group, to oppose the measure, which they succeeded in killing.[2] The San Francisco tax was also defeated, despite the *Nightline* exposé.

The Coalition for an Affordable City was funded by the American Beverage Association, and Coca-Cola is the ABA's top funder. But Coca-Cola's fingerprints were not on the body of the dead tax. The double-front-group strategy—Coca-Cola money laundered through two nonprofits—had succeeded.

A few years later, Coke and its allies would develop a strategy to fight soda taxes in California so obtuse and cynical, and yet so effective, it would make this one appear relatively transparent.

* * *

Taxes were a growing part of the soda-policy conversation the following year, and in late May of 2015, Coca-Cola's Ryan Guthrie had an urgent message for his team: "The Washington correspondent for Cox Media, the parent company of the AJC [*Atlanta Journal-Constitution*], posted a story today on the call for a beverage tax in the 2015 Dietary Guidelines Advisory Committee's report," Guthrie wrote in an email. "The story includes a quote from CSPI's Jim O'Hara and ABA's statement. It references both the Berkeley beverage tax and the failed Bloomberg size restriction. The author implies that a beverage tax recommendation is a certainty when the final guidelines come out. This is not the case. While the 2015 Dietary Guidelines Advisory Committee's report, released earlier this year, made the policy recommendation to tax beverages, USDA officials have publicly commented that the USDA and HHS [Health and Human Services] will stick to the statutory parameters in developing the Dietary Guidelines. Policy recommendations such as a soda tax are considered outside the scope of the agencies' mandate."[3]

What did Coca-Cola intend to do about this threat of taxes? Guthrie had assurances: "The DC team continues to execute a robust campaign with Congress and the agencies to ensure that policy recommendation on a soda tax is not included in the final guidelines." When the final guidelines were released the following year, sure enough, there was no mention of a soda tax. And the strong recommendations from Frank Hu and his colleagues to take specific action on sodas were diluted to reference sugar, more broadly.

The DC team's robust campaign had proven effective, but soda taxes would not go away quietly.

* * *

The following spring, Capricia Marshall was on a train to New York when she got a disturbing email. Marshall had worked as an assistant to First Lady Hillary Clinton, and in the State Department. Now, in April 2016, she was a constant companion to Clinton on the campaign trail as Clinton vied to clinch the nomination for Democratic presidential candidate.[4] Marshall was also a consultant to Coca-Cola.

The problem began a few days before, when Clinton had expressed support for a 3-cent-per-ounce soda tax proposed by Philadelphia mayor Jim Kenney. "I'm very supportive of the mayor's proposal to tax soda to get universal pre-school for kids," Clinton said at a forum.

When Susan Neely of the American Beverage Association heard about this, she emailed her colleagues at Coca-Cola: "Ouch. Our local team in Philly isn't worried about the impact there, but it makes me irritated. Seems totally unnecessary." Coca-Cola's Katherine Rumbaugh replied, "WTF—this seems completely random."

As the news rose up the corporate organization chart, the anger increased. Coca-Cola executive Clyde Tuggle was worrying about how chairman and CEO Muhtar Kent would take the news. Tuggle emailed Marshall to say, "Really??? After all we have done. I hope this has been falsely reported. Pls give me some talking points for Muhtar in the a.m." Riding on the train, Marshall emailed Sara Latham, another Coca-Cola consultant and a senior advisor to the Clinton campaign. "Are you looking at this, and I should sit tight?"

"Yep," Latham replied. "I'll look into this morn, so don't ask HRC —yet . . . ;-)"

Another Coca-Cola executive, Matt Echols, tried to assuage corporate concerns, noting, "Outreach is being made to Secretary Clinton's campaign at the highest levels to clarify."

Beyond the two advisors who were also paid by Coca-Cola, there was yet another indication of the close connections between the corporation and the Clinton campaign. Just a month earlier, Clinton campaign manager John Podesta had included Kent in a long list of possible running mates.

By that evening, Coca-Cola and the American Beverage Association were breathing easier. The campaign insiders had smoothed things over.

Rumbaugh wrote to her Coca-Cola colleagues:

The HRC campaign leadership was caught unaware of the comments about the beverage tax. It was not part of the agenda or planned comments, not part of the policy brief. Here is an end-of-day update on our actions and next steps:

Worked together with campaign comms team to keep story to one day and requested outreach to Mayor with same objective. We also worked to keep GOP from picking up the ball and carrying forward, potentially generating more media. From campaign policy team we have the understanding that this is not a part of the campaign policy agenda and will not be pushed further.

But even that was not enough for Coca-Cola. Rumbaugh said the Clinton campaign would be further "walking this back." Rumbaugh also noted her glee from an unlikely quarter. Senator Bernie Sanders, then battling Clinton for the Democratic presidential nomination, criticized Clinton over the tax. "Frankly, I am very surprised that Secretary Clinton would support this regressive tax after pledging not to raise taxes on anyone making less than $250,000," Sanders said at a rally in Reading. "This proposal clearly violates her pledge. A tax on soda and juice drinks would disproportionately increase taxes on low-income families in Philadelphia."

"I couldn't have said it better myself," said Rumbaugh, wrapping up a long day of damage control.

* * *

Throughout that spring of 2016, Philadelphia mayor Jim Kenney had been pushing his soda tax proposal. Although the tax would improve the health of city residents by reducing their sugar consumption, Kenney focused his efforts on another benefit of the tax: it would provide sorely needed funding for public education.

Some residents had taken Bernie Sanders's view, that the tax would be regressive, because the impacts would be borne disproportionately by lower-income residents. But others pointed out that benefits, too, would accrue to low-income residents.

Kenney, a hardscrabble politician raised in a South Philly row house, fought hard for the proposal. And his campaign attracted some high-profile support. Former New York mayor Michael Bloomberg, whose ban on supersize sodas had failed, kicked in $1.6 million. And Kenney had even had that fleeting statement of support from Hillary Clinton.

But the opposition was fierce. The soda industry spent more than $4 million trying to defeat the proposal. As an indication of the industry's savvy, it had killed a similar tax proposed in 2010 by bartering a $10 million donation to a children's hospital.[5]

On June 16, the city council approved the ordinance. Along the way, Kenney had lowered the tax from 3 cents per ounce to 1.5 cents per ounce. Still, it was a major victory.

And Kenney joined a select club. Although Mexico had passed a soda tax in 2014, dozens of American cities had attempted to pass soda taxes, but only Berkeley had succeeded. Most had been shot down, like the effort in San Francisco that triggered the formation of the astroturf group.

Public health advocates thought the tax might portend a watershed. For Coca-Cola and the American Beverage Association, the tax portended something else: a direct threat to their business model, worth billions of dollars annually.

* * *

Public support for soda taxes grew over the coming months, and both sides waged fierce campaigns. The American Beverage Association had noted Senator Bernie Sanders's position on the Philadelphia tax, and began using his name in ads opposing taxes proposed for San Francisco and Oakland. Sanders pushed back, and sent the ABA a cease-and-desist letter in early October. "I have not taken any position on those ballot items," Sanders said in a statement, "and I have asked the American Beverage Association to stop using my name in connection with this misleading advertising."[6]

November 8 turned out to be a very bad day for the soda corporations, best summed up in the headline over the Bloomberg News wire story: "Coca-Cola, Pepsi Hit with Wave of Taxes as Cities Punish Soda."[7] Voters in San Francisco, Oakland, and Albany, California, and Boulder, Colorado, had approved soda taxes. It was a watershed for soda taxes, a moment of critical mass.

In opposing the taxes, the beverage industry had used the same tactics that had served it well before—organizing a slew of new organizations, all designed to sound like homegrown, mom-and-pop grassroots operations.

But this time the beverage industry lost, despite the American Beverage Association's $38 million in opposition spending.[8]

Seeing the mainstreaming of soda taxes, industry executives worried that more would soon follow, causing soda consumption to fall further. Coca-Cola and its allies in the American Beverage Association began developing a plan to head future taxes off at the pass, starting with California.

36

California governor Jerry Brown stood by the elegant staircase in the governor's mansion, its hardwood floors shining, paintings in gilt frames on the walls. It was June 6, 2018, a year and a half after a handful of cities approved soda taxes. Brown was surrounded by ten dinner guests, the men in business suits, the women in neat dresses. The guests wore unrestrained, ear-to-ear grins. But Brown and his wife, Anne Gust, wore the sort of forced half smiles associated with hostage videos.[1]

The guests had every reason to smile. They were executives from Coca-Cola, Pepsi, and the American Beverage Association, and they had convinced the governor to support legislation preventing any municipality in California from enacting a new soda tax until 2030. This was a major victory for Coca-Cola, and a huge setback for California's public health community. And it was part of a long game, you might say, or a long con.

Starting in April, earnest canvassers had fanned out all across California, hustling to gather enough signatures to place an initiative question on the November ballot. The initiative would have changed state law to require any municipality to get the approval of two-thirds of voters before implementing any local tax change. It would be hard not to want to sign the petitions, given the campaign's name: Californians for Accountability and Transparency in Government Spending, Sponsored by California Businesses.

But this anodyne-sounding campaign was funded by Coca-Cola and Pepsi, through the American Beverage Association. The soda industry spent more than $8 million on the project.[2] The beverage companies had specifically designed this measure in the most shrewd, or cynical, manner imaginable, depending on whose side you were on. Whatever interest

Coca-Cola had in the stated aims of the initiative, it was more interested in crafting something so abhorrent to municipalities and unions that California lawmakers would do anything to make it go away.

When Coca-Cola and its allies had the signatures in hand, they went to Sacramento, ready to negotiate. That's when they joined Governor Jerry Brown at the governor's mansion for a meal. (Though Brown's spokesperson said they did not discuss the initiative.)

The beverage companies knew that legislators hated this measure, so they swung a deal. We'll withdraw the initiative, they said, in exchange for a law banning new taxes on groceries, including sodas, through 2030. Legislators pushed that bill through as a rider on a budget bill in late June.[3]

This strategy of banning new taxes statewide is known as preemption, because it preempts the possibility of local taxes. Some legislators called it extortion. "In a truly vile move, the soda industry aimed a nuclear weapon at CA by funding a ballot measure to make it nearly impossible for cities to raise revenue," said state senator Scott Wiener. "The ransom to withdraw the measure? Requiring the Legislature to pass a 12-year ban on new local soda taxes to protect health."

In a series of tweets, he wrote, "To be very clear: The soda corporations—Coca Cola, Pepsi, Snapple, Red Bull—are now a rogue industry. They're willing to burn down the house to protect their bottom line & ability to sell dangerous products that give kids diabetes." He encouraged Californians to direct their anger not at the legislature but at the soda industry. It was not Wiener's first fight with soda. As a member of the San Francisco Board of Supervisors, he had advocated for health warnings on soda ads, which, as we'll see later, wound up in court.

But not all legislators were so outraged. Assemblyman Matthew Harper, a Republican from Huntington Beach, conspicuously sipped a soda, through a straw, during the floor debate. His beverage of choice? A Coca-Cola, of course, in the classic twelve-ounce can.

To the beverage industry, the preemption campaign was a bargain. It had spent more than $30 million to oppose local soda taxes in 2016 alone and could not afford to fight each brushfire as it ignited. Already eight cities across the United States had implemented soda taxes, including four in California. And the taxes were having their intended effect—reducing soda consumption and raising money for public health initiatives.

Laura Schmidt, a professor of health policy at the UCSF School of Medicine, noted in a 2019 paper that the soda industry took its preemption cues from tobacco.[4] Starting in the 1980s, the tobacco industry embarked on campaigns to encourage unified state smoking regulations, instead of patchwork local regulations. "As of 2018," Schmidt wrote, "25 states have enacted state laws that preempt tobacco regulation at the local level."

The gun industry had followed tobacco's lead on preemption, and then came soda. Other states were following California's lead—Arizona, Michigan, and Washington also preempted soda taxes by 2018.

In addition to the California preemption campaign, the soda industry scored another coup in June. After expressing strong support for significant soda taxes, particularly through its former director general Margaret Chan, a WHO panel backed off on plans to recommend soda taxes. The fly in the ointment was the United States, specifically panel member Eric Hargan, appointed by President Trump to serve as deputy secretary for Health and Human Services (HHS). "Deputy Secretary Hargan opposed endorsing increasing taxes on sugary drinks in the commission report," HHS spokesperson Caitlin Oakley told the Associated Press. Oakley said there was not enough evidence that the taxes were beneficial.[5]

The International Food and Beverage Alliance, the global corollary to the American Beverage Association, praised the decision.

37

With concerns growing about sugar-sweetened beverages, the World Health Organization was playing an ever-greater role in the debate. In March 2015, WHO had released its sugar guidelines, which greatly disappointed the soda industry. "A new WHO guideline recommends adults and children reduce their daily intake of free sugars to less than 10% of their total energy intake," the WHO advised. "A further reduction to below 5% or roughly 25 grams (6 teaspoons) per day would provide additional health benefits."

The WHO guideline was similar to the recommendations issued four months earlier by the Dietary Guidelines Advisory Committee, which also advised limiting added sugars to 10 percent of total calories.[1] The report and an accompanying press release specifically singled out sodas for criticism. "A single can of sugar-sweetened soda contains up to 40 grams (around 10 teaspoons) of free sugars," it said.

Meanwhile, WHO director Margaret Chan became a high-profile voice supporting soda taxes. This set off a frantic bout of conversations among Coca-Cola and its allies. Correspondence from June 2015 shows that the Coca-Cola team had hoped that the Global Energy Balance Network, then at its apex, or an ally at the Centers for Disease Control could provide an antidote.

Alex Malaspina, the former Coca-Cola staffer and founder of the International Life Sciences Institute, concerned by the anti-soda position of the WHO, began emailing his colleagues: "Please see report on WHO. This is getting a lot of publicity. We must find a way of some one such as a famous scientist arrange to pay her a visit. May be Jim Hill or some one of similar stature or a US Government scientist."[2]

Beyond endorsing Hill to carry water for Coca-Cola, Malaspina recounted his access to the former directors general of the WHO, when he was leading ILSI, in a series of anecdotes that provide a glimpse of how effectively ILSI had infiltrated health organizations—not only on behalf of the soda industry, but also on behalf of genetically modified organisms (GMOs). "As the President of ILSI I had a special and productive luncheon with the former DG Dr. Nakajima in 1995 at his private dining room in the WHO Geneva Headqurters [*sic*] to tell him about ILSI and how the two organizations could work with each other," Malaspina wrote. "In 1999 I visited with the new DG Mrs. Brutland in Geneva, when I invited her on behalf of The World Economic Forum, to come to the Davos meeting of 1999, and be the Keynote Speaker at the Food Governors special dinner, where she discussed that GMO foods are not only safe but could be very useful in feeding a hungry world. By the way, the future Coke President, Mr. Neville Isdell attended that dinner with me."

But mostly, Malaspina was focused on protecting the interests of Coca-Cola from the possibility of soda taxes. "In summary I am suggesting that collectively we must find a way to start a dialogue with Dr. Chen [*sic*]," he wrote. "If not, she will continue to blast us with significant negative consequences on a global basis. This threat to our business is serious, Warmest regards. Alex"

Jim Hill replied the same day:

> Alex,
>
> I agree that we need to do something to try and prevent WHO from taking a completely anti-food industry stance in the obesity field. This will not be easy given where Dr. Chen [*sic*] seems to be going. Maybe we could visit with her and explain about the Global Energy Balance Network and why we feel effective public-private partnerships are essential if we are going to solve the obesity problem.
>
> All the best
>
> Jim

Malaspina then roped Barbara Bowman, a high-ranking officer with the Centers for Disease Control, into the conversation. A series of emails the year before, when Malaspina was encouraging a dinner meeting for one of his Coca-Cola associates, showed how close the two were. In one email, Malaspina asked how Bowman was. She replied: "I'm doing well.

Am now the Director of the Division for Heart Disease and Stroke Prevention at CDC, our budget doubled this year to about $155 million. I cannot tell you how often I think of how much I learned from you at Coca-Cola, and how often I think to myself, 'How would Alex handle this.'"[3]

In another email exchange that year, Malaspina forwarded a news story about former Coca-Cola executive Donald Keough. Bowman replied, "Thank you for this. I read about it in today's paper. I will never forget meeting Mr. Keough as he walked through the employee cafeteria one day. He definitely inspired confidence among the ranks. I am very much looking forward to meeting you this evening."[4]

The messages made it clear that Bowman and Malaspina had a long-term relationship, forged as Coca-Cola coworkers and as friends. More interesting was that the person in charge of the CDC division dealing with critical aspects of chronic disease was a former Coca-Cola employee, who was still tight with Coca-Cola and ILSI—even as Coca-Cola was among the greatest dietary contributors to chronic disease.

Those chummy 2014 emails gave an appearance of foxes guarding the henhouse, if not actually anything untoward. But Bowman's replies to Malaspina's request for help with WHO raised red flags.

On June 26, 2015, Malaspina wrote, "Dear Barbara: How are you? Are you having a nice summer? Any ideas on how we can have a conversation with WHO? Now, they do not want to work with industry. Who finds all the new drugs. Not WHO but industry. She is influenced by the Chinese Govt and is against US. Something must be done. Warmest regards, Alex."

Bowman replied inside of an hour. "Am wondering if anyone with ISLI China, perhaps Madame Chen [Chen Junshi, of ILSI China], might have ideas. Another thought, perhaps someone with connection to the PEPFAR [the U.S. President's Emergency Plan for AIDS Relief] program. Or Gates and Bloomberg people, many have close connections with the WHO regional offices. Perhaps an issue of defining legacy."[5]

Malaspina replied the next day, in an email copied to Jim Hill and John Peters of the University of Colorado, several Coca-Cola executives including Clyde Tuggle, and ILSI staff and board members. "Dear Barbara, You gave me some very good leads. I like the one especially about having Mr. Bill Gates help. Our Chairman knows him well. I will explore this idea with Clyde [Tuggle]. We would want WHO to start working with ILSI again, with the GEBN, and with the food industry in general, to resolve issue of food safety and nutrition and for WHO to not only consider sugary foods as the only cause of obesity but to consider also the life style changes that have been occurring through out the Universe."

This string of emails looked worse. They were not just chummy. It was a federal public health official, charged with overseeing key aspects of chronic disease, advising Coke and ILSI on how to circumvent WHO policies designed to fight chronic disease. They would soon become a major headache for Bowman, a career-defining blunder.

* * *

These close ties between the Coca-Cola team and the Centers for Disease Control became public in June 2016. Carey Gillam of US Right to Know uncovered the details by poring through correspondence acquired through FOIA requests.

Gillam's article for HuffPost detailed the cozy relationship between the CDC and Coca-Cola.[6] More specifically, it noted the previous year's correspondence between Bowman and Malaspina, over WHO's stance on sugar. The emails certainly gave the appearance of conflict. Gillam wrote that it was not surprising that the soft drink industry was fighting back against the wave of anti-soda sentiment. "But what is surprising is one of the places where the beverage industry has sought, and apparently garnered, some help—from a top official with the Centers for Disease Control and Prevention, whose mission in part is to prevent obesity, diabetes, and other health problems," Gillam wrote. Bowman tendered her resignation from the CDC just after HuffPost published the story.

The Malaspina-Bowman correspondence was emblematic of Coca-Cola's deep ties to CDC. The agency is not headquartered in Washington, DC, as many might imagine. It is in Atlanta. Its Georgia roots can be traced to a disease of warm climes, malaria. The region was once "the heart of the malaria zone," according to the CDC. The agency started modestly in a small Atlanta building in 1946. The next year, a local entrepreneur and civic booster arranged for Emory University to sell fifteen acres of land to the fledgling agency. That is, to this day, its campus.[7]

The entrepreneur was Robert Woodruff, president of Coca-Cola. Woodruff already had deep ties to Emory, and the campus now feels like a memorial to late Coca-Cola executives. The business school is named after former CEO Roberto Goizueta. And the Robert W. Woodruff Library, one of several prominent buildings named for him, features a bronze statue of Woodruff smoking one of his beloved cigars.

The CDC and Coca-Cola have shared close links over the years. By one account, a 1960s regulatory conflict over the caffeine in Coca-Cola was resolved when President Lyndon Johnson tapped a CDC veteran who was a Coke ally to lead the FDA.[8] "Johnson was happy to consult with the Coca-Cola Company before making an appointment," Frederick Allen recounted in *Secret Formula*, "and in due course he picked James Goddard, an assistant surgeon general who happened to be the director of the Centers for Disease Control in Atlanta, where he was on friendly terms with several company officials."

The company remains proud of its founding connection and friendly ties to CDC. But by the time of the Bowman dustup, those friendly ties were chafing. A group of concerned CDC staffers, writing under the name CDC SPIDER (Scientists Preserving Integrity, Diligence and Ethics in Research), drafted a letter later that summer over ethical concerns at the agency.[9] "Another troubling issue at the NCCDPHP [National Center for Chronic Disease Prevention and Health Promotion] are the adventures of Drs. Barbara Bowman and Michael Pratt (also detailed in national media outlets)," the CDC employees wrote. Michael Pratt was a CDC staffer doing triple duty: he was also affiliated with Emory and with ILSI. "Both seemed to have irregular (if not questionable) relationships with Coca-Cola and ILSI representatives," the CDC employees' letter continued. "Neither organization added any value to the good work and science already underway at CDC. In fact, these ties have now called into question and undermined CDC's work. A cloud has been cast over the ethical and excellent work of scientists due to this wanton behavior. Was cultivating these relationships worth dragging CDC through the mud?"

After Bowman stepped down, her boss Ursula Bauer sent a memo to CDC staffers: "While the article appears to be fairly accurate, it omits an important fact that Alex Malaspina and Barbara Bowman are family friends of many years. It's not unusual for Barbara—or any of us—to correspond with others who have similar interests in our areas of work (nutrition, in this case)."[10] And she had an admonition for other staffers—to be careful not just about relationships with industry, but about putting such relationships in writing. "This blog serves as an important reminder of the old adage that if we don't want to see it on the front page of the newspaper then we shouldn't do it (or write it, in this case)," Bauer wrote. "That pertains to our work email and our personal email messages. With current technology, we have no control over where our messages end up."

38

As the World Health Organization guidelines on added sugars became more widely accepted and influential, a team of British researchers analyzed the text to see if it had been modified to satisfy the food industry. They found the guidelines were little changed, "despite strenuous efforts by industry to modify it."[1] Their assessment, published in May 2016, was a succinct review of strategies used by Coca-Cola and others in the sugar industry. "Many of the sugar industry's arguments were characteristic of denialism, which is widely practiced by the tobacco and alcohol industries to thwart effective public health interventions," they wrote. "The overarching strategy was to promote doubt and, thereby, undermine the case for changing the status quo."

The sugar industry had used several methods. David Stuckler and colleagues wrote:

> One was to attempt to confuse: the relationship between sugar and health outcomes was complicated by, for example, discussing different types of sugar and whether added or total sugar was more important. Another was to set unrealistic expectations for scientific research—the results of observational studies were discounted by arguing that confounding was "certain." . . . A third method was to divert attention to other risk factors, such as a lack of physical activity, which excused the sugar industry from responsibility. . . . A fourth method, which is widely used by the alcohol industry, was to shift attention from measures to reduce sugar consumption towards measures to avoid harm: for example, the prevention of dental caries by water fluoridation and the use of fluoride toothpaste.

Promote doubt. Suggest the science is shoddy. Divert attention elsewhere, say, to physical activity. And suggest Band-Aids for the harms. The decades-old strategy was familiar. The surprise was that it had not had its intended effect of influencing the WHO guidelines.

* * *

The National Academy of Medicine invited a high-profile public health expert to deliver the keynote address at its annual meeting in October 2016: Dr. Margaret Chan, director general of the World Health Organization. Chan's topic: "Obesity and Diabetes, the Slow-Motion Disaster." Her direct and powerful talk was the polar opposite of the address Jim Hill had delivered at the same academy just eighteen months earlier.[2] "Members of the National Academy of Medicine and your distinguished guests, ladies and gentlemen. The world has 800 million chronically hungry people, but it also has countries where more than 70% of the adult population is obese or overweight."

Chan noted that under-nutrition was the primary concern in developing countries until the late twentieth century. But the world now faced the entirely different crisis of obesity. It soon became clear why Coca-Cola allies like Alex Malaspina and Jim Hill had been worried enough about Chan to ask the CDC for help. "One of the strongest recommendations of the WHO Commission on Ending Childhood Obesity calls on governments to implement an effective tax on sugar-sweetened beverages," Chan said. "WHO recommends that, to be effective, a tax should increase the price by at least 20%."

There it was, a substantial soda tax, recommended by the head of the world's leading health organization. And Chan was not finished. She then took a jab at the myths that Coca-Cola and its allies had been spending millions of dollars each year to promote. "Ladies and gentlemen, I have a final comment," Chan said. "When crafting preventive strategies, government officials must recognize that the widespread occurrence of obesity and diabetes throughout a population is not a failure of individual willpower to resist fats and sweets or exercise more. It is a failure of political will to take on powerful economic operators, like the food and soda industries. If governments understand this duty, the fight against obesity and diabetes can be won. The interests of the public must be prioritized over those of corporations. Thank you."

39

If the Global Energy Balance Network fiasco had not already confirmed a broad, deep soda industry conspiracy, research published in October 2016 did.

A pair of Boston University researchers attempted to quantify the influence of Coke and Pepsi on national health policy. Their paper for the *American Journal of Preventive Medicine* surveyed records of philanthropy and health spending by soda companies from 2011 to 2015.[1]

The results were striking. Coca-Cola and Pepsi had sponsored at least ninety-six health organizations in those five years. Concurrently, the soda companies had lobbied against twenty-eight bills or regulatory proposals. This included legislation to restrict items that could be purchased with Supplemental Nutrition Assistance Program (SNAP) funds (food stamps), implement soda taxes, restrict advertising, and improve soda labeling. "In 28 of 29 cases (97%), the positions of the soda companies were antagonistic to public health," the authors wrote, "calling into question a sincere commitment to improving the public's health. By accepting funding from these companies, health organizations are inadvertently participating in their marketing plans."

They noted that the Academy of Nutrition and Dietetics had declined to support New York mayor Michael Bloomberg's effort to limit soda serving sizes, while taking hundreds of thousands of dollars from Coke. The NAACP was in the same boat. And Save the Children, a nonprofit that had previously supported soda taxes, flipped its position at the same time it accepted $5 million in donations from Coca-Cola and Pepsi.

Some of the recipients of soda funding were surprising, like the American Diabetes Association. Others were quite predictable, like ILSI, the

International Food Information Council, and the American Council on Science and Health, another industry front group. The spending was significant. Coca-Cola, the authors pointed out, was spending more than $6 million to influence health policy annually. Adding in spending by the American Beverage Association and Pepsi brought the total to $10 million annually. And the authors said they likely missed some soda spending. Although Coca-Cola had pledged to be transparent about such donations in the wake of the Global Energy Balance Network scandal, Pepsi had not.

Their conclusion cited the precedent of most health organizations refusing tobacco industry funds, suggesting they do the same with soda funding: "Leading the way in this effort are the Academy of Nutrition and Dietetics, the American Academy of Pediatrics, the American Academy of Family Physicians, and the American College of Cardiology, all of which did not renew contracts with Coca-Cola at the end of 2015." The researchers noted the University of Colorado's example of returning $1 million to Coca-Cola after their complicity was exposed.

Coca-Cola let the American Beverage Association take the heat for this one. "Yes, we may disagree with some in the public health community on discriminatory and regressive taxes and policies on our products," the ABA said in a statement. "But, we believe our actions in communities and the marketplace are contributing to addressing the complex challenge of obesity. We stand strongly for our need, and right, to partner with organizations that strengthen our communities."

40

The evidence was steadily stacking up against sugar. That's why it was interesting to see this December 2016 paper in the *Annals of Internal Medicine*, a well-respected, peer-reviewed journal: "The Scientific Basis of Guideline Recommendations on Sugar Intake: A Systematic Review."[1] The paper was essentially a takedown, a systematic deconstruction, of the growing body of research showing the health risks of sugar consumption. "Guidelines on dietary sugar do not meet criteria for trustworthy recommendations and are based on low-quality evidence," the authors wrote. "Public health officials (when promulgating these recommendations) and their public audience (when considering dietary behavior) should be aware of these limitations."

The conclusion could not have been better even had the study been bought and paid for by industry. Which, it turned out, it was. The paper was written by a cluster of industry-friendly scientists. Where did they get their funding? From the International Life Sciences Institute, ILSI. But this time ILSI seemed to have overstepped. The paper was such an overt case of industry allies using industry funding to present industry-favorable science that it even drew criticism from a high-profile ILSI member.

Associated Press reporter Candice Choi wrote a story: "Snickers Maker Criticizes Industry-Funded Paper on Sugar." "Mars—which is also a member of the group, the International Life Sciences Institute—said Wednesday the paper undermines the work of public health officials and makes all industry-funded research look bad," Choi reported. "Company spokesman Matthias Berninger said the study, published by the *Annals of Internal Medicine*, creates more doubt for consumers rather than helping them make better choices."[2]

The research paper was laced through and through with conflicts of interest. Joanne Slavin, one of the authors, had not disclosed her own financial ties to Coca-Cola, which had both funded her research and paid for her to talk to dietitians about "The Confusing World of Dietary Sugars." "They're hijacking the scientific process to sow doubt and jeopardize public health," Dr. Dean Schillinger told *New York Times* reporter Anahad O'Connor.[3] Schillinger, chief of the UCSF division of general internal medicine at San Francisco General Hospital, also cowrote an editorial to accompany the ILSI-aligned research paper, with his colleague Cristin Kearns, the dentist and sugar researcher.[4] "It is important to note that the North American branch of the International Life Sciences Institute (ILSI North America) funded the review," they wrote. "ILSI North America is a trade group representing The Coca-Cola Company; Dr Pepper Snapple Group; The Hershey Company; Mars, Inc.; Nestlé USA; and PepsiCo, among others. In essence, this study suggests that placing limits on 'junk food' is based on 'junk science,' a conclusion favorable to the [food and beverage] industry."

Then Kearns and Schillinger noted that the tobacco industry had made similar claims. And they gently chided the journal: "To combat the tobacco industry's influence over scientific discourse, leading journal editors recently refused to be passive conduits for articles funded by the tobacco industry," they wrote. "Accordingly, high quality journals could refrain from publishing studies on health effects of added sugars funded by entities with commercial interests in the outcome."

This was a bit much for Christine Laine, the editor who'd invited the review. She told Nina Teicholz, writing for the *Atlantic*, that Kearns and Schillinger's tone was unusually strident. And Laine requested that they modify their disclosure statements to note their advocacy for the UCSF SugarScience program, which educates the public about the risks of sugar. In essence, Laine was accusing them of intellectual conflicts of interest. Laine told Teicholz, "It's shown me that conflicts of interest are not only financial, but also intellectual."[5]

It was an argument with echoes of white-hat bias.

* * *

Conflicts of interest in science can seem straightforward. A corporation like Coke funds research. The research findings are often favorable to the corporation, which touts them directly or through their surrogates. And then, when the funding becomes clear, critics cry foul, and the researchers take umbrage at having their good names sullied. It's a well-known pattern. But a paper published in 2017 highlighted an interesting nuance.[6]

Bennett Holman and Justin Bruner pointed out a specific type of bias by "industrial selection." "The primary concern about industry funding has heretofore been that a researcher will face a conflict of interests and either intentionally or unintentionally place corporate profits over truth," they wrote. "The same conception also leads industry-funded researchers to vehemently assert that their research has not been corrupted by corporate sponsorship."

Their point is that industrial selection—that corporate entities are choosing which projects to fund, and which research questions to answer—has the effect of biasing the body of science, if not the individual study. "Our claim is that it is entirely possible for every individual researcher to remain unaffected by industry funding and for the community as a whole to be biased," they said. In one instance, "Industry was able to survey the community, identify those research methods that were most economically beneficial, and then increase the amount of research done with these methods, and this, the probability that those researchers would attain positions of influence."

This strategy of industrial selection describes well one of the patterns that was becoming ever clearer as critics reviewed the research being produced by Coca-Cola's allies in the science community.

41

Speaking at a conference in San Francisco in July 2017, Kimber Stanhope noted that there was still some controversy over the science of sugar.[1] Or at least it appeared that way to many Americans. On a video screen, Stanhope showed the conclusions from two papers, both published in 2016. The first read: "Evidence suggests that excessive intake of added sugars has adverse effects on cardiometabolic health, which is consistent with many reviews and consensus reports from WHO and other unbiased sources."

The second reached the opposite conclusion: "We conclude based on high quality evidence from randomized controlled trials (RCT), systematic reviews and meta-analyses of cohort studies that singling out added sugars as unique culprits for metabolically based diseases such as obesity, diabetes and cardiovascular disease appears inconsistent with modern, high-quality evidence and is very unlikely to yield health benefits."

The first paper was by University of North Carolina obesity researcher Barry Popkin. The second was from James Rippe, of the University of Central Florida. "Of course, the savvy person might notice who the author of the second conclusion is and say, 'Oh, that's the guy that gets $500,000 a year from the corn refiners, maybe that's why he's saying that,'" said Stanhope. But other laypeople, Googling for information, might easily come to Rippe's work and become convinced that sugar is benign. Especially because of Rippe's productivity. "Ten reviews in the past year, and seventeen sugar-related publications," Stanhope said, "So what is a person who doesn't know the background going to think?"

Stanhope went on to deliver a very technical talk about the metabolic pathways of fructose versus glucose. It was well suited to her audience, dozens of sugar experts gathered for a symposium titled "Diet & Cardiometabolic Health—Beyond Calories." The event brought together some of the leading lights of the movement. The organizer? CrossFit. The nutrition conference was part of the fitness company's growing focus on the health risks of sodas.

In her talk, Stanhope discussed one of her more interesting studies. She had adult subjects consume either fructose- or glucose-sweetened beverages for eight weeks, along with their normal diets. Both groups gained weight and body fat. But the metabolic effects were quite different. The subjects consuming glucose, as expected, had higher post-meal blood sugar and insulin levels. Those consuming fructose, on the other hand, experienced increased liver fat, increased visceral fat, reduced fat oxidization, and decreased insulin sensitivity. (It's worth noting that Stanhope did related research that was contracted by Pepsi, which she disclosed.)

The key difference is in the liver. The liver gets first rights to glucose but usually takes up only about 10 percent, and passes along what it does not need, which ends up circulating through the body. The liver is much better at straining out fructose, nearly 90 percent of it, which it always tries to metabolize, whether it needs it or not.

Stanhope likes the analogy of workers in a factory. The worker loading the glucose on a conveyor belt is in constant communication with the workers at the other end, and places more glucose on the belt as it is needed. But the worker on the fructose conveyor belt has no line of communication, and just keeps piling the fructose on the belt whether the factory needs it or not.

Stanhope's was one strong example of how calories are distinct from one another. Not only are sugars distinct from, say, proteins or fats, but each type of sugar is metabolized differently. Stanhope's research also showed that even when subjects' caloric expenditures were rigorously calculated, and sweetened drinks were substituted for 25 percent of their typically daily diet, subjects drinking glucose solutions and fructose solutions both gained weight. In this case, the sweetened drinks were not additional calories, but calories substituted for solid foods.

Speaking before a chart showing the global rise in obesity, Laura Schmidt, the UCSF School of Medicine professor who has researched soda tax preemption, posed the key question of the day. "Do some foods and beverages contribute to obesity and cardiometabolic disease independent of the calories they contain?" she asked. "Is weight control simply a matter of balancing calories in and calories out? Can we exercise away the health risks of a poor diet?" She continued, "We have all been steeped in this notion that weight control is simply a matter of balancing the calories we take in, through food, with the calories we put out, through exercise and physical activity. If we want to lose weight, we just need to eat less and exercise more. This is called the energy balance paradigm. But the experts today in this room who do research on nutrition are suggesting that there is more to this story. And if so, I truly believe that this will have profound implications not just for our own individual health, but also, more broadly, for public policy."

Schmidt and Stanhope are affiliated with the UCSF SugarScience program, which claims to be the "authoritative source for evidence-based, scientific information about sugar and its impact on health." Robert Lustig is another high-profile member of the group, as are the investigative dentist Cristin Kearns and Dean Schillinger. It was this affiliation that that prompted the *Annals of Internal Medicine* editor to request the intellectual conflict of interest statement from Kearns and Schillinger.

Schmidt mentioned that one reason it is challenging to look beyond energy balance is because food and beverage companies work so hard to promote the concept. This was a direct challenge to Coca-Cola's long-term, multimillion-dollar campaign to promote energy balance. It was a direct challenge not just to Coca-Cola, but also to one man, sitting in the audience, quietly taking it all in. This was Jim Hill, once an architect of and spokesman for the disgraced Global Energy Balance Network.

42

Speaking before the three judges of the United States Court of Appeals for the Ninth Circuit on April 17, 2017, was a slender, neatly dressed, silver-haired, and bespectacled attorney.[1] This was Rick Bress, representing the American Beverage Association. Two years earlier, San Francisco had passed a city ordinance requiring warnings on ads for soft drinks.[2] Now Bress was trying to reverse it. And he was just the man for the job.

A Pittsburgh native and still a Steelers fan, he'd argued several cases before the US Supreme Court, where he once clerked for Antonin Scalia. Bress was a go-to lawyer for corporations using the courts to fight restrictive ordinances. He'd won cases for Monsanto and for DuPont. For Lorillard tobacco, he once killed a Massachusetts ordinance that restricted cigarette advertising. And for the American Beverage Association, he'd helped to kill New York City's ban on supersized sodas (which he said raised "the question of what makes us American, the right to choose"[3]).

The San Francisco ordinance posed a special threat to the soda industry by establishing a precedent. The proposed wording on soda ads, which would be enclosed in a black box that would occupy fully 20 percent of the ad, was as follows:

WARNING: Drinking beverages with added sugar(s) contributes to obesity, diabetes, and tooth decay. This is a message from the City and County of San Francisco.

On approving the measure in 2015, San Francisco supervisor Scott Wiener had praised it. "Today, San Francisco has sent a clear message that we need to do more to protect our community's health," Wiener said. "These health warnings will help provide people information they need to make informed decisions about what beverages they consume. Requiring health warnings on soda ads also makes clear that these drinks aren't harmless—indeed, quite the opposite—and that the puppies, unicorns, and rainbows depicted in soda ads aren't reality." (It was Wiener, as a state legislator in 2018, who was so critical of the soda tax preemption campaign.)

The ABA had challenged the San Francisco ordinance in federal court, on First Amendment grounds. Failing to win an injunction, it had appealed that decision to this court. Now, speaking before the judges in San Francisco, Bress said the warning was false and misleading because it didn't talk about energy balance. "The warning just says, 'Drinking sugar sweetened beverages contributes to obesity, diabetes, and tooth decay.' The problem there is that it's not true, unless your overall caloric intake—counting the sugar-sweetened beverages but [also] everything else—is more than your overall caloric expenditure. . . . For most San Franciscans, and most Californians who drink sugar sweetened beverages, the warning is actually false, because it won't contribute, because overall they are not taking in more calories than they are expending."[4]

Attorney Christine Van Aken, representing San Francisco, stated the city's case. Two-thirds of Americans are obese or at risk for obesity, she said. Reducing added sugar is important, and soda is the single largest source of added sugar in the American diet. She noted that a single twenty-ounce serving would put an adult over the recommended daily limit for added sugars. "The reason the city has started with sugary beverages is because there is wide consensus that this is a leading contributor to the obesity epidemic. . . ." Van Aken said. "There is no other product that is marketed and sold the same way, where a single serving puts you over this daily limit. And where . . ."

Judge Michael Seabright interrupted Van Aken, "I think I could eat enough ice cream to take me over."

"Well, but most people don't have a bowl of ice cream with every meal," Van Aken replied. "But that's how sodas are marketed. That's the intended consumption of sodas, based on its marketing. So if sodas were marketed as an occasional treat. . . . But they are not; they are marketed to refresh your thirst, to quench your thirst. Because they are marketed as if they were water, and because many people consume them as if they were water, then the city has singled that out. So if people read the warning, and take away the message that 'I should be particularly careful about this product,' that is not misleading in light of the evidence the city has been put in the record, about the extent to which these products, in particular, are overconsumed."

The judges seemed skeptical, because not everyone will overconsume the products and experience health risks, and because other sources of added sugars are not required to have warnings. Judge Sandra Ikuta asked Van Aken if the city was saying that sugar-sweetened beverages are uniquely unhealthful. Van Aken said no. "The warning doesn't make claims about the actual nature of the drink," she said. "The warning tells people that they should be concerned; when they choose to drink soda, they should undertake that with special caution, because of the contribution soda and other sugary beverages make to these diseases."

Van Aken agreed that a person could also consume ice cream to this same extent but said that's not what the city's evidence shows. Judge Ikuta mentioned that other items with warnings, such as tobacco and pharmaceutical products, did not seem comparable to a food item. "It's true that I don't have another food item that I can point to that has had a warning like this," Van Aken said. "But I also don't have another food item whose overconsumption has had such dramatic health effects."

When Bress had time for rebuttal, he said, "What the city is really arguing is that there is a behavioral problem, that many people are misusing this product as they misuse other products, and therefore we've got a reason to attack it in this warning. The problem is that the warning doesn't talk about behavior, it doesn't talk about overconsumption as compared to other things, it singles out this product as inherently more dangerous, metabolically more dangerous, and that's misleading."

Among those paid to provide expert testimony to support the ABA's position was Richard Kahn, the former chief scientific and medical officer of the American Diabetes Association. His stance was unequivocal: "There is no scientific consensus that sugar (including added sugar in beverages) plays a unique role in the development of obesity and diabetes."[5] Kahn also referenced a paper he had recently published with a compelling title: "Dietary Sugar and Body Weight: Have We Reached a Crisis in the Epidemic of Obesity and Diabetes? We Have, but the Pox on Sugar Is Overwrought and Overworked."[6] His coauthor? The University of Toronto's John Sievenpiper.

43

More and more mainstream health organizations began speaking out on the risks of sugar, and now it was the American Medical Association's turn. The AMA specifically focused its June 2017 statement on sugar-sweetened beverages. "Excessive sugar consumption has been linked to some of the nation's most debilitating diseases," said AMA board member William E. Kobler, MD,[1] "and limiting the consumption of sugar-sweetened beverages will go a long way toward helping people prevent the onset of these diseases, improve health outcomes, and rein in health costs associated with chronic diseases."

It was slightly awkward, because just two years earlier the American Beverage Association had lauded the AMA when it developed a policy designed to fight quackery: "We support AMA in its efforts to encourage factual reporting of science," the ABA had said. "It is the responsibility of medical professionals—regardless of their presence in the media—to provide people with accurate information."[2] In this case, the factual reporting did not bode well for the beverage association. And it wasn't just the AMA speaking out.

In May, the American Heart Association had published a scientific statement on added sugars and cardiovascular disease risk in children, in the journal *Circulation*. "Associations between added sugars and increased cardiovascular disease risk factors among US children are present at levels far below current consumption levels," wrote Miriam Vos, an associate professor of pediatrics at Emory University School of Medicine. "Strong evidence supports the association of added sugars with increased cardiovascular disease risk in children through increased energy intake, increased adiposity, and dyslipidemia."[3]

Vos and colleagues also noted that higher consumption of sugar-sweetened beverages is linked to higher skin-fold thickness, waist circumference, and excess body fat in children. And they said the inverse is true—reducing soda consumption leads to decreased fat in children and adolescents. And that timing plays a role—sugar-sweetened beverage consumption in infancy was associated with obesity at age six. For all of these reasons, the American Heart Association recommended that children and adolescents have no more than one eight-ounce sugar-sweetened beverage per week. They also recommended that children have no more than twenty-five grams of added sugar daily (in total, not just from sugar-sweetened beverages). And that children under two, who are especially vulnerable to the effects of sugar, have no added sugars at all.

The authors also noted a research gap: "Is there a threshold of added sugars below which there are no negative effects on cardiovascular health?" The question was intriguing. What level of soda consumption is safe? Evidence was stacking up to show that as little as one twelve-ounce can of soda daily was associated with a wide variety of health risks. So how much Coca-Cola could a person drink and not be at risk for health problems? Clearly, that number was somewhere between zero and twelve ounces daily, but more research was needed.

IV

COKE IN COURT

44

A paper published in the *American Journal of Public Health* had a surprising finding—posting signs about the caloric effects of sugar-sweetened beverages reduced soda sales.[1] Sara Bleich and colleagues from the Johns Hopkins Bloomberg School of Public Health studied soda purchases in four corner stores in low-income, predominantly Black neighborhoods in Baltimore for the 2012 paper. The goal was to see if any of three types of signs affected soda sales.

The research was an early indication that the 2010s would see a greater focus on soda's disproportionate impact on communities of color and low-income communities. This included more research in places like Jackson, Mississippi, and more outrage, which would come in the form of a court case filed in Washington, DC, in 2017.

Bleich was well suited for the work. She'd earned a BA in psychology from Columbia and a PhD in health policy from Harvard. She had already been studying obesity-related behavior and racial disparities in health care for five years. And Bleich grew up in Baltimore. "I'm very interested in obesity policy, that's where I come at this," Bleich told me in an interview at Harvard, where she is a professor with the Harvard T. H. Chan School of Public Health and the Radcliffe Institute for Advanced Study, while also on the faculty at the Harvard Kennedy School. "I've just always been interested in soda because, from a public standpoint, people get what that is," Bleich said. "People don't understand junk food, they don't always understand fast food. But they know what a soda is. And it's the largest source of added sugar in the diet. And the consumption is highest among low-income populations. For me, it's always been this category, which, it's easy to isolate, it's easy to study, and in my mind it's low-hanging fruit. If you want to move the needle, and the goal is to pull calories out of the diet, trying to get people to drink less soda is one of the easiest ways to do it."

Among Bleich's interests is why soda consumption is higher among lower-income, less-educated people, a pattern similar to cigarette smoking. Why does that variation exist, Bleich has asked, and why don't we care? A big part of the answer, she said, is dictated by what people see and hear in their neighborhoods, and while they are shopping. More broadly, she said, the Coca-Cola team is masterful at marketing. "It is striking to me the way that Coke, more so than any other brand, feels like family, in the way it advertises itself. Like its ads during Black History Month, its ads during the holidays. It has such slick and skillful marketing that you almost feel like, 'It's part of me. It's who I am, I'm American and it's part of being in this country,'" Bleich said. "And I don't think Pepsi does that as well, and other companies do it as well. And so I think for that reason, it becomes very hard to separate the bad stuff about Coke from the good ways that it makes us feel, because it's a feel-good soda."

More generally, Bleich said, many Americans don't understand the ubiquity of soda advertising, partly *because* of its ubiquity. "It's like wallpaper," Bleich said. "You can't take a step and not see it everywhere. It's so common that it'd be weird not to see soda marketing everywhere. And people generally have no appreciation for how in-your-face it is." She continued, "It's really remarkable the amount of real estate that stores dedicate to just trying to sell soda. And from a business standpoint, I get it. It's highly lucrative, so you pay these slotting fees and you can get a huge amount of money. It just makes it so irresistible that it's not surprising that customers drink so much of it."

The bottom line, Bleich said, is that marketing works. "I think what the average person doesn't appreciate is how much our behavior is manipulated all the time," she said. "So if you say to someone, 'Why did you take that bag of chips and not the other bag of chips?' what they will probably tell you is, 'Oh, because I wanted that one.' But in reality, so much of our wants are based on the environment that we walk into, and how things are pushed toward us as consumers. People may not appreciate both how easily manipulable we are as human beings, and how even more dollars flow toward populations who are just at higher risk for the diet-related conditions that come along with all of the types of the consumption that all of this marketing is supporting, like sugary beverages, like unhealthy snacks, and so on."

So a person's environment is important, and the research from the Baltimore corner stores focused on that environment. Bleich's paper showed that a specific type of caloric information was most effective at reducing soda purchases. Signs that noted that you would have to jog for fifty minutes to burn off the 250 calories in a twenty-ounce soda, for example, were more effective than signs that simply noted the number of calories in a soda. Bleich's research showed that messaging about soda and exercise could be effective. But such messages were few and far between in the places that needed them most.

45

On the north side of Jackson, Mississippi, just past the intersection where KFC, Rally's, and McDonald's vie for the attention of passersby, a defunct shopping mall now serves as the Jackson Medical Mall. JCPenney is gone, replaced by a cancer institute. The Landmark Theater is now part of a conference center. And about midway along the long corridor, the Jackson Heart Study occupies a suite of offices.

This is where Arnita Norwood, PhD, MPH, RD, analyzes the data from a large group of people researchers have been following since 2000. The Jackson Heart Study is modeled after the Framingham Heart Study, a large-scale, long-term study in Massachusetts designed to better understand cardiovascular disease. But in the Jackson study, the subjects are all African Americans.

Norwood, a vigorous, slender woman, grew up nearby, and remembers shopping and going to movies at the mall. Now she is particularly interested in kidney disease. She said the African American community faces unique challenges, including some that are genetic. For example, about a third of African Americans have a genetic variant known as APOL1, which puts them at great risk for kidney disease.

Norwood said sugar-sweetened beverages play a key role in kidney disease. Sodas contribute to the common progression to obesity and hypertension that often leads to chronic kidney disease. Additionally, she said, there are risks caused by the fructose in sodas that can contribute to urate production. This is also linked to increased risk for kidney disease. Norwood and colleagues even quantified the risk, in a 2019 paper. Following three thousand Black men and women in the Jackson Heart Study for eight years, they found that "higher consumption of sugar-sweetened beverages was associated with an elevated risk of subsequent CKD [chronic kidney disease] in this community-based cohort of Black Americans." More specifically, the top consumers of a group of beverages, including soda, sweetened fruit drinks, and water, were 61 percent more likely to develop chronic kidney disease than those who consumed fewer sugar-sweetened beverages.[1]

Norwood said it is important to understand the health challenges in Mississippi, partly because the state is the exemplar of chronic disease. "When you think about chronic disease, we really are the epicenter," she said.

For a grim trifecta of health and diet statistics, Mississippi is among the worst states in the country. It is routinely near the top of the list in rates of obesity, spending for soft drinks, and reliance on SNAP, better known as food stamps. The latter plays a role because sugary drinks are the top items purchased with food stamps—generating about $6 billion in annual revenue for the beverage industry.[2]

Norwood said Mississippi deserves scrutiny for another reason: it serves as an indicator of public health scenarios other states will soon be facing. "We're early adopters," Norwood said. "Nobody, not even Colorado, is trending downward in obesity. We all still have work to do."

One challenge in downtown Jackson, according to Norwood, is a dearth of good grocery stores. Kroger and Whole Foods are on the other side of the interstate, in an area that's not easy to reach with public transportation. On this side of the highway, the only grocery store is a Save a Lot. The Save a Lot is a soda lover's dream. There are four soda machines outside the store—two Coke and two Pepsi. Inside the store, a paltry produce section is squeezed between two huge Coke displays. There is an aisle full of warm soda, of course. At the back of store are four displays at the ends of aisles—premium displays called endcaps—two for Coke and two for Pepsi. At front of the store, on the opposite side from the produce section, there's another Coke cooler. And on the way out are three coolers between the registers, full of assorted sodas.

Dr. Dan Jones has a name for this type of food environment. He calls it a food swamp. He prefers this to the better-known phrase "food desert," because in a food swamp enough calories are available, but they are not nutritious. "Underweight is a rare problem in this state, but there are many people who are overweight and undernourished," said Jones, on a summer morning at his office in the University of Mississippi's Guyton Research Center. "Because they have access to cheap high-calorie foods, but they don't have access to nutritious foods."

Jones is well versed in the subject. He is the Sanderson Chair in Obesity, Metabolic Diseases and Nutrition at the University of Mississippi in Jackson. He started his career studying hypertension at a mission hospital in South Korea. When he returned to Mississippi, he had a revelation. "It kind of hit me in the face here that if I was interested in hypertension, I had to be interested in obesity," he said. Obesity and high blood pressure go hand in hand and are components of metabolic syndrome. Studying obesity, in turn, made Jones interested in sodas. "Sugar beverages are a big part of the obesity epidemic in our country, and this is the epicenter of it, primarily due to the poverty," he said. "Bad health issues enter a population in the wealthy and then settle in the poor, and obesity is the ultimate example of that. People who have access to education and access to wealth begin to change their habits, and have access to healthier food. And people who have less money have less access to those healthy foods and have less access to the education about what's good for health."

Jones was a founding investigator of the Jackson Heart Study. He said there are health disparities along racial lines in Mississippi. "The vast majority of the health differences, including in obesity, between Blacks and whites, is socioeconomic," he said, "with influences of politics and influences of culture." And there are less tangible societal elements that may affect health. "We know that there is a relationship between psychological stress and eating habits," Jones noted. "The psychological stress of constant discrimination is a very difficult thing to measure; we've made attempts at the Jackson Heart Study. I personally think it's an issue. It's hard to be a Black person, it's hard to be a person of color in this country."

Some of the most conspicuous symbols of the health care challenges in Jackson are the dialysis clinics that seem to be on every corner. Dr. Richard deShazo, former chairman of the department of medicine at the University of Mississippi Medical Center, mentioned them in a TEDx talk. "Fifty percent of diabetes and about 50 percent of hypertension in Mississippi is undetected, and by the time we get the patient, we have end-stage disease," deShazo said. "And that's why dialysis units in Mississippi are growing faster than dollar stores. They are literally everywhere, and they are just getting started."[3]

Back at the medical mall, Norwood said both her mother and grandmother developed type 2 diabetes late in life, and she remembers accompanying her grandmother to some of her three-times-weekly dialysis appointments. She said some people just assume they will get diabetes, because so many of their friends and family do. And once they have the disease, some do little to change their lifestyles. Norwood knows people with type 2 diabetes who continue to drink soda and compensate for the rush of sugar by taking more insulin.

Down the mall from Norwood's office is a dialysis clinic, one of a dozen in Jackson. In the clinic, tubes are connected to ports affixed to the patients' arms in spots where doctors have fused veins and arteries to create bulbous blood sacs known as fistulas, which look like huge varicose veins. The tubes pump the patients' blood through a machine that extracts the toxins their failing kidneys can no longer filter. A steady stream of mostly Black patients comes and goes all day long.

This is the end point of what Norwood said are two of the health challenges in Jackson. "Lack of access to health care, and great access to sugary beverages," Norwood said. "In the most inner of inner cities, and the most rural of rural America, you can always get a Coke."

46

Americans of color are among the biggest consumers of Coke, and Dr. Yolandra Hancock says this is by design. A pediatrician who researches obesity at George Washington University, Hancock's specialty is working with Black and brown families, and helping them achieve healthier lifestyles. "When it comes to sugary drinks, and the soda industry specifically, there is targeted marketing of African Americans," Hancock said in an interview in her office at George Washington University's Milken Institute School of Public Health, where a steady stream of students and colleagues seems ever waiting to see her. "Black children see twice as many soda ads as white children. It isn't that our children are watching more TV. It's that on BET and these other 'Black channels' you're going to have the industry buying more ad time."

Hancock grew up in Tangipahoa Parish, Louisiana, and has some personal experience with sodas. She developed a taste for them at five, while eating the frozen Pepsi pops her grandmother made as treats for her when they watched *Mutual of Omaha's Wild Kingdom* on TV. "I got hooked. I loved it," she said. "I drank Pepsi like it was water growing up."

When Hancock was in college, she had a checkup and found her calcium levels were low. Studies have shown an association with reduced bone density and an increased risk for fractures among women who drink colas, though not among those consuming other carbonated beverages. It appears that the phosphoric acid in colas binds calcium and decreases serum blood calcium, but more research is needed. "I cut soda that day, we broke up," said Hancock. "I started taking my calcium supplements because I didn't want to have the bones of an old lady, in my twenties."

Hancock believes sodas should bear warning labels like cigarettes. And she said soda's effects on children's dental health, from both its sugars and its acidity, do not get the attention they deserve. "Cavities are the most common chronic medical condition in pediatrics," Hancock said. "People assume it to be asthma and all of these other things. It truly is dental caries."

She said it is not surprising to see the cavities, given the amount of sugar in the diets of most children. "The average child is consuming about ten teaspoons of sugar a day," Hancock noted. "We know that little ones drink about thirty-two gallons of sugary drinks a year, which can fill up a tub. When you expose the body, at such a young age, to that much sugar, we're not talking about the development of risk factors for diabetes, hypertension, heart disease, cancer in their forties and fifties, we're talking ten, fifteen."

"My youngest patient that I diagnosed with type 2 diabetes was nine years old," she said. "And it was all lifestyle and dietary related. Nine years old. Can you imagine the parent and the child having to manage type 2 diabetes while just trying to grow up? And the earlier a child develops these chronic diseases, the higher the risk of complications, and the higher the risk of early death." She continued, "It's very important for people to truly understand the role that sugar plays in increasing risk of diabetes, high blood pressure, and heart disease. We know that just drinking one sugary drink a day increases your risk of developing type 2 diabetes by 25 percent. And especially for people of color, we're already at higher risk. So we're at higher risk at baseline, and then we increase our risk by an additional 25 percent."

Hancock said the discussions about obesity hold special relevance for Black women, of whom 80 percent, across socioeconomic levels, experience overweight or obesity. She said this is a specific demographic that Coca-Cola has targeted with brilliant marketing at the Essence Festival, the nation's largest event for African American women. "You go to Essence, you walk in, you get your gift bag," Hancock said. "Coca-Cola is on one side. Guess what's on the other side? McDonald's. It's not by accident that they are the biggest supporters of Black events. Why would an organization, an institution, about Black women, position a product that is known to increase my risk of chronic diseases and death? It's counterintuitive."

Hancock said examples of the targeted marketing abound. "When Tyrese [Gibson] is on the bus, singing about Coke, 'Oh oh, yeah,' when there are billboards placed in our communities with our pictures on them, but not in Bethesda, there's a connection there, a purposeful targeted marketing that makes Coke part of family," she said. "You have a cookout—'Who's bringing the Coca-Cola?' No one says, 'Who's bringing the RC? Who's bringing the Dr Pepper?' It's 'Who's got the Coke?' Black folks weren't loyal to Philip Morris. Newport, maybe. But the company, the establishment in general? Not at all," Hancock said. "But Coca-Cola, there's a relationship."

Hancock mentioned another related issue: When you ask people not to drink soda, you have to be able to tell them what they can drink that's safe and free. That means addressing the social justice issues related to water, by routinely assessing tap water quality so that communities of color know they can trust it. "When Flint, Michigan, is still waiting for this issue to be addressed," Hancock said, "even Beyoncé could be on a commercial saying, 'Hey everybody, get yo tap water in,' and they're going to look at Beyoncé with some side eye. They're going to say, 'Beyoncé, you don't live in my neighborhood. Come over here to Detroit and drink the water, let me see how you like that. Bring Blue Ivy over here and have her drink our tap water when it comes out brown first, and then talk to me about not drinking soda and instead drinking water.'"

Hancock feels that one way to dramatically decrease soda consumption, not just among people of color but across the board, would be through powerful public health campaigns, like the compelling TV ads about the dangers of smoking. "When that woman had to speak out of her trachea—oh my gosh, I never want to smoke, because she's talking out of her throat!" Hancock said. "You don't see that same thing with sugar. Show them the man that I saw at Shoppers, double amputee with two packs of Pepsi [in his grocery cart]. Let him talk about what sugar did."

47

A November 2016 USDA report shed some light on a murky corner of the soda world: the money spent on sugar-sweetened beverages through SNAP. The Supplemental Nutrition Assistance Program is more commonly thought of as food stamps, though the funds are now administered through electronic cards. The report synopsized data from a major grocery chain for 2011.[1] Soft drinks were the number one purchase, of 238 commodities tracked by the USDA. This was a taxpayer-funded windfall of $3.7 billion for Coca-Cola, Pepsi, and other bottlers. Add in other sugar-sweetened beverages like sports drinks, energy drinks, and juices, and the figure grew to more than $6 billion.

Critics have long pointed out the irony in spending taxpayer dollars to purchase soft drinks, which can lead to health problems paid for by taxpayers through Medicaid. But efforts to limit the purchase of soft drinks with food stamps have met stout resistance from the soda industry.

In his book *Saving Gotham*, former New York City health commissioner Tom Farley noted that the federal funds spent on sugary drinks in 2010 were five times the size of the CDC's budget for the prevention of chronic disease. That October, Governor David Paterson and New York mayor Michael Bloomberg requested permission from the USDA for a two-year pilot program to eliminate soda from SNAP. "The day after our announcement, Coca-Cola CEO Muhtar Kent sent a letter to Bloomberg, calling the idea 'unjustified and discriminatory,'" Farley wrote. "PepsiCo CEO Indra Nooyi, writing the same day, was more threatening. 'When we met earlier this summer,' she told the mayor, 'we let you know that as we restructure our business, we are redoubling our commitment to retain and increase investment in New York City and New York State. But apparently commitment and loyalty is a one-way street in New York.'"[2]

That proposal went nowhere. Legislative efforts to limit SNAP funds for sugar-laden foods were also killed in Florida and Maine after stiff opposition from the soda industry. In Maine, the opposition also included advocates for Mainers with low incomes, who felt that limiting purchases stigmatizes people who are already marginalized.

Amplifying the effects of the SNAP purchases, retailers promote sodas more heavily on the days after the benefits are issued.[3] And many stores, and even drugstores, place window stickers on the soda coolers, to remind consumers that they accept SNAP funds.

Yolandra Hancock, the George Washington University pediatrician, knows the SNAP issue inside and out. "I grew up as a recipient of SNAP, and WIC, all that stuff, as a little girl," she said. "I used to use food stamps when you had to tear them out of a book. So I have my own personal biases from having grown up in the system. But I also have a bias because I'm a pediatrician and an obesity specialist, and I've seen the impacts it has on our children, and on our adults, particularly in communities of color."

Although the current system has taxpayers paying twice—for the SNAP-purchased sodas and for the Medicaid funding to address the associated health problems—Hancock thinks any reform of the system needs to be thoughtful.

Sara Bleich, the Harvard researcher, has studied the Supplemental Nutrition Assistance Program. And she said the issue is fraught. "This is one of the most third-rail issues in nutrition right now," Bleich said. "I'm a former SNAP baby, and there's a piece of me that's like, 'Let families do what they want with the money. It's theirs, you're giving it to them, why be paternalistic?' But there's a piece of me that's thinking that these same families are probably on Medicaid. And if you're allowing government dollars to be put toward things like sugary beverages, you are driving up the cost of health care. And what outweighs what?"

In order to develop an effective policy, Bleich said, it would be important to have research about how soda consumption patterns change when limits are placed on SNAP purchases. But in order to do that, Congress would have to authorize a pilot program, or the USDA would have to grant a waiver to a state. "If I had a magic wand, I would say we need evidence, authorize a pilot, and let's go from there," Bleich said. "The biggest challenge in this area is that there are incredibly strong opinions, and there is zero empirical evidence, because a waiver has never been granted."

In the meantime, American tax dollars are subsidizing the business models of Coke and Pepsi. The USDA will not divulge the exact amount of SNAP money spent on sugary beverages. (It even withstood a legal challenge from the South Dakota *Argus Leader* over shielding the information, which was decided in the US Supreme Court.)

Bleich thinks the total could be close to $10 billion. "It's huge, it's huge," Bleich said, "and soda is a big moneymaker."

48

In a forty-one-page complaint filed in the Superior Court of the District of Columbia in July 2017, three plaintiffs filed suit against Coca-Cola and the American Beverage Association, "for their deceptive marketing, labeling, and sale of Coca-Cola's sugar-sweetened beverages." The suit had echoes of those the tobacco industry had fought in the 1980s. In a bit of a twist, two of the three plaintiffs were pastors.[1]

William Lamar was the leader of Washington's 179-year-old Metropolitan African Methodist Episcopal Church. Delman Coates led Mt. Ennon Baptist Church, a ten-thousand-member megachurch in Clinton, Maryland. Both claimed their congregants were suffering the health consequences of sugar-sweetened beverages and were being deceived by Coke's advertising and public relations campaigns.

The third plaintiff was more traditional—the Praxis Project, an Oakland-based nonprofit organization dedicated to health equity and justice, led by longtime health advocate Xavier Morales. Crucially, the lawsuit noted, each of the three plaintiffs had purchased a Coca-Cola product in DC.

The organization that catalyzed the lawsuit was less surprising. It was the Center for Science in the Public Interest. Michael Jacobson, the executive director of the center and a thorn in Coca-Cola's side since 1972, had used litigation over the years to challenge many large food companies, including McDonald's and Kellogg's. And the organization had even challenged Coca-Cola over Enviga and its "negative calorie effect" claims. It had also successfully sued Coca-Cola over Vitaminwater, stating, "VitaminWater is not a beneficial fortified drink—it is just another flavored sugary snack food like Coca-Cola, except that defendants chose not to carbonate it."[2] But this time it was after something bigger.

"We tried to think of some ways to use litigation to really get at the soda issue writ large," Jacobson said later. "Coke was kind of the natural target. So we looked at their marketing practices, the science, and came up with this lawsuit." The lawsuit itself was writ large. It alleged false, deceptive, and misleading advertising, under DC's Consumer Protection Procedures Act. The allegations were powerful: "Aware of the science linking sugar-sweetened beverages to obesity and obesity related conditions, including type 2 diabetes and cardiovascular disease, and of growing public concern over this link, Coca-Cola and the ABA have engaged in an aggressive campaign to protect profits earned from the sale of sugar-sweetened beverages by flooding the market with countervailing representations that obscure this link between the beverages and disease."

The suit was not only ambitious in its targets; it was ambitious in its remedies. It sought to prevent further deceptive marketing. And it requested that the court fund a corrective public education campaign. That campaign would counter the misinformation that all calories are equal and clarify "that science has linked sugar-sweetened beverages to obesity, diabetes, and cardiovascular disease, and that light exercise does not offset the potential harm caused by routine consumption of sugar-sweetened beverages."

Jacobson's organization laid out its case for the lawsuit in a press release and videos. "This is, for me, an issue of paramount importance, and a justice issue, because in the District of Columbia, where I work, where I live, where I pay taxes, more people die from diabetes-related illnesses than AIDS, cancer, and homicides combined," said Lamar. "The link between the consumption of sugary beverages and death is appalling, and we don't hear about it. And much of that is because of the amazing and powerful marketing regime of Coca Cola, linking consumption of their beverages with fun, and with health. This type of mendacity from corporate leaders makes it difficult for me to do my job of not only dealing with people's spiritual health, but dealing with people's physical health. The two go together."

Coates said his congregants are suffering from disease and early death related to the consumption of sugar-sweetened beverages. "I am the one who goes to the hospital rooms, who presides over the planning and preparation of funerals in our congregation," he said. "So as a part of my work, it's become important, for me, to help people understand the relationship between their consumption of Coca-Cola and sugar-sweetened beverages, and the illnesses they experience today. That work is challenged by the range of deceptive statements and deceptive marketing that comes from Coca-Cola . . . and I'm a part of this effort to end these deceptive practices of Coca-Cola and the deceptive marketing that is devastating the African American community, and the community I serve."

In announcing the lawsuit, the plaintiffs' attorneys explicitly echoed the tobacco battles. "When defendants argue that a calorie is a calorie, they are pointing people away from more nutritional products," Andrew Rainer said. He noted that it was a familiar campaign of disinformation: "That is exactly what the tobacco companies did for 50 years."

"For decades, the tobacco industry engaged in a systemic campaign of deception to cast doubt on the science connecting smoking to lung cancer," said attorney Maia Kats. "Today Coca-Cola and the ABA are conducting their own campaign of deception to hide the science connecting sugar-sweetened beverages to obesity, and obesity-related diseases like diabetes and heart disease."

One odd aspect of the case was that Kats and colleagues had first filed a very similar suit in federal court in California, six months earlier. That suit featured the nonprofit Praxis as the only plaintiff. Although the Center for Science in the Public Interest issued a press release when it filed that suit, it got no press when it quietly withdrew it after only two months. Typically, attorneys take such an action when shopping for a more favorable outcome elsewhere—a more sympathetic court, and a more sympathetic judge. It may not have been the best calculation.

49

On a bright morning in mid-March 2018, a few blocks from the National Mall in Washington, DC, a series of dark town cars discharged a small parade of well-dressed lawyers outside a courthouse. But this was not the stately United States Supreme Court, a mile east on the other side of the Capitol. Nor even the more modest US District Court that handles federal cases, a couple of blocks away. This was the DC Superior Court, a complex of granite and limestone buildings on Judiciary Square.

It's a court that most often sees low-level offenders accompanied by public defenders. But today it was hosting some of nation's top attorneys. The legal team gathered in the tall hallway, with its harsh fluorescent light, marbled wall, and composite stone floor, and waited.

When the doors to Judge Elizabeth Wingo's courtroom opened, the legal teams walked in, some carrying banker's boxes full of files, others pulling rolling cases. The matter before the bar was the lawsuit filed by the California nonprofit group Praxis Project and Pastors Delman Coates and William Lamar against Coca-Cola and the American Beverage Association, alleging false advertising.

The pastors claimed that their congregants, and many people of color, were targeted by Coca-Cola and deceived by its advertising. Growing data backed up the claim of targeted marketing. One study found that Black children and teens saw twice as many TV ads as their white counterparts in 2018.[1]

For the defense, a heavy legal contingent turned out, the absolute A-team of corporate law, there to defend the soda industry against the civil suit. The soda team included Steven Zalesin, representing Coca-Cola. Tall, sharply dressed, with a full head of salt-and-pepper hair, Zalesin is a trial lawyer focused on protecting corporations like Hershey and pet food giant Blue Buffalo from legal claims. In 2016, Zalesin won a major victory for Coca-Cola in a seven-year case brought by POM Wonderful alleging false advertising on a Coca-Cola juice blend. The case went all the way to the US Supreme Court. When Zalesin won, the *American Lawyer* highlighted him as "litigator of the week."

Joining Zalesin was attorney Jane Metcalf, who worked alongside him at Patterson Belknap Webb & Tyler. They sat with Rick Bress, representing the American Beverage Association. Bress was the attorney who was concurrently battling the San Francisco ordinance requiring warnings for soda ads, also for the ABA.

As Zalesin and Bress prepared their files, the benches behind them filled up with more legal heavies on the soda team. Anthony Pierce was there, a large mustached Black attorney and a partner with the Akin Gump group, a power player in DC law. Behind him was the American Beverage Association's in-house counsel, Amy Hancock. She sat with Coca-Cola's Russell Bonds, a Georgia lawyer who also writes historical nonfiction about the Civil War and reviews history books for the *Wall Street Journal*.

It was a legal showing worth many thousands of dollars in billable hours. The investment was an indication that Coca-Cola and the American Beverage Association took the suit very seriously.

The other side of the room could not have been more different. The attorneys before the bar included Maia Kats, litigation director for the Center for Science in the Public Interest. A graduate of the University of Michigan and Michigan Law School, she'd once gone head-to-head with Coca-Cola's Russell Bonds in the case over the health claims for Vitaminwater, and won.

Next to Kats stood Massachusetts attorney Andrew Rainer. A Princeton graduate, Rainer had represented whistleblowers and civil rights plaintiffs and fought polluters for the state of Massachusetts. He once challenged R. J. Reynolds in court over a Florida woman's emphysema and was partly successful. Rainer had also sued soda companies over the benzene in soft drinks, prompting Coca-Cola and others to reformulate some of their beverages as part of a 2007 settlement.[2]

But it was the audience seated on the benches behind Kats and Rainer that painted the strongest contrast with the corporate team just across the aisle. The benches were full of mostly Black men and women, many of whom were congregants of the plaintiffs' churches. The Reverends Coates and Lamar were seated there, too. Yolandra Hancock, the pediatrician and obesity researcher at George Washington University, was among the group. As was Michael Jacobson, the grizzled warhorse of the soda wars, who had recently stepped down from the helm of the Center for Science in the Public Interest.

There was also a contrast between the corporate legal muscle on one side of the room, and the room itself. If not shabby, the courtroom was certainly well worn, with perfunctory wood paneling, wall-to-wall carpet, and, just behind the rail on the plaintiff's side, a large floor fan on a pedestal, with two feet of dusty duct tape waving in its breeze.

When the arguments began, Judge Wingo tried to keep the discussion focused on the matters at hand. A graduate of Yale Law School with light brown hair going gray, and reading glasses, Wingo looked serious. There were five pre-trial motions to consider. And they could become complicated. "I was revisiting this for basically the entirety of the last week," Judge Wingo said. Because almost every argument was multiplied by four, given two plaintiffs and two defendants, "there is a truly astonishing number of legal issues raised in these five motions."

But the most important matter before the judge was the issue of standing. This is the determination of whether the plaintiffs had experienced sufficient harm to have legal status to sue Coca-Cola and the ABA over their health claims. This launched a long, arcane discussion between Wingo and the attorneys, with many references to precedent-setting legal cases. But it inevitably veered from procedural matters to the substance of the case.

Rainer argued that Coca-Cola was deluding people into buying non-nutritional calories. The products contain "virtually zero nutritional value, lots of carbs, and lots of sugar," he said. "When defendants argue that a calorie is a calorie, they are pointing people away from more nutritional products." In essence, Rainer said, Coca-Cola is deluding consumers. "That is exactly what the tobacco companies did for fifty years," he said.

The discussion eventually circled back around to standing, which basically had two prongs. On one, the pastors each purchased Coca-Cola products, to show, essentially, that they were engaged. Zalesin was not buying this. They did not test the product, to determine its healthfulness or otherwise. He said there was no precedent for "simply saying we read the label and we put it in context." A consumer has to have injury in fact, Zalesin said; it's not enough to say the consumer bought the product. He characterized Rainer's argument as this: if you are a consumer, you have an abstract right to truthful statements, and if it's violated, you can bring an action. This, Zalesin said, is absurd.

The plaintiffs also claimed standing based on the diversion of resources. In essence, the pastors and the California nonprofit argued that they had been prevented from doing the work that was their mission because they had to spend time helping people who had become ill due to consumption of Coca-Cola and other sodas.

Zalesin argued that you can manufacture standing neither by buying something nor by claiming resource diversion. Growing exasperated at one point, Zalesin referred to a precedent decided by the highest court: "The Supreme Court right down the street here, Your Honor."

Listening to the lawyers, Wingo looked alternately engaged and pensive. She said she appreciated everyone's exhaustive arguments, and that she would have to make a decision on standing before anything else could happen. After two hours of animated jousting, Judge Wingo noted the knottiness of the legal questions the case involved. "I was trying to make a chart of all the issues, it's so complicated," she said. "It's a very interesting case." Still, she told those assembled not to expect fireworks in the courtroom. She warned the audience that the next hearing would likely be just as dull as this one.

50

Judge Elizabeth Wingo came walking down the tall, bland hallway of DC Superior Court on September 18, 2018, in slacks and moderate heels. She was pulling a roller bag and clutching a stack of binders and papers, reading material for the next hearing in the Praxis case.

Plaintiffs' attorneys Maia Kats and Andrew Rainer arrived, and chatted with their colleague Matt Simon in the hall. Then came Steven Zalesin with his colleague, Jane Metcalf. Rick Bress soon strolled in, carrying an umbrella and hauling a roller bag. He joked easily with Rainer and Kats, then huddled with Zalesin and Metcalf.

Bress soon took a seat at a bench off to the side and reviewed a thick three-ring binder labeled:

> ARGUMENT BOOK
> PRAXIS 2
> AMERICAN BEVERAGE ASSOCIATION

The attorneys were gathered for the second hearing in the lawsuit pitting two pastors against the American Beverage Association and Coca-Cola. When the courtroom doors opened, the attorneys walked in, took their seats, and waited. Zalesin and Bress chatted and laughed, while Rainer looked at his laptop, and Kats reviewed notes in a binder.

Pastors Lamar and Coates came in and sat down to observe the proceedings. Both in their mid-forties, with shaven heads and crisp suits, Coates and Lamar cut striking figures in the courtroom. But the courtroom was much more subdued than in March. The congregants were not there, nor healthy foods firebrand Mike Jacobson. Coca-Cola attorney Russell Bonds had not made the trip, nor ABA attorney Amy Hancock.

Judge Wingo began the hearing by announcing that she'd not made a ruling on standing. In other words, it was still not clear that the plaintiffs were in a position to bring the lawsuit. This was a surprise. And Judge Wingo seemed a bit apologetic. She noted that the plaintiffs could have interpreted the case moving forward to mean that they had standing. Wingo asked the attorneys if they had anything they wanted to discuss.

Zalesin spoke first. Perhaps feeling generous, he told Judge Wingo that if she were to dismiss the case on any grounds, Coca-Cola would take its anti-SLAPP motion off the table. One of the many legal maneuverings in this case, the anti-SLAPP motion was a cynical legal strategy for Coca-Cola, one that inverted the natural order of things. Strategic lawsuits against public participation, or SLAPPs, are generally thought of as corporate strategies to intimidate and silence their critics. In essence, a large corporation with a lot of legal firepower will challenge a citizen or nonprofit that is its nemesis—knotting them up in court and burdening them with legal fees.

These SLAPP lawsuits have become so popular and effective that many jurisdictions have enacted anti-SLAPP laws, efforts to protect activists and nonprofits against frivolous corporate legal cases. DC has such a law. It allows the subject of a SLAPP lawsuit to file a special motion to dismiss. Typically, an anti-SLAPP motion would be filed by a grassroots activist being silenced by a large corporation's SLAPP lawsuit. Creatively, Coca-Cola flipped this in this case. Here it was Coca-Cola filing an anti-SLAPP motion, alleging the Praxis case was a SLAPP lawsuit.

In discussing the motion, Judge Wingo took umbrage at attorney Maia Kats's characterization that the anti-SLAPP motion would "threaten plaintiffs with financial destruction." Wingo admonished Kats to tone down her language.

Kats replied that her claim was accurate, because the plaintiffs were two individual pastors and a small nonprofit.

"To the extent that arguments can be made without hyperbole or expressing evil intent," Wingo said, "it will be helpful."

Coca-Cola attorney Jane Metcalf said the anti-SLAPP motion was perfectly appropriate, because the plaintiffs were trying to silence Coca-Cola by keeping it from participating in the discussion over sodas and health. "The crux of the argument is that Coca-Cola must be excluded from the debate," Metcalf said. And that, she said, is a "dramatic and absurd" point of view.

In response, Kats respectfully asked that the anti-SLAPP motion be dismissed. "I would suggest that Coca-Cola, which is a large multinational with revenues in excess of $35 billion, is not intimidated by the plaintiffs," she said. She also suggested that the American Beverage Association was sophisticated and aggressively litigious. She made the case that the pastors and Praxis were modest. "Are these the silencers?" said Kats of the pastors. "Do they intimidate Coca-Cola and the ABA? I would suggest not, Your Honor."

Before long, as it always seemed to, the discussion veered from the specifics of the anti-SLAPP motion to the broader underlying themes of the legal case: the impacts of sugar-sweetened beverages on human health. "This is what the whole debate is," said Judge Wingo. "They do not concede that what they are disseminating is false. There is some science on their side, there is some on your side."

No, said Kats, the science is firmly on the plaintiffs' side.

"The science on your side is a little shaky," said Judge Wingo, referring to Kats's assertion that sugar-sweetened beverages are more unhealthful than other elements of the diet. And there, once again, they were into the weeds, into the particulars of the case, while still trying to resolve pre-trial motions.

Kats referenced a statement by Katie Bayne, then Coca-Cola's president of sparkling beverages for North America. In a 2012 *USA Today* interview about New York mayor Michael Bloomberg's proposal to limit soft drink serving sizes, Bayne told journalist Bruce Horovitz, "There is no scientific evidence that connects sugary beverages to obesity."[1]

But Judge Wingo asked: At the time they said that, six years ago, was there such scientific evidence? Kats said there absolutely was. She referred to a 2011 statement from the Centers for Disease Control. But Judge Wingo remained skeptical of the soda science. "I don't want you to overstate what you are doing," Judge Wingo said. "I don't think it helps your argument." Again, Judge Wingo asked Kats: Can you link to obesity, in 2012? Kats seemed exasperated at the breadth of the judge's inquiry. She said the matter under consideration was an anti-SLAPP motion, "not a motion for summary judgment." The defendants are trying to intimidate the plaintiffs, Kats said. The idea that Coke could apply an anti-SLAPP motion to them "is the world turned upside down."

As they recessed for lunch, Metcalf was feeling good. "It's looking more and more optimistic," she said to a colleague. After lunch, Metcalf responded to Kats. For starters, she said, there was some debate about whether Katie Bayne actually said there were no links between sugary beverages and obesity. This may have been paraphrased, Metcalf said, in response to a question about obesity. "It was in response to that that she allegedly said, 'There is no scientific evidence that connects sugary beverages to obesity.'" By using the word *allegedly*, Metcalf suggested *USA Today* journalist Bruce Horovitz's reporting was inaccurate. But Coca-Cola, though well aware of the statement at the time, had not asked *USA Today* for a correction.

This debate put Coca-Cola in a delicate position. On one hand, it would appear unseemly, and might even put the company in legal jeopardy, if its formal position was that sugary beverages are not linked to obesity, despite the large and growing body of scientific evidence. On the other, its proxies did routinely suggest that this was the case.

When Bress finally got a chance to argue that the American Beverage Association should be dismissed from the case, he persuasively argued that it was just a trade association. The ABA, he argued, was merely doing promotional work. "We're not a merchant. We don't make things. We don't sell things," Bress said. "And we're being sued for speaking out."

In response, Andrew Rainer said that the ABA was very much a part of the sales of a product. He pointed out that the ABA logo adorned Coca-Cola's Mixify ads, part of a $20 million campaign to emphasize activity over diet. "I know you tire of hearing comparisons to the tobacco industry, but I'm going to ask you to endure a few more," said Rainer.

He said that when the science about the health risks of smoking became increasingly clear, the whole tobacco industry denied science, created science, and spoke to the media to say, "It has not been shown." "The science here is not like this"—Rainer held his hands level, at either side. "The science is like this." He reached one arm up to the air, the other nearly to the ground, to show how lopsided it was. "They say on their website today there is no science," Rainer continued. "It's just like the tobacco companies."

Rainer said the ABA was so connected with Coca-Cola that "they refer to it as 'our product.'" This sank the ABA argument, he said, and they shouldn't get to take themselves out of it. The ABA, Rainer said, was trying to have a screen of disinterest while doing the bidding of its members. He mentioned correspondence from Coca-Cola basically saying, "There are concerns about our product, we're going to work it out through the ABA."

Coca-Cola had been criticized over this very point the year before, when executive Ryan Guthrie, discussing a flap over artificial sweeteners, had written, "This has gotten next to zero news coverage. Should that change, ABA will run point."[2]

Responding to Rainer, Bress seemed mildly peeved. "They refer to tobacco and they refer to tobacco all day," he said, "and I've kind of had it up to here with tobacco, Your Honor." Bress said the ABA had never denied that soft drinks contain calories, or that some people over-consume calories from products, including soft drinks. Those issues were exactly the reason for the campaigns like Mixify. "When we say sugar-sweetened beverages don't cause obesity, we mean it, and we have a lot of science to prove it," Bress said. "Correlation doesn't mean causation." He continued, "They are seeking to shut us up. They don't like the fact that we are disagreeing with them on our blogs and our newsletter."

By now it was getting late, and Judge Wingo had said she didn't want to go past 4 p.m. But she had not gotten to all of the issues—not even close.

Speaking for Coca-Cola, Zalesin said, "It's important to my client that we have the opportunity to present our motion to dismiss." He did not get to do so, but that was just one of the major issues left on the bench. Judge Wingo had still not ruled on the matter of standing. As Judge Wingo tried to firm up next steps, Zalesin, Bress, Rainer, and Kats convivially compared their calendars and conferred about schedules. It was increasingly apparent that the case was not going to be resolved quickly.

51

Just a week later, on September 25, Rick Bress was in another courtroom, this one in Pasadena, California. This time he was before an eleven-judge panel of the United States Court of Appeals for the Ninth Circuit.[1] At issue was the San Francisco ordinance requiring warnings on soft drink ads.

Bress, his cuff links flashing as he gestured in a measured way, told the judges that the proposed warnings were misleading and, because of their size—20 percent of an advertisement—unduly burdensome. "Obesity and related conditions are serious health problems," he started. "The causes and best means of prevention are hotly disputed. The city is entitled to have and to share its view—that drinking beverages with added sugars contributes to these conditions more so than consuming equivalent calories from other foods and beverages. The FDA, and we, are entitled to believe otherwise. What the city can't do," Bress continued, "consistent with the First Amendment, is force us to convey its controversial view. Yet that is exactly what the city is doing here with this warning, by singling out advertisements for beverages with added sugar."

Here several judges jumped in to ask about the accuracy of the proposed warning, which would read: "WARNING: Drinking beverages with added sugar(s) contributes to obesity, diabetes, and tooth decay. This is a message from the City and County of San Francisco." Specifically, would the warning withstand scrutiny, under the First Amendment, if the phrasing were literally accurate, including the distinction between type 1 and type 2 diabetes?

No, Bress said. "We don't just look at the literal accuracy of a warning," he argued. "We look at what it conveys to consumers." And singling out sugar-sweetened beverages as unique contributors to disease conveyed the wrong message. "If you look at alcohol, for example, the government doesn't require, on its bottles, a warning about the danger of birth defects to pregnant women, or the danger from driving while impaired, only on wine, only on beer, or only on hard liquor." Gesturing broadly, he said, "It puts it across the product category. Similarly with tobacco, Your Honor, once science progressed to the point that people understood that all the different tobacco products raised the same problems, they required the warning across the board."

The judges were aggressive in their questioning, often cutting Bress off in mid-sentence. In a spirited back-and-forth, Bress argued that it was wrong to single out soft drinks when consumers could overindulge in any type of food. "I think in this case, to be accurate, you'd have to include all caloric foods and beverages," Bress said.

But when Judge William Fletcher asked, "Are you saying that the calories from a sugared soda are the same as the calories from, say, broccoli?" Bress replied, "Not only am I saying that the calories for purposes of obesity and diabetes type 2, Your Honor, are the same as the calories from broccoli—" Here the judge interrupted to ask if Bress was saying there should also be a label on broccoli.

"Your Honor, the FDA has told us, and the city has not disputed this, that calories from sugar-sweetened beverages do not contribute any more than calories from any other energy source," Bress said. "And so if you wanted to be accurate, what you'd really tell people—"

"Don't contribute more to what?" asked Judge Morgan Christen. "You have to finish the sentence. Don't contribute more to what?"

"More to obesity and diabetes," he said, "and we're talking about diabetes type 2, Your Honor."

At questioning about the lack of nutrition in sodas, Bress pointed out that sugar-sweetened beverages account for only about 4 percent of Americans' overall diets. And that, accounting for juices, sodas make up just 3 percent of the overall diet. Bress said his core argument was that the city was trying to address the complex problem of "the overconsumption of calories in society," so the warning could not be fixed by just changing the wording. "No, I don't think you can address that, in a constitutional way, by requiring warnings on only one product," Bress said. "Because I think inevitably, you are going to be sending misleading messages by doing that."

His presentation was more persuasive because he rarely referred to notes, instead focusing directly on the judges, and yet had the material so committed to memory that he could refer them quickly to a quotation on, say, "paragraph 28 at ER 353."

Judge Fletcher asked: If the 20 percent size was unduly burdensome, then what would happen to tobacco warning labels?

"Your Honor, I don't think it would affect the warnings on tobacco products—"

"But they're 20 percent."

Bress reviewed the legislative history, noting that cigarette warnings were soon to increase in size, to 20 percent, essentially because consumers had gotten used to them. This soda warning was novel, so it ran no such risk. Further, he said, "In this case, there has never been a warning on an ad for a food or beverage item that is generally recognized as safe, in the history of regulation."

Next up was Jeremy Goldman, of the San Francisco City Attorney's Office. (Goldman had taken over the case from Christine Van Aken, who had been appointed a superior court judge.) The judges quizzed Goldman on the accuracy of the statement. Was it overly broad? Had the wording "cigarette smoking causes cancer" been challenged? Because, clearly, in some cases it does not. Who was the target audience? How was health literacy among city residents?

"There is a striking association between consumption of sugary beverages and health literacy," Goldman responded. "The people who are most likely to consume sugary beverages are the people least likely to know the health risks associated with sugary beverage consumption."

Chief Judge Sidney Thomas asked if a warning label might deter a type 1 diabetic from consuming soda when going into insulin shock, when it would be beneficial. The concern was that the label did not distinguish between the types of diabetes. "You have to concede it's inaccurate," he said to Golden. "Your position is it doesn't matter."

"It is inaccurate, as to type 1 diabetes," Goldman said. "If that's the court's only concern with the language of the warning, the city can fix that."

Judge Fletcher said, "This is inaccurate with respect to diabetes, if we're talking about this from an analytic standpoint, in the same way the tobacco warning is inaccurate. It says causes cancer. Now, I'm not a doctor, or a medical researcher, but I suspect there are some forms of cancer that are not caused by the use of tobacco."

Then Judge Christen questioned the science. She referred to the website of the American Diabetes Association. "With respect to type 2, it says type 2 is not caused by sugar," Christen said, "but by genetics and lifestyle factors." Did that not make the label misleading or uncontroversial?

Goldman responded, "The American Diabetes Association does not dispute the evidence showing that sugary beverage consumption is associated with higher risk of type 2 diabetes, it absolutely does not dispute that. And in fact the 2015 [Dietary Guidelines Advisory Committee] report said that there is strong evidence of this association, and it isn't fully explained by body weight. So there is no dispute about that association."

By the time Goldman wrapped up, the complexities of the case were clear. The hearing illustrated the challenges of something as apparently simple as a warning label. How big was too big? What wording was accurate and appropriate? Were sodas uniquely harmful? Did lawmakers have any right to impose their will on the soda industry?

As the hearing wound down, Bress had time for a rebuttal. It had been precisely a week since he had stood in a DC court and expressed his frustration with tobacco analogies. But this time, it was Bress who used the analogy. "If I might end on the differences between this and tobacco, because I think a lot's been made of the tobacco warnings and this warning," Bress said. "The tobacco warning says cigarettes cause cancer. We do think that a reasonable person understands that as a warning about an inherent risk of a problem. A consumer would say if I smoke cigarettes, I increase my risk of getting cancer. And that's absolutely true, that they are increasing their risk of it, because there is no safe level."

The wording of the soda warning was insufficient, he continued. "The word *contributes to* is not better than *cause* because it's weaker," Bress said. "It's worse than *cause* because it's weaker, because it's more easily misunderstood."

With that, the chief judge declared the session in recess, and with a hammer of the gavel, the clerk said, "All rise." The judges filed out through a curtain behind their bench.

Bress appeared to exhale slightly. Then he turned to shake Goldman's hand.

52

When Judge Wingo convened the next hearing in the Praxis case, in February 2019, one attorney was conspicuously absent. In January, Rick Bress had gotten the American Beverage Association dismissed from the Praxis case. He had successfully argued that the ABA could not be liable under the DC statute because it did not actually sell any products.

Bress had certainly earned his keep in January. In addition to disconnecting from the Praxis case, his arguments in September had convinced the California appeals court to issue a preliminary injunction against the San Francisco soda-warning ordinance and remand it. In that ruling, the court found that the warnings, covering 20 percent of soda ads, would be "unduly burdensome" and would "offend Plaintiffs' First Amendment rights by chilling protected speech."

With Bress gone, it was only Coca-Cola squaring off against Kats and Rainer, and their plaintiffs. The first thing Judge Wingo did was to discuss standing—the matter of who was sufficiently connected to the alleged harm, and thus had the right to sue Coca-Cola. "I was struggling for some time with the standing issue," Wingo said.

Wingo denied standing for all three plaintiffs on the basis of the diversion of resources, and as testers (the assertion that they bought the Coca-Cola products to test their healthfulness). Wingo also considered standing under DC law stating, "A consumer may bring an action seeking relief from the use of a trade practice in violation of a law of the District." But even here, under this narrow definition, Coates failed to pass muster, because his complaint neglected to specify that the Coca-Cola products he purchased were sugar-sweetened, and because he did not state that his purchase was influenced by Coca-Cola's advertising.[1]

Finally, Wingo had determined that one plaintiff, Pastor Lamar, had standing on the basis of a violation of statutory rights. Although Wingo had determined that only one plaintiff had standing, this was sufficient to move the pastors' case forward.

After addressing standing, Wingo began to dissemble the case, systematically and very quickly. For starters, she said, anything that occurred prior to 2015 would be thrown out, due to a statute of limitations. This meant that the many items of alleged Coca-Cola deception from before 2015 that were listed in the lawyers' complaint would not be admissible.

Wingo also accepted Coca-Cola's argument that it had not been in control of the Global Energy Balance Network. At one point, Coke's Rhona Applebaum had sent Jim Hill and Steve Blair an email saying Coca-Cola needed to be "hands off" once the network was established. While critics of the corporation had used the interaction to point out its duplicity—that it was orchestrating the program but did not want its fingerprints on it—Judge Wingo accepted it at face value, as an indication that the network was independent of Coca-Cola.

Wingo said the public relations campaigns organized by the American Beverage Association would also be inadmissible: Coca-Cola held just a fraction of the board seats on the ABA, not enough to control its actions. And unlike the tobacco cases, Wingo said, there was no indication that Coke and Pepsi, for example, were conspiring on science.

This meant that many of the key items in the lawsuit would be thrown out. Rhona Applebaum's comment about Coca-Cola hydrating, from her talk in Vancouver? Out, for the statute of limitations. Steven Blair's comment about there being "really virtually no compelling information" tying junk foods to obesity? Out, because the Energy Balance Network was independent of Coca-Cola, in the judge's view. The Be OK and Coming Together ads that the attorneys claimed were deceptive? Out, for the statute of limitations.

Wingo was moving along quickly now. She seemed increasingly skeptical of the pastors' case. The hearing was scarcely twenty minutes old, and Maia Kats and Andrew Rainer could see their case being gutted before their eyes.

Kats and Rainer had every reason to be discouraged. With each hearing, the case had become gradually diminished. And today looked especially bad. Technically, it was a hearing on Coca-Cola's motion to dismiss. But Judge Wingo was quickly dismissing key elements of the plaintiffs' case.

Rainer stood to suggest to the judge that she was moving along too quickly. On the contrary, Wingo replied, the entire case had been moving along far too slowly.

Kats then rose. "My concern, Your Honor, is that we are separating everything when what we are alleging is an overarching—"

Judge Wingo interrupted Kats to say that maybe an overarching scheme worked with RICO—the Racketeer Influenced and Corrupt Organizations Act—but not in this case.

Kats asked for clarification: "I'm not understanding—"

Judge Wingo interrupted Kats in mid-sentence. "Hold on," she said, "I'm going to stop you there." Judge Wingo accused Kats and Rainer of unduly complicating the case. She said the "scattershot approach" that they took "created an incredible amount of extra issues that we have to go into. . . . We wasted a whole lot of time on things that are just irrelevant."

Rainer replied that it was all relevant, that this case could not be picked apart piecemeal; it referred to "an overall deceptive scheme," as in tobacco, as in global warming. "I try tobacco cases every year, Your Honor, and this is exactly the same thing," said Rainer.

"Minus the industry-wide agreement," said Wingo.

"How do you know that?" said Kats.

"This is not a fishing expedition," said Wingo.

Rainer rose to his feet now, his voice raised: "Coke is trying to pick items off one at a time."

Judge Wingo, increasingly frustrated, replied, "Just because you say it's like tobacco doesn't mean it's like tobacco."

After an increasingly heated exchange between Rainer and Wingo, Coca-Cola attorney Steven Zalesin, who'd been patiently waiting to speak, said to Rainer, "Please sit down, and don't interrupt me for once."

"He is right," said Judge Wingo, "you need to stop standing up while he is talking." Eventually, Judge Wingo called a lunch break, her exasperation with the case, and with Kats and Rainer, showing. "I would like everybody to take a deep breath," Judge Wingo said. The break could be a chance to cool down.

Rainer, unable to leave well enough alone, asked the judge to ponder something else over lunch, whether this was a "campaign to deceive," he said, "an overarching campaign by Coca-Cola to hide what it knew."

When the hearing reconvened an hour later, there wasn't much collegiality. Pierce sat talking with a colleague among the benches. Metcalf scrolled through her phone. Zalesin arranged papers. Kats and Simon talked quietly. Rainer fiddled with a PowerPoint deck: Praxis, Third Hearing. The courtroom was quiet, just the hum of the fluorescent lights and the hushed whispers of the lawyers.

Entering the courtroom, Judge Wingo said she'd spent her lunch hour trying to decide whether it made sense to go forward without a discovery rule. This rule asserts that a statute of limitations does not begin to run until the harmed party discovers the injury.

Wingo said the discovery rule raised more than one issue. What do you do when you have two different plaintiffs? "It's just not anywhere in the briefs," Wingo said. "It's not something we've discussed at all."

She said that it was very clear that as of 2012 the link between sugary drinks and health was of such concern that New York mayor Michael Bloomberg was trying to limit the size of sugary drinks. But she said you might have a different application of discovery for the individual plaintiffs, who would be less versed in these matters, versus Praxis, whose job it is to stay on top of health issues.

Zalesin said he could provide a brief on discovery, if it would help the court.

"I feel the plaintiffs are talking multiple bites of the apple. When one thing doesn't work, they try another," Wingo said. "That's not the way litigation is supposed to work."

Zalesin told Wingo that there was no indication that Lamar was influenced by Coca-Cola's Mixify ad campaign, or the bloggers' statements on the company's behalf, or anything else. The bloggers Zalesin referred to were dietitians whom Kats and Rainer had noted in their complaint, who had been paid by Coca-Cola to promote its products.

One such dietician was Robyn Flipse, a longtime paid ally of Coca-Cola and the ABA. In a 2015 article pegged to American Heart Month, Flipse had listed soda as a sensible snack: "Select portion-controlled versions of your favorites, like Coca-Cola mini cans, packs of almonds or pre-portioned desserts."[2]

Procedurally, Zalesin said he wanted any further hearings to be very focused. It seemed as though he was providing Wingo with a prescription of how to move forward with the case. "We're here today, and prepared to address those remaining ads today," Zalesin said.

Judge Wingo thought quietly for a long time, staring at the ceiling. "I am concerned with the approach here," Wingo said to Kats and Rainer, "which is the multiple bites of the apple." The judge asked for a five-page brief on discovery. But she said that when she received briefings from the plaintiffs, they often had exhibits that were not in the original complaint. "It's unusual to put in, when I asked for a brief, items that amend the complaint."

Wingo soon returned to the dietitian's statement. Zalesin said he believed there was nothing actionable in the statement. Wingo again sat in silence, looking over her glasses at Zalesin.

Zalesin noted that the defendant's experts said some people tend to consume too many, but that sugar-sweetened beverages themselves were not uniquely harmful. "That's why Coke runs ads that say everything counts," he said.

Again, the discussion had veered into the meat of the case, which was far beyond the matter at hand. "I'm a bit lost here," Kats said, "because I'm focused on the discovery rule."

Wingo asked, "But your position is that sugar-sweetened beverages are uniquely harmful?"

Kats said the primary matter, in their complaint, was that Coke has muddied the waters. "But it wasn't our intention to get into a battle over science," she said.

Zalesin said the case had morphed: "This is a very different case." It started out as public interest actors, then was narrowed to one individual who claimed that Coke failed to disclose the definitive links between sugar-sweetened beverages and obesity and disease.

"We completely disagree, Coca-Cola does, that there is a so-called 'definitive link,'" said Zalesin, making air quotes with his fingers around the phrase.

After a bit more tussling about the total calories versus the nutritional value of a bag of almonds, Wingo set a tentative schedule for moving the case forward, then left the courtroom.

53

It had been more than two years since Maia Kats had filed the lawsuit on behalf of the pastors and the Praxis Project. Now, in October 2019, Judge Wingo finally ruled on the five motions before the court. The judge's order formalized in writing some of her statements from the hearing in February. Coke won a bit of a reprieve, but the pastors' case at least stayed alive.

Coke, in its motion to dismiss, had argued that its statements were protected by the First Amendment, that the plaintiffs did not have standing to sue, and that the plaintiffs had not made a claim under the District of Columbia's Consumer Protection Procedures Act. Judge Wingo partly denied and partly granted the motion.

Perhaps the most notable finding was that Judge Wingo tightly limited the scope of actions Coke could be responsible for. This was not a big surprise, after her comments from the bench at the last hearing. The judge said Coke could not be held accountable for the actions and statements of the American Beverage Association, the Global Energy Balance Network, and the European Hydration Institute. This was a big victory for Coke, given how frequently it used such organizations as proxies to carry its messages.

In addition, Judge Wingo ruled that the statute of limitations barred any statements made before July 13, 2014.

In a win for the pastors, Judge Wingo denied Coke's anti-SLAPP motion. And in another victory for the plaintiffs, Judge Wingo confirmed and clarified the fact that they had standing to bring the action. This had seemed tenuous. And the judge's ruling showed the slender thread by which the case hung. She denied the pastors' standing based on the so-called tester standard. This is because the plaintiffs did not conduct any scientific testing on the sodas they purchased, or on their own blood sugar levels after consuming it. Further, "there was no evaluation of anything even remotely relevant to the question of whether 'a calorie of Coke is nutritionally equivalent to a calorie of any other food.'"

Judge Wingo also denied the pastors standing on the basis of diversion of resources. This was the argument Kats put forth on behalf of the pastors and the Praxis Project: that they had less time to dedicate to their primary work because the people they serve, having been misled by Coke and suffered the health consequences, were ailing, and even dying, requiring more of the pastors' attention.

But Judge Wingo did grant standing based on a violation of the plaintiffs' statutory rights: "the Court is persuaded that at least Plaintiff Lamar has standing, given his allegation that he would not have purchased Defendant Coca-Cola's products, specifically Sprite, had Defendant disclosed the link between the sugar-sweetened products and obesity, type 2 diabetes, and cardiovascular disease." Given Lamar's standing, the judge ruled, "The Court need not consider the standing of the other plaintiffs." Put another way, Lamar's standing alone met the threshold for keeping the plaintiffs' case alive.

The case could now creep forward. Judge Wingo ordered that the plaintiffs file an amended complaint. But Wingo would not be reading them. She had been reassigned to another court, and was passing the case on to a colleague, Judge José López. It had taken more than two years just to resolve preliminary motions and standing.

* * *

As time went on, the ambitious court case brought by the pastors in Washington, DC, was ground into finer and finer legal dust. In the fall of 2019, the attorneys for the Center for Science in the Public Interest withdrew from the case entirely. Maia Kats had left CSPI by then and was continuing to litigate the case while working for a private law firm. The case was moving at a snail's pace. The grand ambitions health advocates once had for the case were drying up.

V

THE NOOSE TIGHTENS

54

When Coca-Cola sales began to take off in 1906, its owner Asa Candler built a suitably noble skyscraper on Peachtree Street to house its headquarters. At seventeen stories, the Candler Building was the tallest in Atlanta, built with the finest white marble from northern Georgia. The ornate and elegant structure has, set in its cornerstone, a Bible, several newspapers, a portrait of Candler, and a bottle of Coca-Cola.

A luxury hotel now occupies the building, which Coca-Cola long since outgrew. Corporate headquarters are now on a large campus a mile and a half to the northeast, dominated by a utilitarian-looking twenty-nine-story building, topped on four sides with the iconic red logo.

That is where CEO James Quincey was speaking to a key group of analysts and shareholders on November 20, 2017, at Coca-Cola's first Investor Day since 2009.[1] Quincey had recently replaced Muhtar Kent as CEO, but Kent remained chairman of the Coca-Cola Company.

A British man who'd been with the company since 1996, Quincey brought some new ideas with him. But he stuck to the company line about energy balance.[2] "When we talk about obesity, a calorie is a calorie. The experts are clear—the academics, the government advisors, diabetes associations—we need to have balance in the calories," he'd said in 2013. "And if you're taking in too many, or burning them off, that is a problem; wherever they're coming from, a calorie is a calorie."

Now facing the investors, looking trim and healthy in a pale-blue, open-collared, button-down shirt, dark jeans, and low-heeled cowboy boots, Quincey strode the stage like a TED talker. A lavalier mic was clipped to his lapel and linked to a wireless unit clipped to his medium-wide, perfectly weathered leather belt. The stage was spare, empty but for a small, round white table, with a bottle of water perched on top. In one hand Quincey held the clicker he used to run through his deck of slides.

Quincey began by mentioning the company's global dominance, starting with sodas, known to the industry as sparkling beverages. "We are number one in sparkling beverages, which of course everyone knows and expects, but also the number one company across any RTD—nonalcoholic ready-to-drink," Quincey said. "We're the number one juice, dairy, and plant company. We're the number one hydration company. We're the number one tea and coffee company."

Put more simply, Coca-Cola's position as the world's top beverage company was secure indeed. The company had twenty-seven million customer outlets. And its global portfolio was balanced, Quincey said, with roughly a quarter of its revenue coming from each of four operating groups: North America, Latin America, Asia Pacific, and Europe/Middle East/Africa.

One important metric to Coca-Cola is billion-dollar brands—those that generate more than $1 billion in revenue annually. Quincey, appearing energetic but with bags beneath his eyes hinting at the stress of the job, said the company had twenty-one billion-dollar brands, and those had more than doubled in a decade. They range from Minute Maid orange juice to Vitaminwater to Georgia coffee (huge in Japan). But atop the multibillion-dollar heap are sugary standbys like Fanta and Sprite. And at the very top of the sales peak, of course, is Coca-Cola.

So it seemed appropriate that Quincey pivoted from overall corporate health to the soda wars. "The food and beverage industry is certainly coming under the microscope for more regulation around the world," Quincey told the investors, continuing his TED talk two-step—two slow steps left, two back, two to the right—and gesturing gently with the clicker in his hand.

"There are instances of taxation, particularly on sugared beverages, and sometimes broader, but including sugared beverages," said Quincey. "And we have to confront these realities. We have clear points of view, and beliefs about why and when taxation is a useful vehicle and how it should be implemented, depending on the objective. Depending on whether the objective is to generate funds for the government or to try and help solve the obesity problem. We're clear we need to be part of the solution. We have a clear strategy. We obviously have a clear view, as well, on narrow taxation not being effective. But we think we can help solve the obesity problem."

It was true that Coca-Cola had a clear strategy, at least in terms of fighting taxation. Just a month earlier, Coca-Cola and the American Beverage Association had successfully repealed a Cook County, Illinois, soda tax.[3] Their $3 million campaign featured an ad blitz, a front group called the Can the Tax Coalition, and anti-tax "protesters" hired for $11 per hour.

Quincey moved on to discussing the future of the company, which sounded futuristic. "Digitizing the enterprise" is critical, Quincey said. "If you used to like the old phrase, our products need to be within 'an arm's reach of desire'; maybe in the future that needs to include, they need to be within 'a click's reach of desire.'" Quincey used Coca-Cola's new motto, or catchphrase, "Beverages for Life."

Coca-Cola spends more than $4 billion on advertising annually. Over the years, the gist of the ads has been the same—sparkly, happy people doing fun things and drinking Coke. But the taglines seem to be getting shorter. Things Go Better with Coke. It's the Real Thing. Have a Coke and a Smile. Open Happiness. Each presented with an image of Coke. This new motto, Beverages for Life, seemed every bit as vaguely wonderful as anything ever to drip from a copywriter's pen.

Quincey discussed different sales strategies for the more than 200 countries in which the company operates. He said volume was still driving revenue in many parts of the world, especially in emerging markets. "It's not like volume disappeared from the equation," he said. "It's just, let's get clear, we want revenue, and whether that's places like the US, which is more price mix and not much volume, or places like India which is much more volume and less price mix."

That's a bit of soda jargon that is worth breaking down. Price mix is the strategy that includes, for example, selling smaller cans of Coca-Cola, which fetch a higher cost per ounce. This is a way for Coca-Cola to maximize profits in markets like the United States where consumers are starting to react to the flood of soda science, and seeking smaller servings. Volume is the old strategy of pushing more ounces into more stomachs more often. Whatever lip service Coca-Cola was offering about reducing calories in the United States did not apply, apparently, in India.

"We're clear that we need to push it harder," Quincey said. "We're clear that in order to drive a total beverage company we need to be much simpler with people and say, 'Look, it's about growth.' We need to have a growth orientation." He left off by assuring the investors of his long-term growth model. "So I think it's going to be an exciting journey," Quincey said, "an exciting new phase of growth, with a culture that underlines that expectation that we can turn this into a successful and grand future."

55

When he spoke to investors, Quincey had another reason to feel some confidence about avoiding the regulatory bullets that were starting to fly. A key Coke ally had been tapped to lead the Centers for Disease Control, just a few months earlier.

When US Department of Health and Human Services secretary Tom Price was looking for someone to run the CDC in July 2017, he picked a doctor already well known in Georgia: Brenda Fitzgerald, commissioner of the state department of health.

Price issued a press release trumpeting her substantial qualifications.[1] "Having known Dr. Fitzgerald for many years, I know that she has a deep appreciation and understanding of medicine, public health, policy and leadership—all qualities that will prove vital as she leads the CDC in its work to protect America's health 24/7," Price said. "We look forward to working with Dr. Fitzgerald to achieve President Trump's goal of strengthening public health surveillance and ensuring global health security at home and abroad."

Twitter had a split-screen response to Price's announcement. Rhona Applebaum, the former Coca-Cola staffer, simply tweeted: "An excellent choice!"

But CrossFit's Russ Greene tweeted this: "Trump's new @CDCgov director Brenda Fitzgerald was involved in 2 @CocaCola partners that received >$1.4mill." Greene linked to Fitzgerald's column posted earlier on Coca-Cola's website, "Solving Childhood Obesity Requires Movement," which did not include the words "diet" or "sugar." Greene was the first to note Fitzgerald's Coca-Cola connections after her appointment. But the story soon drew broader interest. The *Intercept* quickly ran a story about

Fitzgerald's Coca-Cola ties. Sheila Kaplan then wrote a front-page story for the *New York Times*.[2] Kaplan's story also noted Coca-Cola's donations to the CDC foundation, totaling more than $1.1 million over two years.

Although Fitzgerald's Coca-Cola connections attracted some attention, her undoing would come from another angle, and soon enough. A January *Politico* story ran under a dramatic headline: "Trump's Top Health Official Traded Tobacco Stock While Leading Anti-Smoking Efforts." The story, by Sarah Karlin-Smith and Brianna Ehley, cast Fitzgerald in a poor light.[3]

Fitzgerald had bought stock in Japan Tobacco after her appointment to the CDC and sold it a few months later. *Politico* also reported that Fitzgerald had owned stock in five other tobacco companies while leading the Georgia Department of Public Health. Fitzgerald resigned the next day.

In a *New York Times* story about the resignation, Sheila Kaplan noted Fitzgerald's close ties to Coca-Cola in Georgia. "As the state's public health chief, Dr. Fitzgerald made fighting childhood obesity one of her highest priorities," Kaplan wrote. "But she drew criticism from public health officials for accepting $1 million for Coca-Cola to pay for the effort. Her program drew heavily from the soda giant's playbook, emphasizing Coke's contention that exercise—rather than calorie control—is key to weight loss."[4]

Although Fitzgerald's Coca-Cola connections had drawn some fire, it was tobacco, not soda, that brought her down.

56

The transparency initiative Coca-Cola had rolled out after it was caught secretly funding the Global Energy Balance Network had won praise from some clean governance advocates. But it wasn't long before a researcher in England found evidence that its health funding was still as opaque as a two-liter bottle of Coke.

Writing in *Public Health Nutrition* in March 2018, the University of Oxford's Paulo Serôdio and colleagues analyzed Coca-Cola's research money and found that most was not declared.[1] Helpfully, they created visual maps of research nodes and connections. Lines fanned out from Steven Blair's node at the University of South Carolina, of course. Another node radiated from John Sievenpiper, at the University of Toronto. Jim Hill, the University of Colorado researcher, anchored another node. As did Carl Lavie, the Louisiana doctor.

In all, Serôdio found 389 articles, in 169 journals, written by 907 researchers who cited funding from Coca-Cola. But Coca-Cola, in its efforts toward transparency, had listed only forty-two of these authors. In other words, Coca-Cola had left 95 percent of the researchers off its list. And even this high percentage is clearly an undercount, because it did not capture any Coca-Cola–funded researchers who had not disclosed the funding.

"The Coca-Cola Company appears to have failed to declare a comprehensive list of its research activities. Further, several funded authors appear to have failed to declare receipt of funding," the authors wrote. "Most of Coca-Cola's research support is directed towards physical activity and disregards the role of diet in obesity. Despite initiatives for greater transparency of research funding, the full scale of Coca-Cola's involvement is still not known."

The paper came two years after Coca-Cola admitted that that its first transparency declaration had left out $14 million in health science funding. Now Serôdio was suggesting the corporation had omitted far more.

In a related blow for corporate-funded science, Mars, Inc., announced in March that it had decided to leave the International Life Sciences Institute. It was not a great surprise, after the corporation had criticized the ILSI paper on sugar that attracted so much criticism. Mars staffer Matthias Berninger said, "We do not want to be involved in advocacy-led studies that so often, and mostly for the right reasons, have been criticized."[2] It was a harsh rebuke. Mars could have left more quietly.

57

A paper published in the journal *Progress in Cardiovascular Diseases* in May 2018 seemed a long-awaited corrective to the cascade of research showing the health risks of sugar.[1] Edward Archer, the author, took a contrarian view. Archer said sugar was getting short shrift. "Therefore, given the unscientific hyperbole surrounding dietary sugars, I take an adversarial position and present highly-replicated evidence from multiple domains to show that 'diet' is a necessary but trivial factor in metabolic health, and that anti-sugar rhetoric is simply diet-centric disease-mongering engendered by physiologic illiteracy," Archer wrote. "My position is that dietary sugars are not responsible for obesity or metabolic diseases and that the consumption of simple sugars and sugar-polymers (e.g., starches) up to 75% of total daily caloric intake is innocuous in healthy individuals."

It was lively writing, and an interesting premise. And Archer is an interesting guy. In addition to the pages of research experience, his packed CV shows stints as a fitness consultant, a sporting goods designer, a project manager for a Long Island residential construction company, and a professional polo player competing for seven years in the United States, France, Australia, and Argentina. Archer had earned a PhD in exercise physiology from the University of South Carolina, where he had worked on Steven Blair's energy balance study. And he had served on an ILSI panel. To top it off, he had wound up at the University of Alabama, a vortex of Coca-Cola funded research, where his mentor was David Allison. But it gets better.

Who might publish such a contrarian view on sugar? It turns out that the editor of the journal that published the article was Carl Lavie, the doctor who was one of the scientists attending the Coca-Cola-sponsored press conference at the National Press Club. Lavie had been criticized for having accepted funding from Coca-Cola,[2] and now, as editor of this journal, he'd chosen to publish Archer's article.

Archer, Blair, and Lavie had been cooperating for years by now. In 2013, Archer, Blair, and Gregory Hand had written a paper that criticized the validity of the National Health and Nutrition Examination Survey.[3] The data from NHANES, as it is known, kept revealing associations that looked bad for the soda industry. Then the trio of researchers systematically critiqued it. Archer was the primary author of the paper they wrote for *PLOS One*, but he declared that the authors had no competing interests. Not only had Blair and Hand separately received funding from Coca-Cola, as a correction to the paper pointed out, but the study itself was funded by Coca-Cola.

Archer, Blair, Hand, and Lavie had also collaborated on a paper, for the same journal, that purported to show that the weight gain in women was driven by women doing less housework due to automation (which Jim Hill had joked about at the National Academy of Medicine).[4] That paper, too, was funded by Coca-Cola.

Now Archer's journal article for Lavie underscored a surprise about the exposé of the Global Energy Balance Network. While some people felt that they had been treated shabbily, everyone seemed to land on their feet. Sure, Jim Hill had left Colorado under a cloud, but he had landed a fine job at the University of Alabama. Gregory Hand had been forced out of his role as dean of the West Virginia School of Public Health, but he had assumed another role at the university. Steven Blair and Rhona Applebaum had quietly retired from the University of South Carolina and Coca-Cola, respectively, after long careers.

Meanwhile, industry-funded science just kept gushing out of the journals, like Coke from a soda fountain.

58

Speaking to a crowded auditorium in Boston in July 2018, Frank Hu was measured in his assertions. Americans consume twenty-two grams of added sugars daily, he said, most of that from sodas. That is 350 calories, every day. The added sugars constitute 15 percent of the average American's diet. When Hu went from looking at the broader issue of sugar to the specific issue of soda, the statistics became shocking: one serving of soft drinks daily is associated with a 30 percent greater risk of cardiovascular disease mortality. Dietary sugars affect blood pressure and serum lipids, even independent of body weight.

The audience was attentive, but likely not shocked. Hu was preaching to the converted. In fact, this was the national brain trust of sugar scientists, there for the annual conference of the Nutrition Obesity Research Center at Harvard. This year's theme: Sugar: The Epidemic. The fuller title was wonky and ambitious: "Epidemiologic, Physiologic, and Policy Consideration of the Sugar Epidemic."

The schedule was packed with some of the top researchers in the field. Sara Bleich talked about preemption and the food industry's efforts to debunk science. Barry Popkin of the University of North Carolina discussed the revolution of caffeinated sugary drinks that have conquered the world. Kelly Brownell of Duke University, a longtime soda tax advocate, gave a keynote speech about connecting sugar science to social and policy change. And Kimber Stanhope of UC Davis was there to describe her research on the metabolic effects of glucose and fructose.

In his presentation, Hu continued to cite dramatic statistics. Over ten years, sugar-sweetened beverages are responsible for nearly two million new cases of type 2 diabetes in the United States. And sugar-sweetened beverages magnify genetic risk of obesity. The best substitutes, to reduce weight gain? Water and coffee.

Not all fructose is created equally, Hu said. Liquid fructose—the kind found in high-fructose corn syrup—is strongly associated with a higher risk of type 2 diabetes. Fructose in solid form, as found in whole fruits like apples, blueberries, and grapes, is associated with lower risk of type 2 diabetes. Fruit juice is better for you than sodas, he said, but worse for you than whole fruit.

Wrapping up, Hu mentioned the USDA Dietary Guidelines Advisory Committee that he'd served on. While some of the committee's recommendations had been adopted—including a front-of-package calorie label, and the recommendation that added sugar make up no more than 10 percent of total calories—other key recommendations had been eliminated. Notably missing from the final guidelines were the recommendations specific to sugar-sweetened beverages, and soda taxes.

"Most of the recommendations have not gone anywhere," Hu noted diplomatically, "due to very challenging political conditions."

59

A few months later, in a lecture hall at the University of California, San Francisco, Marion Nestle told a crazy tale that started with Russian president Vladimir Putin, Hillary Clinton, and an email leak.[1] That politically motivated information dump, known as DC Leaks, turned out to have a lot of information about Coca-Cola, and about Nestle herself.

Nestle is a New York University professor, a longtime advocate for healthy foods, and the author of *Food Politics, Soda Politics*, and other books. After the DC Leaks dump, Nestle said she'd been contacted by CrossFit's Russ Greene, who told her that Coca-Cola executives mentioned her in some emails, which he blogged about. In fact, Coca-Cola had been closely monitoring her lectures and public appearances. Nestle said the emails provided the backbone for the first chapter of her latest book, *Unsavory Truth: How Food Companies Skew the Science of What We Eat*.

Nestle had mentioned the emails to UCSF professor Laura Schmidt. She was glad she did, because the DC Leaks site was taken offline soon after it had served its purpose of weakening Clinton's bid for the presidency. By then, Schmidt had arranged to have the Coke emails archived.

"So here they are at UCSF," Nestle said. "Thank you to all of you." Nestle was speaking at the November 2018 launch of UCSF's Food Industry Documents Archive, an online database with thousands of documents. The archive joined similar archives for the tobacco, drug, and chemical industries, all cross-referenced and often overlapping, collected in the UCSF Industry Documents Library.

Nestle was followed by Stanton Glantz, whose tobacco papers had catalyzed the archive. "It's a really unique role that we're playing here," Glantz said. "No other university that I know of has been willing to stand up to industries in this manner. The university got sued twice over this, thanks to the work we're doing, and we won twice. It just shows that if you stand up to bullies, you can, with a little help, beat them."

Nestle and Glantz, gray-haired veterans of the battle against the corporate manipulation of science, were followed by a relative upstart, Cristin Kearns. The food industry archives were the culmination of much of the work she'd done since hauling her documents to California in a U-Haul.

Kearns talked about her research journey from those Great Western Sugar Company files she discovered in Colorado to more papers at the University of Illinois and the University of Florida. She told the audience about how the Tobacco Documents Archive showed her how the sugar industry's PR campaign was related to the tobacco industry's. She said she knew of collections of thousands of pages of documents that had yet to be archived. "I do wonder how many more file cabinets and how many more basements are there out there, to find this material," she said.

When it was time for questions, an audience member asked Kearns what she thought were industry's biggest and worst offenses in hiding sugar's impacts on health. "I think the story is going to be a sort of larger story of all of these actions coming together," Kearns said. "It's a comprehensive set of strategies and tactics, and it's hard to pick out any one. I think that the enormity of just the scale of the work that they've undertaken, to me, that's the biggest piece. It's really hard to point to just one document or one event and say, 'It's this.'"

60

Up in the hills above Santa Cruz, CrossFit's global corporate headquarters shared a building with Dakota Ultrasonics, ReGeneration Church, and Robert Slawinksi Auctioneers in a small, modern office park tucked among redwoods between the freeway and a rifle range.

The administrative offices upstairs were trimmed out in industrial chic—a lot of exposed Douglas fir and a lot of glass. Downstairs was a big gym, with doors opening onto the parking lot for warm-weather workouts. And at one end of a corridor was a small conference room with a polished concrete floor and about fifty padded metal chairs. On this day in December 2018, the chairs were full of visitors, there for one of the semi-regular symposiums CrossFit had been hosting for doctors. Their goal was to deputize the 20,000 or so doctors who do CrossFit as warriors in the battle against chronic disease.

Sarah Hallberg was just finishing a talk about a controversial idea: the notion that an extreme low-carbohydrate diet can not only slow but also reverse type 2 diabetes. The concept is as crazy as it is true. Hallberg works for Virta Health, founded by Sami Inkinen, whose work was first roundly and fiercely criticized but eventually gained broad acceptance.

The assembled doctors also heard from Malcolm Kendrick, a doctor whose views on cholesterol got him kicked off of Wikipedia (for his CrossFit workout that afternoon, he wore a T-shirt reading "Wikipedia deleted my page and all I got was this lousy T-shirt"), and from Dr. Michael Eades, a low-carb proponent.

In each case, the message was similar. Much of the accepted science wisdom is not just wrong, but dangerously wrong. And this has happened due to systemic flaws and corruption within the field of research. There was a whiteboard in the lecture hall and a few general-interest talks. A self-defense seminar included a discussion about "situational awareness." A trainer discussed the nuances of training older people and less fit people. "A squeaky knee is not the reason you are going to avoid a squat, but the reason you are going to do it," he said. "Life demands a squat. Life demands a deadlift. Life demands a burpee."

Another contrarian spoke late that afternoon. Jason Fung, a Toronto nephrologist and author, talked about conflicts in medical research. Fung discussed the ways that financial conflicts of interest affect research: through industry funding of doctors, biased reporting of results, and selective publishing. "We need to save doctors from themselves," he said. "More and more people are talking about this. You have a bunch of corrupted journals; you have a bunch of corrupted research."

Fung discussed some of the myths perpetuated by the influence of industry. With opiates, there was the idea that when you're in pain, you can't get addicted. For tobacco, there was the lie that smoking doesn't cause cancer. More recently, he said, there has been the myth that fructose is a health food. Fung referred to a 2017 paper by a University of Toronto professor touting the benefits of fructose. "Well, now I see why you think Coca-Cola is a health food, put it next to the kombucha," Fung said. "This is the problem; they can just pay researchers to say, 'See, it's not that bad.'"

Fung mentioned the importance of transparency, of divulging the source of research funds. "Then the story would be: 'Coca-Cola physician says Coca-Cola is good for you.' Nobody would pay any attention to that," Fung said. "Instead you say, 'University of Toronto professor says Coca-Cola is good for you.'" The University of Toronto professor Fung referred to was John Sievenpiper.

61

Four weeks after the CrossFitting doctors had gathered near Santa Cruz, John Sievenpiper walked through the bright lobby of the Wyndham Grand hotel in Clearwater Beach, Florida. The Wyndham sits on a touristy barrier spit in the Gulf of Mexico, tethered by a causeway to Tampa. It was a coolish day, and the hotel was hosting a large, raucous group from Big Frog, a local T-shirt company made big. A man played a steel drum nearby, accompanied by a drum machine. Sievenpiper walked past a stack of complementary *New York Times* newspapers on a table in the lobby and headed toward a quieter gathering taking place among the conference rooms arrayed along a wing of the deluxe new resort.

The occasion was the annual meeting of the International Life Sciences Institute. A group of about a hundred mostly middle-aged people in business-casual dress loitered in the hall, where urns of coffee were diplomatically flanked by cans of Coke, Pepsi, and Dr Pepper. Each of the corporations had sent staffers to the meeting. But as has been the pattern since ILSI's inception in 1978, Coca-Cola representatives outnumbered Pepsi staffers two to one.

And that day, just as the conference opened, the attendees had an in-your-face criticism from those newspapers stacked in the lobby. There, on the front page of the *New York Times*, was a story titled, "With Obesity Rising in China, Coke Helps Set Nutrition Policy."[1] The story, by Andrew Jacobs, was based on research by Harvard's Susan Greenhalgh, showing that Coca-Cola had used ILSI to infiltrate and influence national health policy in China.

"In the decade after Coca-Cola launched its obesity campaign, the focus of China's obesity science and interventions shifted markedly from diet to physical activity, aligning them with the company's message," Greenhalgh wrote in the *Journal of Public Health Policy*. "In putting its massive resources behind only one side of the science, and with no other parties sufficiently resourced to champion more balanced solutions that included regulation of the food industry, the company, working through ILSI, re-directed China's chronic disease science, potentially compromising the public's health."[2]

Chen Junshi, the architect of ILSI's China campaign, was there in Clearwater. But nobody was panicking about the *Times* story, and the mood was mellow. The conference theme was ambitious: "A Brave New World in Nutrition and Food Safety."

Back along the hallway, Arti Arora, Coca-Cola vice president of scientific and regulatory affairs, was huddling on a couch with Clare Thorp, the newly tapped executive director of ILSI North America. Nearby, Sievenpiper and James Hill were laughing over their coffee. They had been Applebaum's co-conspirators in the Global Energy Balance Network, which was ingloriously disbanded after its Coca-Cola origins were exposed. But in Florida, Sievenpiper was far from a pariah—he was the chair of the science symposium planning committee.

Hill had left his job as director of the University of Colorado's Anschutz Health and Wellness Center after the Global Energy Balance Network scandal,[3] but he had recently landed on his feet. He was the new chair of the University of Alabama at Birmingham Department of Nutrition Sciences, and director of the UAB Nutrition Obesity Research Center.[4]

That was the whole point of the ILSI confab. Sievenpiper could chat comfortably in the hallway with Hill. And he could sit next to a Coca-Cola executive who was, at that moment, finalizing details for Coca-Cola to host the mid-year meeting of the International Food Information Council in Atlanta. (IFIC is the food industry front group that ILSI founder Alex Malaspina called "kind of sister entity to ILSI.") The conference held the food industry's brain trust of corporate spin.

In a small gathering for first-time visitors to the conference, an ISLI representative ran through a slide show and projected a soft-focus, warm-and-fuzzy video about the organization's work. One mind-numbingly arcane slide showed a flow chart of ISLI's seventeen divisions and foundations, illustrating the international scope of the organization.

The money slide was very simple. It was a Venn diagram, showing circles representing industry, government, and academia. That center area, the grayed-in area where the circles overlapped, was labeled "ILSI." This is the pattern that ILSI prides itself upon, and the pattern that critics view as an unholy alliance.

But it wasn't unholy, said ILSI's Andrew Roberts, because ILSI was all about transparency. "In our day and age, people are very wary of private sector funding," Roberts told the first-timers. "We do advocate that people should be informed by good science." A Coca-Cola employee sat nearby and took it all in, sipping from a bottle of water.

Over the meeting's several days, ILSI working committees on bioactives, sodium, and, of course, caffeine held members-only meetings. And members attended big lectures about microbiota, nanotechnology, and sustainability in the food industry. There were presentations about feeding compost to cockroaches in China, for example, then using them for chicken feed.

One speaker, Richard Williams, said the way we eat is about to change radically, but "consumers don't want to eat technology." Then he took a stab at naturalistic dietary advice, like the phrase, "If you can't pronounce it, you shouldn't eat it." And he paraphrased a John Prine song ("Blow up your TV, throw away your paper, go to the country, build you a home. Plant a little garden, eat a lot of peaches") as an illustration of simplistic hippie-think. Citing nutritionist Marion Nestle's assertion that foods from nature are healthy, Williams said he views nature as indifferent and capricious. From his perspective, natural food leaves something to be desired.

"Actually, I believe we can make foods much better than nature," he said. He touted 3-D food printing to treat obesity, because you can print out the right portion for everyone in the house. And you can 3-D print your food, drugs, and vitamins all together, and control the portions of fat, for example, and carbohydrates. For obvious reasons, Williams said he hates the term "Frankenfoods."

Karl Friedl of the US Army Research Institute of Environmental Medicine gave a keynote speech titled "New Technologies and the Fifth Industrial Revolution." Friedl talked about all of the emerging technologies that might improve fitness: integrated wearable systems, functional fibers, and "smart eyeglasses" that can tally food consumption. And he said such technology is needed, and soon, to address a growing problem for the military. "We have a shrinking number of recruits because they are overweight and they are already unfit," Friedl said. He displayed a still image from the movie *WALL-E*, showing blobs in recliners, sipping soda-like beverages. "This is a sort of dystopian view of where we're going."

Friedl's was a fascinating talk that also perfectly illustrated the manufactured complexity of the obesity conversation among industry-funded researchers. (Friedl himself had been a member of a working group on healthy food choices, funded by Coca-Cola, Pepsi, and others.) What Friedl did not say, what nobody at the conference said, was this: although obesity is complex, one critical remedy is simple—stop drinking soda.

Alex Malaspina, the Coca-Cola executive who had founded ILSI, did not attend, but he was well remembered in Clearwater. Malaspina remained the guiding light of ILSI long after his retirement, and ILSI acknowledges his service through its Malaspina International Scholars Travel Award. This is a Coca-Cola–funded program to support the work of young scientists from outside the United States. Indeed, Malaspina scholars from several continents roamed the halls, some looking a little stunned to be at a swanky resort hotel in the United States.

At an evening poster session and wine and beer reception, Chen Junshi stood by a poster illustrating ILSI China's recent work, including three Exercise Is Medicine trainings in 2018. The China example served to illustrate the point of critics like CrossFit's Russ Greene—that Exercise Is Medicine is primarily a Coca-Cola organization, and that the American College of Sports Medicine serves to legitimize the program. In the United States, Coca-Cola had transferred the reins of Exercise Is Medicine to the nonprofit organization. In China, Coca-Cola had opted to use ILSI as its front group. The effect is the same—Exercise Is Medicine is a massive, global organization, and few understand that it is a program conceived of and promoted by Coca-Cola.

Standing nearby, Jim Hill downplayed that day's *New York Times* story. He said he had been to some of the trainings in China, and they had not emphasized movement over nutrition. Hill, ever affable and engaging, a twinkle in his blue eyes, said it was also untrue that the Global Energy Balance Network had downplayed nutrition. "There is so much misinformation in the soda-health world," he said, growing animated, gesturing with his plastic cup of red wine.

But how about Steven Blair's comment, in the video for the network: "Blaming fast foods, blaming sugary drinks, and so on, and there's really virtually no compelling information that that is, in fact, the cause"? Hill dismissed this, too. "That was just Steve Blair."

And why is it that the people who agree with Hill, who emphasize energy balance, tend to also be those who are paid by the soda industry? Hill said there are plenty of others who agree with him. But people who share his views tend to keep their heads down, to avoid criticism. Overall, Hill said he was frustrated that the conversation had become personal and not focused on science.

As the conference ground on, attendance fell off. So there were plenty of empty seats when Clare Thorp took the podium. Thorp had newly assumed the position of executive director of ILSI North America. She talked about scientific integrity ad nauseam. The emphasis seemed a corrective, an effort to reinforce the message among the membership. Because for an organization that prides itself on independence and integrity, ILSI kept getting caught doing the bidding of its members, over and over again. It just couldn't seem to rein itself in.

It wasn't just that ILSI's Applebaum, Hill, and Sievenpiper had become the public faces of pseudoscience. Thorp also referenced the Mars situation. The corporation had first criticized ILSI-funded science, then left the group entirely. "Our membership comes with some major challenges and opportunities," Thorp said. "We've lost a major member. It happens. We keep going."

Unwittingly, Thorp worked doggedly to prove the aforementioned axiom, that the degree to which you have scientific integrity is inversely related to the number of times you claim it. "I have a passion for sound science. . . . I come from a family of scientists, whether practitioners or academics," she said. The science statements came out in torrents. "Unbiased and credible research . . . Scientific integrity is not something we made up overnight; it's a journey." She displayed a slide touting the Scientific Integrity Consortium, in partnership with the USDA, which she called "a coalition of the willing." "We are not an advocacy or a lobbying organization. But we are actually something entirely different," she said.

"ILSI is an industry-funded organization where these companies support research that doesn't directly serve their private interests. They agree to be hands-off . . . and they bravely commit to publishing the data, no matter what it says. This is very scary. And then, why would they do it? . . . It's actually altruistic. They genuinely believe it's important. They also believe that having a collaborative forum where everyone's voice can be heard is really necessary."

But it wasn't enough to just focus on the science. Thorp also considered the public perception of ILSI. She said she wanted to communicate their work more broadly, to step outside this circle of friends and take a more proactive approach. "We need to have a better understanding of who ILSI North America is, and what we do, and how we do it." In response, ILSI was developing more communications materials, she said, and new website graphics.

Then she displayed a slide showing an elaborate, graphically elegant word cloud. Some of the big words in the center of the cloud: "science," "truth," "food," "unsavory," "industry," "Nestle," "Marion." It turned out that the nonprofit had chosen to spend some of its money to hire a media tracker to follow the press coverage of Marion Nestle's recent book *Unsavory Truth*. The book focused on corporate influence in nutrition policy. The word cloud represented an analysis of the press coverage. And here, Thorp was actually pleased. "The themes of manipulation, deception, and conspiracy that Nestle is promoting are not coming through as main themes in the media coverage."

Thorp said that one of ILSI's challenges was the public perception that it's an industry front group, and that gets onto the web. "We are working very hard to get our Wikipedia page updated, and then it gets changed again, and then we have to update it again, but it's important," she said.

Leading ILSI had become a tough gig. Thorp would not last a year at the helm.

62

The next month, Coca-Cola and ILSI's machinations drew the ire of federal lawmakers. US representatives Chellie Pingree (Democrat from Maine) and Rosa DeLauro (Democrat from Connecticut) wrote to the inspector general of the US Department of Health and Human Services in early February, requesting an investigation.[1] At the heart of their concerns were Alex Malaspina and Rhona Applebaum—ILSI and Coca-Cola.

"The CDC has an essential mission," they wrote:

> Its pursuit of evidence-based public health policy is fundamental to the safety and well-being of all Americans. As we face an unprecedented obesity epidemic, we must ensure that the public can trust the agency to promote quality and objective data—particularly when it conflicts with powerful industry interests. Therefore, in your capacity as Inspector General, we ask that you investigate the relationship between the CDC and Coca-Cola outlined in this report, determine whether there is a broader pattern of inappropriate industry influence at the agency, and make recommendations to address this issue.

The letter referred to a report published the week before by several researchers, including Gary Ruskin of US Right to Know. Using Freedom of Information Act requests, they had revealed more about the cozy ties among Coca-Cola, ILSI, and the CDC.[2] "It is unacceptable for public health organizations to engage in partnerships with companies that have such a clear conflict of interest," they wrote. "The obvious parallel would be to consider the CDC's working with cigarette companies and the dangers that such a partnership would pose."

In one instance, a CDC official emailed Applebaum, inquiring about a job at Coca-Cola for a friend. Pingree and DeLauro also noted the time that Malaspina had complained to Barbara Bowman, of the Centers for

Disease Control, about WHO director general Margaret Chan, and called Chan's support of soda taxes "a global threat to our business."

By this point, Applebaum had left Coca-Cola and ILSI, after the public relations disaster of the Global Energy Balance Network. Bowman had resigned from the CDC, after her close ties to Coca-Cola and ILSI were exposed. And Malaspina, ILSI had made clear, had not held any formal post with the organization for years. Still, Pingree and DeLauro wanted assurances for the future.

Even as lawmakers pushed back, an event in DC that same month showed that ILSI's influence remained strong. The annual meeting of the American Association for the Advancement of Science bills itself as the world's largest general scientific gathering. Thousands of researchers and hundreds of journalists attend annually. The February 2019 meeting, held in DC, included a panel on scientific integrity.

The panel featured the researchers who had recently drafted a paper titled "Scientific Integrity Principles and Best Practices: Recommendations from a Scientific Integrity Consortium."[3] It got a bit of notice on social media under the hashtag #scientificintegrity. The session was organized by ILSI, which was a member of the Scientific Integrity Consortium. One panelist described it like this: "The focus will be extensively on the promotion of rigor, reproducibility, and transparency in research with examples drawn largely, but not exclusively, from the domains of nutrition and obesity research."

Who was this panelist, the expert on integrity in nutrition research? It was David Allison,[4] the Coke-funded researcher who coined the term "white-hat bias" to discredit the work of researchers who raised concerns about sugar. It was Allison who was the subject of the ABC News exposé in 2011. Now Allison was lecturing on scientific integrity, on an ILSI-organized panel, at the world's largest science conference.

63

In late April 2019, Muhtar Kent stood on the stage in a sun-drenched room before a crowd of Coca-Cola's most important, most engaged shareholders and raised a bottle of Coke. It was a toast to them, and a toast to him, as they celebrated his legacy. It was his last meeting as chairman, and he had delivered the goods, in spades.

Former US senator Sam Nunn, a Georgia Democrat who had gotten to know Kent well through his service on Coca-Cola's board, noted Kent's work on behalf of the shareholders. "From the time Muhtar became CEO in 2008 through today, the company returned $91 billion to shareowners," Nunn said, "$55.3 billion in dividends and $35.7 billion through share repurchases—this during a period of significant currency pressure."[1]

There was a bit more self-congratulatory corporate speak. But there was also a fly in the ointment on Kent's last day on the Coca-Cola stage. The shareholders considered five proxy questions, mostly run-of-the-mill queries such as approving a slate of board members and ratifying Ernst & Young as an independent auditor.

But when Ray Rogers rose to speak on a proxy item, Muhtar Kent and incoming chairman James Quincey knew what to expect.[2] Rogers had been a burr under Coca-Cola's saddle for years. "Thank you, Mr. Kent, I'm here representing John Harrington," Rogers began in a thick Boston accent. "Before I introduce John Harrington's proposal on sugar and public health, I want to ask two remarkable women, who have traveled long distances to be at this meeting, to stand up and be recognized. Dr. Esperanza Cerón, please stand up. Dr. Cerón has come here from Colombia. And Rebecca Berner is here representing Mexico's leading consumer organization, El Poder del Consumidor. Rebecca, over there, thank you.

No countries have been harder hit than Mexico and Colombia with skyrocketing rates of obesity, diabetes, and other serious health issues attributed to high consumption of sugar, especially what's referred to as liquid sugar found in soda, energy, and sports drinks."

Rogers was speaking on item five on the list of proxy questions. It was simply titled "Shareowner Proposal on Sugar and Public Health." In formal terms, the issue was this: "The Proponent, John C. Harrington, submitted a Proposal relating to the rapidly advancing scientific understanding that a national health crisis is being caused by sugar consumption in our national diet."

Harrington was asking the shareholders to "request the board of directors issue a report on Sugar and Public Health, with support from a group of independent and nationally recognized scientists and scholars providing critical feedback on our Company's sugar products marketed to consumers, especially those Coke products targeted to children and young consumers."

Coca-Cola had fought hard to keep the question away from its shareholders. The previous December, A. Jane Kamenz, Coca-Cola's securities counsel, wrote a thirteen-page letter to the Securities and Exchange Commission essentially arguing that the question was moot. It was a thoughtful, detailed letter. But the SEC disagreed.[3] So the question was on the proxy. And Ray Rogers was standing to address Kent and Quincey.

Rogers is a sharp-elbowed activist, with a full head of wiry gray hair, who began working on union campaigns soon after graduating from the University of Massachusetts in 1967. His father was a union lathe operator who had gone on strike against General Electric. As an activist shareholder, Rogers had been a steady presence at Coca-Cola's annual meetings. In 2004, after protesting Coca-Cola's links to murderous, anti-union, paramilitary forces in Colombia, he'd been ejected from the annual meeting in Wilmington, Delaware. But this year he had a different angle.

"There is mounting scientific evidence showing that there is a national and worldwide health crisis caused by overconsumption of sugar," he said, "and that the Coca-Cola Company, following the playbook of the tobacco industry, is trying to downplay the crisis and the scientific evidence." Developing momentum, Rogers continued assertively.

"Harrington, who heads up an investment company, is also trying to wake up and warn investors, and potential investors, in Coca-Cola, that if the company continues along the path of keeping its head in the sand and trying to deceive the public by funding front groups and producing junk science and bogus reports downplaying the detrimental effects of sugar consumption on health, the company's overall value could be at risk, and plummet," he said.

With a ringing bell indicating that his time was up, Rogers mentioned that Coca-Cola had lost the battle with the Securities and Exchange Commission over adding this question to the proxy statement. For more details, he asked shareholders, "Please visit our newly revamped website, www.KillerCoke.org."

Kent responded in a lower voice, a slower cadence, and very measured tones. "Thank you, Mr. Rogers," Kent said. "You actually talked about really what is our board's position on this proposal. This proposal requests, specifically, that the board issue a report on sugar and public health, with support from a group of independent, nationally recognized scientists and scholars." Kent said the Access to Nutrition Foundation, "a respected nonprofit organization, based in Holland, funded by the Bill & Melinda Gates Foundation, the Dutch Ministry of Foreign Affairs, and the Robert Wood Johnson Foundation," had already issued such reports, as recently as 2018. Any additional report would provide no new useful information.

"Importantly, though," Kent continued, "let me just again stress that we certainly recognize the role our company must play in addressing health challenges. This proposal might lead you to believe that our company is not a responsible player in this area, and nothing, nothing, could be further from the truth. Our company fully comprehends that people should not eat, or drink, too much sugar. We're taking, also, specific and meaningful actions, to help make consumers more aware about, and more easily control the consumption of added sugar," he said. "Just to give you a couple of bullet points: 425,000 tons of sugar have been removed from the market through product reformulations and packages. Only in 2018, last year, 400 products were reformulated alone, bringing the total to 800. Products with no sugar, that we have, are growing double digits, like Coca-Cola Zero Sugar. And 40 percent, now, 40 percent of our sparkling soft drink brands in the US come in eight-and-a-half-ounce mini cans. And North America last year saw 30 percent growth in its mini cans. And we finally, we finally support the WHO recommendation in limiting added sugar to 10 percent of the total diet. We support that. Publicly we've said that. So those are just a few bullet points."

The WHO guidelines that Kent said the corporation supported are the same guidelines it had fought vigorously against. As it had with soda sales in schools, Coca-Cola was quick to turn a policy it had vigorously fought to one it seemed always to have wanted, and to have voluntarily embraced.

Turning to James Quincey, Kent said, "And I don't know if our CEO James would like to add anything."

"I think you've covered it," Quincey said.

The effort failed. Votes representing three billion shares were cast against it, and a mere 5 percent—152 million—were cast in favor.

64

Several months later, on a soccer field in Lyons, France, in the second half of a nail-biting game, Megan Rapinoe sunk a penalty kick to put the American team ahead of the Netherlands. It was the final match of the FIFA Women's World Cup. Seven minutes later, Rose Lavelle added to the team's lead. A crowd of thousands soon roared as the American women took the crown.

Photos of the event will show two things: the jubilant team, so bold, so strong, so charismatic, so all-American. And, just behind them, the entire perimeter of the field illuminated by brilliant red-and-white Coca-Cola signs. It was a good advertising investment. Forget the thousands cheering in the stands. The event was broadcast to more than a billion soccer fans worldwide.

Coca-Cola's marketers are all-stars, in a league of their own, and they are especially good at marketing to sports fans. The marketing reaches a crescendo every four years when the World Cup and the Olympics roll around. Tobacco advertising has been banned from both events since the 1980s, but Coke is still a primary sponsor. It has sponsored the Olympic Torch Relay for three decades. (Steven Blair, who led the Global Energy Balance Network for Coke, was among the torchbearers for the London Olympics in 2012.)

In February 2018, figure skater Adam Rippon looked straight into the camera and talked about his Olympic experience in South Korea, and his feud with the vice president over gay rights. "I don't want my Olympic experience to be about Mike Pence," he said. "I want it to be about my amazing skating, and being America's sweetheart."[1] The breakout star of that year's Winter Olympics appeared in the video looking handsome, fit, and trim. The only other item in the frame was a bottle of Coca-Cola, placed front and center.

The brilliant Olympic marketing especially rankles Eva Twardokens, who was on the US ski team for twelve years. She stood on the podium at World Cup races, and represented the United States in the Olympics. (Twardokens was also a CrossFit pioneer.) "I'm watching the commercials for the Olympics and seeing 'Games sponsor, Coca-Cola, McDonald's.' And I'm like WTF?," Twardokens said. "For someone who is an Olympian, and that's part of my DNA, to see freaking Coca-Cola, and all of these junk foods sponsoring, it kills me."

Coca-Cola also invests in men's soccer, its logo adorning the jerseys of superstars like Lionel Messi. In India, Coke sponsors cricket.

"In the US it is very cleverly associating Coca-Cola with sporting events, national events," Melissa Mialon said. "And they are exporting the practices they have developed in the US, and it's very damaging to the other countries." Mialon is a researcher who has traveled the world to study the commercial determinants of health—the notion that companies such as Coke and Philip Morris play key roles in shaping the health of consumers. Mialon said that in developing countries, people have less awareness of the health risks associated with sugary beverages. "They are still at the stage where they think, this is nice—having a car, drinking a Coke, smoking a cigarette," she said. "People don't see Coca-Cola, for example, as a bad company, like Monsanto or the tobacco companies."

At home in the United States, Coke has long sponsored Major League Baseball, National Football League, and National Basketball Association teams. Hoops star LeBron James even developed his own line of Sprite with Coca-Cola. It also sponsors athletic venues like Coca-Cola Field, a minor league baseball park in Buffalo, New York.

Coca-Cola has also tried to tap into the athletic ethos with Bodyarmor SuperDrink and Powerade, knockoffs of Pepsi's Gatorade. All of these so-called sports drinks are primarily brand extensions for Coke and Pepsi, other vehicles for the soda companies to sell sugar-sweetened beverages.

In all, the advertising dollars have had their intended effect. Sports fans are awash in soda advertising, and the association of athleticism and sugary beverages endures. Watching the highlights reel from that 2019 World Cup, millions of fans have seen Rapinoe in the foreground, back arched and arms raised triumphantly, in a field literally surrounded by ads for Coke brands—Smartwater, Fuze Tea, Minute Maid, PowerAde, and, of course, in that iconic red-and-white script, Coca-Cola.

65

With each passing month, the scientific noose was tightening around the necks of the soda deniers. A 2019 paper by Vasanti Malik, Frank Hu, and colleagues pulled it a bit tighter, by looking at a specific risk posed by sugar-sweetened beverages: the risk of death.

The team analyzed twenty years of data in two studies, totaling more than 100,000 adults. They found that sugar-sweetened beverages were associated with an increased risk of early death.[1] Their analysis found the association between soda consumption and death even after adjusting for diet and lifestyle factors. Compared with people who rarely drank sugar-sweetened beverages, those who drank two or more servings daily had a 21 percent higher risk of early death. And those who only had two to six sugary beverages per week still had a 6 percent increased risk of an early death. The association was graded—the higher the consumption, the greater the risk. "Each serving per day increment in SSB was associated with a 7% higher risk of death," they wrote.

The sodas posed a greater risk for cardiovascular disease than for cancer, but the risks were significant for both. The cancer mortality appeared to be driven by increased incidence of breast and colon cancers. As in previous analyses, the researchers found that sugar-sweetened beverages were associated with weight gain and with higher risks of hypertension, type 2 diabetes, coronary heart disease, and stroke. Adjusting for body mass index did not alter the estimates. In other words, while sugar-sweetened beverages increased the risk of both weight gain and early death, the two seemed to be independent of each other.

In all, it was a strong enough indictment of sugar-sweetened beverages to prompt an accompanying editorial: "Last Nail in the Coffin for

Sugar-Sweetened Beverages," by Alice Lichtenstein of Tufts University.[2] "Rather than generating more data on the adverse effects of SSBs, we need to move on to the harder task and aim to make greater strides in understanding what the motivation is for choosing SSBs despite knowledge of the risks," she wrote. "What is important is that we have identified a problem, and we need to focus a concerted effort on fixing it permanently."

It was a strong argument: the case is closed, sugar-sweetened beverages are very harmful, let's work together to minimize the risks.

The research and the editorial were more powerful for where they appeared. *Circulation* is not the sort of second-tier, pay-for-play journal in which some of the Coca-Cola-funded research had appeared; it is the official journal of the American Heart Association.

* * *

That December, the scale of the obesity crisis added another prospective data point, according to the calculations of a team of researchers from the Harvard T. H. Chan School of Public Health. By the year 2030, nearly one in two American adults would have obesity. The analysis for the *New England Journal of Medicine* tried to compensate for a chronic problem in self-reported data: many people say they are taller than they really are, and weigh less than they actually do. Both conspire to skew body mass index (BMI) readings for the better. Zach Ward, Sara Bleich, and colleagues estimated that the prevalence of obesity would be greater than 50 percent in twenty-nine states, and not below 35 percent in any state. More notable still, the number of adults with severe obesity—those who are more than one hundred pounds overweight—was projected to climb dramatically. By 2030, one in four Americans would have severe obesity.[3]

"We also find that some demographic groups are at much higher risk for severe obesity," Ward said, discussing his grim findings in a video. "So we find nationally that severe obesity will become the most common category; it used to be very rare, but we're projecting that it will become the most common BMI category nationally for women, for non-Hispanic black adults, and for low-income adults, adults who make less than $50,000 per year, annual household income."[4]

The news was even more dramatic for the lowest of the low-income Americans, Ward said. "And we find that for very low income adults, those making less than $20,000 annual household income, severe obesity will be the most common BMI category in forty-four states, so basically everywhere in the country," Ward said. "So we find that obesity is getting worse, more people are going to have it in every state, and the degree, the severity, of obesity is also getting a lot worse."

Ward presented one possible remedy: "One of the most effective interventions, and cost-effective interventions, that we've found is limiting the intake of sugar-sweetened beverages."

Sara Bleich, a coauthor on the paper, said it brought a degree of gravity to the research on sugar-sweetened beverages. "If you'd ask people 'Is Coca-Cola bad for you?' I think the average American would say 'Yes,'" Bleich said. "And that's part of the reason we're seeing this decline over the past ten years. If you ask the average American, 'Can drinking soda cause me to get obese and kill me?' I don't think people would understand that. The link between poor health while you're alive, the diabetes and the excess weight, people sort of get that. But this link between diet and death, I don't think people totally appreciate that, particularly young people. And that's where I think there are opportunities for education without scaring people."

* * *

So ended a wild decade in the soda wars. A decade in which the ever-growing science implicating sodas in the national chronic disease crisis was matched by increasingly sophisticated disinformation campaigns by the industry. A decade that saw Coke fly off the shelves, and under the radar of regulators. A decade in which many Americans still had not received the memo about the risks of sugar-sweetened beverages.

EPILOGUE: COKE SLIPS THE NOOSE

In 1949, the San Francisco Board of Education tried to ban sugary drinks from schools. Coca-Cola developed a targeted public relations campaign to fight the proposal, including a visit to the school board by the owner of the local bottling plant. Soon the ban was scotched.

Back in Atlanta, Coca-Cola executive Roy Gentry sent a colleague a file of correspondence about the controversy. He topped it with a brief, handwritten memo: "An interesting file on one of the most dangerous situations yet—San Francisco Board of Education. Glad to report 'Marines have landed and have the situation well in hand.'"[1] The wartime analogy was hardly hyperbolic. People had been gunning for Coca-Cola for years, and they had been left in the mud. So the trend continues. In the decade covered by this book, nearly every jab by the health advocates was parried by Coke and its allies.

In San Francisco, seventy years after the proposed soda ban in schools, the effort to place warning labels on soda ads met equally strong opposition. Reacting to the legal challenge from the American Beverage Association and its lawyer Rick Bress, the San Francisco Board of Supervisors had amended the ordinance. It reduced the warning-label size from 20 percent to 10 percent, and modified the text to clarify the type of diabetes associated with sugary beverages.

The American Medical Association and California Medical Association filed an amicus brief in support of the case, stating, "Although uncontroversial, the facts about sugar-sweetened beverages (SSBs) are not yet known to many San Franciscans—including many people with prediabetes of [type 2 diabetes]—who consume SSBs at high levels."[2] But after still more legal wrangling, the case was dismissed in September 2021 when

San Francisco withdrew even the watered-down labeling ordinance. It was a decisive victory for the soda industry.

The more ambitious court case brought by the pastors in Washington, DC, had been steadily whittled down. Finally, in the winter of 2021, the pastors withdrew their case. Like the tobacco lawsuits, this was a tough legal row to hoe. As Naomi Oreskes and Erik M. Conway wrote in *Merchants of Doubt*, "Although 125 lawsuits related to health impairment were filed against the tobacco industry between 1954 and 1979, only nine went to trial, and none were settled in favor of the plaintiffs."[3]

In a press release, the pastors and their legal team claimed partial victory: "The good news is that, since we filed our suit, Coca-Cola and the American Beverage Association have moved away from claiming that their products have no connection to chronic disease." They also asked for Coca-Cola to stop trying to preempt soda taxes, stop targeting marketing in communities of color, and stop funding research and advocacy to shift blame for obesity away from sugary drinks. "The beverage industry's manipulation to protect their sales, especially in communities of color and communities with lower incomes, is killing us. Literally," they said. "The current Covid-19 pandemic that is extremely lethal in our communities shows that underlying conditions matter. The beverage industry needs to stop hindering our efforts to increase healthy beverage consumption as we seek to decrease the underlying conditions that have made our communities more vulnerable to the Coronavirus."[4]

As the COVID-19 pandemic began sweeping the world in 2020, sickening and killing millions,[5] the deaths were not equally distributed. Old and infirm people were more susceptible to dying from the virus. People with chronic disease were also more vulnerable. And the virus disproportionately infected and killed people of color.

Xavier Morales, executive director of the Praxis Project, one of the plaintiffs in the pastors' lawsuit, was pointed in his criticism of Coca-Cola. "It is their product that is causing the underlying conditions that are making the coronavirus worse in many of these communities that they predatorily market to," Morales said. "We're socializing the health costs, while they are privatizing the profits."

Yolandra Hancock, the George Washington University obesity researcher, said the pattern emerged early in the pandemic. "To those of us in public health, this was no surprise to see this disparity in Black and brown communities," Hancock said. Obesity stood out among the factors associated with greater risk of poor outcomes, including death, following COVID-19 infections.

COVID-19 offered one lens to view chronic disease in the early 2020s, and the emerging science about sugar-sweetened beverages offered another. Researchers had greatly reduced doubt over the ills of sugar-sweetened beverages over the past decade, and mainstream health organizations had increasingly been warning about the health risks. Meanwhile, the costs of chronic disease and obesity were rising steadily. One study found that the obesity epidemic accounted for more than $170 billion in excess medical costs annually in the United States.[6] More than 35 million Americans, nearly one in ten, had developed type 2 diabetes.[7]

At the same time, life expectancy in America was falling. In large part, this was due to chronic diseases like heart disease, liver disease, and type 2 diabetes. And the gap was widening between wealthy and low-income Americans, with the latter having lower life expectancy.[8]

Both data points—increasing health care costs and falling life expectancy—show that it is not enough to treat the symptoms of chronic disease. It's a challenge that must be addressed at its root. And a primary root is the consumption of sugary beverages, and other ultra-processed foods that dominate the Western diet.

It's important to recognize that the epidemic of chronic disease did not just happen. It's the logical end point of industries flooding the market with hyperpalatable foods, hiding their health risks, and evading regulation. As former WHO director general Margaret Chan put it in her address to the National Academy of Medicine, it is a systemic problem, "not a failure of individual willpower to resist fats and sweets or exercise more. It is a failure of political will to take on powerful economic operators, like the food and soda industries."

The Global Energy Balance Network exposé might have seemed a turning point for soda-funded disinformation, but that conclusion seems premature. Coca-Cola has been using academics, researchers, doctors, dietitians, and journalists-for-hire to convey its messages since at least the 1940s, and continues to do so.

The University of Alabama at Birmingham offers one more recent example. Its program Live HealthSmart Alabama aims to help underserved communities. The program happens to be under the aegis of department of nutrition chair Jim Hill, the longtime Coke ally and conduit for Coke funding. When Coca-Cola UNITED, the local bottler, donated $250,000 to the initiative in 2023, its executives posed for a grip-and-grin photo with an oversized check, allowing it to appear to be on the side of health and wellness in underserved communities.[9] Meanwhile, Coke's sales and marketing teams were aggressively pushing sugar-sweetened beverages in those same communities, every day.

By 2020, the International Life Sciences Institute, established by Coca-Cola executive Alex Malaspina, seemed ever more influential. Of the twenty members of the 2020 Dietary Guidelines Advisory Committee, five had strong ties to ILSI.[10] But late that year came an indication that it may have passed its apex. Coca-Cola followed the lead of Mars and Nestle, and quietly decided to stop funding ILSI.[11] It said the decision came after a routine review, but offered no details.

Coke can claim a huge success for another of its projects. Exercise Is Medicine, which Coca-Cola cofounded to shift the conversation from diet to activity, is now well-established globally. You have to look hard to find Coke's fingerprints on it.

Despite Coca-Cola's unparalleled public relations campaigns, it was clear by 2020 that Americans had reduced their soda consumption. And evidence was mounting that soda taxes in places like Philadelphia were contributing to the decline. Research published in early 2024 analyzed soda sales in Philadelphia, Boulder, Seattle, Oakland and San Francisco, from 2012 to 2020. "In this cross-sectional study, SSB taxes led to substantial, consistent declines in SSB purchases across 5 taxed cities following price increases associated with those taxes," the researchers wrote. "Scaling SSB taxes could yield substantial public health benefits."[12]

Meanwhile, aggressive policies to curb soda consumption in Chile, Mexico, and the United Kingdom provided road maps for future policies in the United States. Chile, for example, had passed a 2016 law restricting the marketing of sodas and other foods high in sugar, salt, and saturated fat, and requiring "front of package" warning labels. One study found a 24 percent reduction in consumption of beverages covered by the law.[13]

Both examples—soda taxes in the United States and more aggressive policies abroad—show that Coca-Cola was right to perceive that soda taxes and warning labels threaten its business model, and to fight them tooth and nail. And both examples show that public health advocates were right—thoughtful policy can reduce the consumption of sugar-sweetened beverages, and improve public health. They also illustrate the binary nature of the battle: Coke is on one side, public health the other. There is no middle ground.

By late 2023, momentum appeared to be building for federal policies to improve nutritional labeling on sodas in the United States. In December, US Representative Jan Schakowsky, a Democrat from Illinois, and Senator Richard Blumenthal, a Democrat from Connecticut, introduced the TRUTH in Labeling Act (TRUTH standing for Transparency, Readability, Understandability, Truth, and Helpfulness). "A poor diet is one of the leading causes of preventable disease in the U.S.," Congresswoman Schakowsky said in a press release. "We must do all we can to create transparency in food labeling and empower consumers to make informed dietary decisions."

At the same time, Senator Bernie Sanders, chair of the Senate Committee on Health, Education, Labor, and Pensions, called for a federal ban on junk food advertising to kids. "While diabetes and obesity rates in America soar, while we spend hundreds of billions of dollars to treat diabetes, the food and beverage industry spends $14 billion a year on advertising to make many of their unhealthy products irresistible to the American consumer," Sanders wrote in an op-ed for *USA Today*. And he singled out Coke: "Last year, for example, Coca-Cola Co. spent $327 million on advertising in the United States alone while it raked in more than $9.5 billion in profits. None of their ads will tell you that drinking one or two cans of Coke a day will increase your chances of getting Type 2 diabetes by 26%."[14]

And in a February 2024 letter, Sanders urged the FDA to require warning labels on products high in sugar, salt, and saturated fats. "This is not a controversial idea," Sanders wrote. "Countries like Chile, Colombia, Uruguay, Peru, and others have successfully implemented strong front-of-package nutrient warning labels."

History shows that if the senator hopes to reform food regulation, he ought to pack a lunch and make a day of it. Despite the handful of municipalities that have implemented soda taxes, the beverage industry has successfully averted a broader wave of taxes, and statewide taxes or a national tax still seem far off. Academic institutions in the United States continue to align themselves with Coca-Cola, and nonprofit groups continue to do its bidding. Meanwhile, athletic events like the Olympics, the World Cup, and Major League Baseball teams like the Oakland A's take millions in Coca-Cola advertising dollars, and bear its logos. There are societal failures to hold the industry to account at nearly every level.

The recent decline in soda consumption is absolutely a victory for public health, but it's a qualified success. By 2019, per-capita sugar-sweetened beverage consumption had declined to about the same level as in 1983. But in 1983, health advocates were already decrying the ill effects of sodas. They were doing so in 1972, when soda consumption was far lower. They did so in the 1950s, and even in the 1940s, when Americans consumed perhaps a third as much soda as in 1983. They did so even as far back as 1909, when soda was, for most people, a rare treat. In addition, there's growing evidence that, in some parts of the United States, the drop in soda sales is offset by other types of sugar-sweetened beverages sold by Coke and other beverage giants, including sugar-sweetened juice drinks, coffees, and energy drinks.[15]

Another perspective is that the decline in soda consumption in the United States merely indicated that a century of dramatic growth had come to an end. Coca-Cola remained profitable by enticing consumers to pay more per ounce of soda, and through vigorous growth overseas.

Smoking presents another frame of reference for soda consumption. At the peak, in 1964, 42 percent of Americans smoked. After sixty years of effort, that number is down to 12 percent. About one in nine Americans now smoke.

This, too, is a great victory for public health. And it is also a good example of a shifting baseline. Had America gone from zero smokers, or, say, 1 percent, to 12 percent, it would be considered tragic. The decline from a very high rate of smoking to today's level masks the reality that smoking remains one of the leading causes of preventable death in America.

So, too, with sugary drinks. The reduction in per-capita consumption obscures the reality that as many as one in two Americans drink enough soda to increase their risk for a range of chronic diseases.[16]

While Coca-Cola executives make obtuse calculations about the amount of sugar that is no longer on the market, they will never say, "We are working to reduce the sales of Coca-Cola and other sugar-sweetened beverages." They are not. It is analogous to oil companies that hype renewable energy, but will never say, "We are working hard to keep carbon in the ground, where it belongs." They are not, and campaigns that suggest otherwise are disinformation.

Likewise, Coca-Cola is working, day and night, to increase sales of Coke and its other sugar-sweetened beverages any way it can. Coke chairman and CEO James Quincey's assertion that it is still pushing "volume" in developing countries is one piece of evidence. Another, in the United States, is Coca-Cola's steady introduction of new full-sugar products.

In 2024, Coke introduced a new soda, Coke Spiced. In a February earnings call, Quincey said Coke Spiced "is really aimed at increasing connectivity with Gen Z and the broader consumers, driving engagement, driving reconsideration." He said he wants to reengage consumers with the Coke trademark.

In this case, he's engaging consumers through a product that is actually sweeter, in its standard formulation, than Coke. Spiced has two more grams of sugar per twelve-ounce serving, and ten more calories. It's sweeter, it's deadlier, and it's marketed to a new generation of young Americans. The battle between Coca-Cola and public health rages on.

ACKNOWLEDGMENTS

When I wrote the book *Caffeinated,* I was impressed that sodas are America's favorite caffeinated beverages by volume, not coffee or tea. And the more I learned about the health risks of sugar-sweetened beverages, the more surprised I was at how they are often hidden, by design. It seemed that much of the public was unaware of the severity of those health risks. That led me down the long path to this book, and I'm indebted to those who helped along the way.

Thanks to the dozens of sources who trusted me with their stories, especially the health professionals and researchers who patiently walked me through their findings. The UCSF Industry Documents Library was invaluable in reporting this book, and it has been exciting to watch the library grow and improve. The Robert Winship Woodruff papers at Emory University also proved fruitful. Many people in the CrossFit community were quite helpful when I started this work. Editor Annys Shin helped frame some of that early reporting for a story I wrote for the *Washington Post Magazine*.

Thanks, also, to the many journalists who have covered Coke thoroughly for years, writing the first rough drafts of history. In addition to the works cited, I found helpful background information on Coca-Cola in Constance Hays's *The Real Thing,* and Michael Blanding's *The Coke Machine*. Beth Macy's *Dopesick* was also useful for understanding the opioid epidemic, and David Kessler's *A Question of Intent* gave me a better understanding of the tobacco industry.

My agents Sascha Alper and Larry Weissman helped steer this project from its inception and have been steady hands through sometimes rough seas. The enthusiasm and clear direction of editor Beth Clevenger and her team at the MIT Press have been invaluable. The book also benefited from the sharp insights of fact-checker Julie Tate.

A big thanks to the supportive community of journalists around me—writers, reporters, photographers, and editors—including the team at Maine Public Radio. Also to my friends who've heard a lot about this book over coffee, and while fishing, surfing, and adventuring in the wilds.

Huge thanks to my entire family, including a far-flung network of cousins. My brothers Andrew and Charlie, and mother Sally, offered sage advice, but only when solicited. And the greatest thanks to Margot, Lila, and Romy, who have strongly supported this work from the get-go.

NOTES

PROLOGUE

1. Vicente Javier Clemente-Suarez et al., "Global Impacts of Western Diet and Its Effects on Metabolism and Health: A Narrative Review," *Nutrients*, June 2023, https://pubmed.ncbi.nlm.nih.gov/37375654/.

2. "About Chronic Diseases," National Center for Chronic Disease Prevention and Health Promotion, accessed April 26, 2021, www.cdc.gov/chronicdisease/about /index.htm.

3. "U.S. Overdose Deaths Decrease in 2023, First Time Since 2018," CDC National Center for Health Care Statistics, May 15, 2024, https://www.cdc.gov/nchs/press room/nchs_press_releases/2024/20240515.htm.

4. "Overweight and Obesity Statistics," National Institute of Diabetes and Digestive and Kidney Diseases, accessed April 26, 2021, www.niddk.nih.gov/health-information /health-statistics/overweight-obesity; "Obesity and Overweight," CDC National Center for Health Care Statistics, accessed April 26, 2021, https://www.cdc.gov/nchs /fastats/obesity-overweight.htm.

5. Mascha Koenen et al, "Obesity, Adipose Tissue and Vascular Dysfunction," *Circulation Research*, vol. 128, no. 7, April 1, 2021, https://www.ahajournals.org/doi/full /10.1161/CIRCRESAHA.121.318093.

6. Center for Science in the Public Interest, video accompanying press release, "Lawsuit Alleges Coca-Cola, American Beverage Association, Deceiving Public about Soda-Related Health Problems," July 13, 2017, https://www.cspinet.org/news/law suit-alleges-coca-cola-american-beverage-association-deceiving-public-about-soda -related.

CHAPTER 1

1. Michael Moss, *Salt Sugar Fat* (New York: Random House, 2013), 106.

2. "The Coca-Cola System," Coca-ColaCompany.com, accessed April 23, 2021, https://www.coca-colacompany.com/company/coca-cola-system.

3. "Best Global Brands, 2020," Interbrand.com, accessed April 26, 2021, https:// interbrand.com/best-global-brands/coca-cola/.

CHAPTER 2

1. Bartow Elmore, *Citizen Coke: The Making of Coca-Cola Capitalism* (New York: W. W. Norton, 2015), 77.

2. Murray Carpenter, *Caffeinated: How Our Daily Habit Helps, Hurts, and Hooks Us* (New York: Hudson Street Press, 2014), 109.

3. The details of products shipped to Caribbean Refrescos were gleaned from bills of lading for 2018 shipments to and from the factory via the Port of San Juan.

4. Memo to Congressional Task Force on Economic Growth in Puerto Rico, September 2, 2016, https://www.finance.senate.gov/imo/media/doc/Coca-Cola%20Company.pdf.

5. Coca-Cola Company, marketing materials from Coca-Cola USA Consumer Information Center, March 4, 1991, Industry Documents Library, CSPI Collection, https://www.industrydocuments.ucsf.edu/docs/mtyj0226.

6. Larry Luxner, "Cola War Finds a Battleground in Puerto Rico," *Journal of Commerce*, March 25, 1990, https://www.joc.com/maritime-news/cola-war-finds-battleground-puerto-rico-coke-pepsi-plants-just-miles-apart_19900325.html.

CHAPTER 3

1. Fleet Trax, "The Largest Fleets in America," https://fleettrax.net/largest-fleets-america/; Transport Topics, "Top 100 Private: 2019 Essential Management and Operating Information for the 100 Largest Private Carriers in North America," https://www.ttnews.com/top100/private/2019.

2. Robert Pear, "Senator, Promoting Student Nutrition, Battles Coca-Cola," *New York Times*, April 26, 1994.

3. N. R. Kleinfeld, "Coca-Cola to Go on Sale in China as U.S. Links with Peking Gain," *New York Times*, December 20, 1978, https://www.nytimes.com/1978/12/20/archives/cocacola-to-go-on-sale-in-china-as-us-and-peking-expand-ties-moves.html; The Coca-Cola Company, "Coca-Cola Reports Fourth Quarter and Full-Year 2023 Results," February 13, 2024, https://www.coca-colacompany.com/media-center/fourth-quarter-full-year-2023-results.

4. Cordelia Hebblethwaite, "Who, What, Why: In Which Countries Is Coca-Cola Not Sold?," *BBC News*, September 11, 2012, https://www.bbc.com/news/magazine-19550067.

CHAPTER 4

1. Gordon Frazer, "Gordon Frazer from Italy," *Blue Network*, March 3, 1944, Robert Winship Woodruff papers, box 45, folder 8, Stuart A. Rose Manuscript, Archives and Rare Book Library, Emory University.

2. Jean C. Buzby and Stephen Haley, "Coffee Consumption over the Last Century," Amber Waves, USDA Economic Research Service, June 1, 2007, https://www.ers.usda.gov/amber-waves/2007/june/coffee-consumption-over-the-last-century/.

3. Jeanine Bentley, "Trends in U.S. per Capita Consumption of Dairy Products, 1970–2012," Amber Waves, USDA Economic Research Service, June 2, 2014, https://www.ers.usda.gov/amber-waves/2014/june/trends-in-us-per-capita-consumption-of-dairy-products-1970-2012/.

4. Mark Pendergrast, *For God, Country, and Coca-Cola* (New York: Basic Books, 1993), 367.

5. David F. Gallagher, "Word for Word/Deep Water: 'Just Say No to H2O' (Unless It's Coke's Own Brew)," *New York Times*, September 2, 2011.

6. Michael Moss, *Salt Sugar Fat* (New York: Random House, 2013), 109.

7. "Get the Facts: Sugar-Sweetened Beverages and Consumption," CDC.gov, accessed April 25, 2021, https://www.cdc.gov/nutrition/data-statistics/sugar-sweetened-beverages-intake.html.

8. Sohyun Park et al., "Prevalence of Sugar-Sweetened Beverage Intake among Adults, 23 States and the District of Columbia, 2013," *MMWR Morbidity and Mortality Weekly Report*, February 26, 2016, https://www.cdc.gov/mmwr/volumes/65/wr/mm6507a1.htm.

9. "Mean Body Weight, Height, and Body Mass Index, United States, 1960–2002," National Center for Health Statistics, October 27, 2004, https://stacks.cdc.gov/view/cdc/61483.

10. Cheryl D. Fryar et al., "Mean Body Weight, Height, Waist Circumference, and Body Mass Index among Adults: United States, 1999–2000 through 2015–2016," *National Health Statistics Reports*, December 20, 2018, https://www.cdc.gov/nchs/data/nhsr/nhsr122-508.pdf.

11. Craig M. Hales et al., "Prevalence of Obesity among Adults and Youth: United States, 2015–2016," *National Center for Health Statistics Data Brief* no. 288, October, 2017, https://www.cdc.gov/nchs/data/databriefs/db288.pdf.

12. Sunkyung Kim et al., "Permanent Tooth Loss and Sugar-Sweetened Beverage Intake in U.S. Young Adults," *Journal of Public Health Dentistry*, November 25, 2016, https://onlinelibrary.wiley.com/doi/abs/10.1111/jphd.12192.

13. Quanhe Yang et al., "Added Sugar Intake and Cardiovascular Diseases Mortality among U.S. Adults, *JAMA Internal Medicine*, April 2014, https://jamanetwork.com/journals/jamainternalmedicine/fullarticle/1819573/.

14. Centers for Disease Control and Prevention, "Health & Economic Costs of Chronic Diseases," March 23, 2023, https://www.cdc.gov/chronicdisease/about/costs/index.htm.

15. Centers for Medicare & Medicaid Services, National Health Expenditures 2022 Highlights, https://www.cms.gov/files/document/highlights.pdf.

16. Zachary J. Ward et al., "Association of Body Mass Index with Health Care Expenditures in the United States by Age and Sex," *PLOS One*, March 24, 2021, https://journals.plos.org/plosone/article?id=10.1371/journal.pone.0247307.

CHAPTER 5

1. Jennifer L. Temple, "Sex Differences in Reinforcing Value of Caffeinated Beverages in Adolescents," *Behavioural Pharmacology*, December 2009.

2. Roland R. Griffiths and Ellen M. Vernotica, "Is Caffeine a Flavoring Agent in Cola Soft Drinks?," *Archives of Family Medicine*, August 2000, https://triggered.edina.clockss.org/ServeContent?issn=1063-3987&volume=9&issue=8&spage=727.

3. Russell S. J. Keast et al., "Caffeine Increases Sugar-Sweetened Beverage Consumption in a Free-Living Population: A Randomized Control Trial," *British Journal of Nutrition*, January 8, 2015, https://pubmed.ncbi.nlm.nih.gov/25567475/.

4. Laura A. Schmidt, "What Are Addictive Structures and Behaviours and How Far Do They Extend?," in *Impact of Addictive Substances and Behaviours on Individual and Societal Well Being*, ed. Peter Anderson, Jürgen Rehm, and Robin Room (Oxford: Oxford University Press, 2015), 39.

CHAPTER 6

1. Mark Bittman, "Soda: A Sin We Sip Instead of Smoke?," *New York Times*, February 13, 2010, https://www.nytimes.com/2010/02/14/weekinreview/14bittman.html.

2. Kelly D. Brownell and Thomas R. Frieden, "Ounces of Prevention: The Public Policy Case for Taxes on Sugared Beverages," *New England Journal of Medicine*, April 30, 2009.

3. Christine Spolar and Joe Eaton, "The Food Lobby's War on a Soda Tax," Center for Public Integrity, November 4, 2009, https://publicintegrity.org/health/the-food-lobbys-war-on-a-soda-tax/.

4. University of California Television (UCTV), "Sugar: The Bitter Truth," July 30, 2009, in the series "The American Diet with Robert Lustig, MD," YouTube, https://www.youtube.com/watch?v=dBnniua6-oM.

5. Richard F. Daines and Thomas A. Farley, "No Food Stamps for Sodas," *New York Times*, October 7, 2010, https://www.nytimes.com/2010/10/07/opinion/07farley.html; Anemona Hartocollis, "New York Asks to Bar Use of Food Stamps to Buy Sodas," *New York Times*, October 6, 2010, https://www.nytimes.com/2010/10/07/nyregion/07stamps.html.

6. Sheryl Gay Stolberg, "Childhood Obesity Battle Is Taken Up by First Lady," *New York Times*, February 9, 2010, https://www.nytimes.com/2010/02/10/health/nutrition/10obesity.html.

CHAPTER 7

1. Gary Taubes and Cristin Kearns Couzens, "Big Sugar's Sweet Little Lies," *Mother Jones*, November/December 2012, https://www.motherjones.com/environment/2012/10/sugar-industry-lies-campaign/.

2. Murray Carpenter, *Caffeinated: How Our Daily Habit Helps, Hurts, and Hooks Us* (New York: Hudson Street Press, 2014), 80–85.

3. Edward H. Cary, "What the Medical Profession Thinks of Bottled Carbonated Beverages," American Bottlers of Carbonated Beverages, 1932, Robert Winship Woodruff papers, box 44, folder 12, Stuart A. Rose Manuscript, Archives and Rare Book Library, Emory University.

4. American Medical Association Council on Foods and Nutrition, "Some Nutritional Aspects of Sugar, Candy, and Sweetened Carbonated Beverages," *JAMA* 120, no. 763 (1942).

5. Cristin Kearns, "How Big Sugar Influences Nutrition Science: A First Glimpse at Sugar Industry Documents," CrossFit video, November 19, 2019, https://www.youtube.com/watch?v=TkM4XkU2tE4.

6. Cristin Kearns et al., "Sugar Industry Influence on the Scientific Agenda of the National Institute of Dental Research's 1971 National Caries Program: A Historical Analysis of Internal Documents," *PLOS Medicine*, March 10, 2015, https://www.ncbi.nlm.nih.gov/pmc/articles/PMC4355299/.

7. Robert Hockett, "Application to the TIRC," January 4, 1954, Industry Documents Library, Council for Tobacco Research Records; RPCI Tobacco Institute and Council for Tobacco Research Records; Master Settlement Agreement collections, https://www.industrydocuments.ucsf.edu/docs/mgjn0041.

8. Naomi Oreskes and Erik M. Conway, *Merchants of Doubt* (New York: Bloomsbury Press, 2010), 16.

9. Robert C. Hockett, "Report of the Executive Director to Members of the Sugar Research Foundation," March 2, 1944, Industry Documents Library, Braga Brothers Collection, https://www.industrydocuments.ucsf.edu/docs/jyml0226.

10. Felix Coste memo to Robert Woodruff, June 25, 1951, Robert Winship Woodruff papers, box 44, folder 13, Stuart A. Rose Manuscript, Archives and Rare Book Library, Emory University.

11. C. L. Emerson letter to Roy Gentry, October 30, 1951, Robert Winship Woodruff papers, box 44, folder 13, Stuart A. Rose Manuscript, Archives and Rare Book Library, Emory University.

12. "Soft Drink Tax Urged to Fight Tooth Erosion," *Nashville Tennessean*, via Associated Press, May 11, 1951.

13. Steve Hannagan memo to Robert Woodruff, March 25, 1952, Robert Winship Woodruff papers, box 44, folder 13, Stuart A. Rose Manuscript, Archives and Rare Book Library, Emory University.

14. Ole Salthe letter to O. E. May, June 21, 1950, Robert Winship Woodruff papers, box 44, folder 12, Stuart A. Rose Manuscript, Archives and Rare Book Library, Emory University.

15. Cristin E. Kearns, "Sugar Industry and Coronary Heart Disease Research," *JAMA Internal Medicine*, November 1, 2016, https://www.ncbi.nlm.nih.gov/pmc/articles/PMC5099084/.

16. John D. Morris, "Sugar Industry Will Correct Ads," *New York Times*, August 19, 1972, https://timesmachine.nytimes.com/timesmachine/1972/08/19/79473836.html?pageNumber=32.

17. Andy Kroll and Jeremy Schulman, "Leaked Documents Reveal the Secret Finances of a Pro-Industry Science Group," *Mother Jones*, October 28, 2013.

CHAPTER 8

1. "The Board of Directors of the Coca-Cola Company Elects Dr. Rhona Applebaum as Vice-President," Coca-ColaCompany.com, April 26, 2012, https://www.coca-colacompany.com/press-releases/board-of-directors-elects-dr-rhona-applebaum-as-vp.

2. Betsy McKay, "Defensive Coke Backs Research That Asks: Is Sugar All Bad?," *Wall Street Journal*, October 22, 2004.

3. "New Enviga Proven to Burn Calories," BevNET.com, October 11, 2006, https://www.bevnet.com/news/2006/10-11-2006-enviga.asp/.

4. Mary Bralove, "More Critics Assail Soft Drinks for Ingredients and Labeling, but Makers Call the Attack Unfair," *Wall Street Journal*, January 20, 1972. Also in Food Industry Documents Library, CSPI Collection, https://www.industrydocuments.ucsf.edu/docs/#id=mkdm0229.

5. "CSPI to Drop Litigation over Coke's Faded 'Enviga,'" Center for Science in the Public Interest, August 17, 2010, https://cspinet.org/news/cspi-drop-litigation-over-cokes-faded-enviga-20100817.

6. Vasanti S. Malik, Matthias B. Schulze, and Frank B. Hu, "Intake of Sugar-Sweetened Beverages and Weight Gain: A Systematic Review," *American Journal of Clinical Nutrition*, August 2006, https://www.ncbi.nlm.nih.gov/pmc/articles/PMC3210834/.

7. Stephanie Thompson, "Obesity Fear Frenzy Grips Food Industry," *Ad Age*, April 23, 2007, https://adage.com/article/news/obesity-fear-frenzy-grips-food-industry/116233.

8. "Coca-Cola Unveils Sleek, New 90-Calorie Mini Can," Coca-Cola Company.com, October 14, 2009, https://investors.coca-colacompany.com/news-events/press-releases/detail/574/coca-cola-unveils-sleek-new-90-calorie-mini-can.

9. "American Academy of Family Physicians Launches Consumer Alliance with First Partner, Coca-Cola," AAFP.org, October 6, 2009, https://www.aafp.org/media-center/releases-statements/all/2009/consumeralliance-cocacola.html.

10. "Dr. Walker Resigns Membership in American Academy of Family Physicians to Protest Its Partnership with Coca-Cola," Contra Costa County Health Services, accessed April 26, 2021, https://cchealth.org/healthservices/aafp_protest.php.

11. R. E. Sallis, "Exercise Is Medicine and Physicians Need to Prescribe It!," *British Journal of Sports Medicine*, January 9, 2009, https://bjsm.bmj.com/content/43/1/3.

12. Rhona Applebaum, "Email from Steven N. Blair to Michael Pratt Regarding the IUNS Meeting in BKK," September 16, 2009, Industry Documents Library, NYT Coca-Cola Collection, https://www.industrydocuments.ucsf.edu/food/docs/#id=rsll0228.

CHAPTER 9

1. ILSI Argentina, "ILSI—Alex Malaspina," YouTube, October 1, 2015, https://www.youtube.com/watch?v=okDuV1Uw_Ig.

2. "International Life Sciences Institute Caffeine Workshop," August 31, 1978, Industry Documents Library, William Darby Papers, https://www.industrydocuments.ucsf.edu/docs/fljl0227.

3. "International Life Sciences Institute Meeting of the Board of Trustees, the Coca-Cola Company, Atlanta, Georgia," March 2, 1981, Industry Documents Library, William Darby Papers, https://www.industrydocuments.ucsf.edu/docs/yswm0227.

4. Jane Mayer, *Dark Money* (New York: Anchor Books, 2017), 186.

5. Melanie Warner, "Striking Back at the Food Police," *New York Times*, June 12, 2005, https://www.nytimes.com/2005/06/12/business/yourmoney/striking-back-at-the-food-police.html.

6. Thomas O. McGarity and Wendy E. Wagner, *Bending Science: How Special Interests Corrupt Public Health Research* (Cambridge, MA: Harvard University Press, 2012).

7. "The Tobacco Industry and Scientific Groups, ILSI: A Case Study," World Health Organization Tobacco Free Initiative, February 2001, https://www.who.int/tobacco/media/en/ILSI.pdf.

8. Sarah Boseley, "WHO 'Infiltrated by Food Industry,'" *Guardian*, January 8, 2003, https://www.theguardian.com/uk/2003/jan/09/foodanddrink.

9. ILSI Argentina, "ILSI—Alex Malaspina."

CHAPTER 10

1. Hilary Farmer, "Q & A with New Department Chair Frank Hu," *Nutri News*, January 1, 2017, https://www.hsph.harvard.edu/nutrition/2017/01/01/interview-frank-hu-chair/.

2. Michael G. Tordoff and Annette M. Alleva, "Effect of Drinking Soda Sweetened with Aspartame or High-Fructose Corn Syrup on Food Intake and Body Weight," *American Journal of Clinical Nutrition*, June 1, 1990.

3. David S. Ludwig et al., "Relation between the Consumption of Sugar-Sweetened Drinks and Childhood Obesity: A Prospective, Observational Analysis," *Lancet*, February 17, 2001, https://www.sciencedirect.com/science/article/abs/pii/S0140673600040411.

4. Matthias B. Schulze et al., "Sugar-Sweetened Beverages, Weight Gain, and Incidence of Type 2 Diabetes in Young and Middle-Aged Women," *JAMA*, August 25, 2004, http://jama.jamanetwork.com/article.aspx?articleid=199317&resultclick=3#COMMENT.

5. David Gelles, "Coke and McDonald's, Growing Together since 1955," *New York Times*, May 15, 2014, https://www.nytimes.com/2014/05/16/business/coke-and-mcdonalds-working-hand-in-hand-since-1955.html.

CHAPTER 11

1. "Research Agreement for the Coca-Cola Company," Coca-Cola Company, April 11, 2010, Industry Documents Library, USRTK Food Industry Collection, https://www.industrydocuments.ucsf.edu/docs/#id=grml0228.

2. Bruce Horovitz, "Coke Executive Answers Questions about Sugary Drinks," *USA Today*, June 7, 2012, https://abcnews.go.com/Business/coke-executive-answers-questions-sugary-drinks/story?id=16521709.

3. "Beverage Industry Announces New School Vending Policy," American Beverage Association, August 17, 2005, Industry Documents Library, CSPI Collection, https://www.industrydocuments.ucsf.edu/docs/zrhd0229.

4. "Coca-Cola and UNC, a History of Partnership," *Carolina Public Health*, November 29, 2010, https://sph.unc.edu/cphm/healthy-from-head-to-heels-fall-2010/coca-cola-and-unc-a-history-of-partnership-fall-2010/.

CHAPTER 12

1. Dan Harris and Maggy Patrick, "Is 'Big-Food's' Big Money Influencing the Science of Nutrition?," ABC News, June 15, 2011, https://abcnews.go.com/US/big-food-money-accused-influencing-science/story?id=13845186.

2. The Coca-Cola Company, Transparency Research Report, April 21, 2021, https://www.coca-colacompany.com/content/dam/journey/us/en/policies/pdf/research-and-studies/transparency-research-report.pdf.

3. Stephanie Saul, "Obesity Researcher Quits over New York Menu Fight," *New York Times*, March 3, 2008, https://www.nytimes.com/2008/03/03/business/03cnd-obese.html.

4. Trevor Butterworth, "ABC News Attacks Scientist Who Exposed Bias in Obesity Research," Forbes.com, June 22, 2011, https://www.forbes.com/sites/trevorbutterworth/2011/06/22/abc-news-attacks-scientist-who-exposed-bias-in-obesity-research/#1facd2f73faf.

5. Liza Gross, "How Self-Appointed Guardians of Sound Science Tip the Scales toward Industry," *Intercept*, November 15, 2016, https://theintercept.com/2016/11/15/how-self-appointed-guardians-of-sound-science-tip-the-scales-toward-industry/.

6. M. B. Cope and D. B. Allison, "White-Hat Bias: Examples of Its Presence in Obesity Research and a Call for Renewed Commitment to Faithfulness in Research Reporting," *International Journal of Obesity*, December 1, 2009, https://www.nature.com/articles/ijo2009239.

CHAPTER 13

1. Michael M. Grynbaum, "New York Plans to Ban Sale of Big Sizes of Sugary Drinks," *New York Times*, May 30, 2012, https://www.nytimes.com/2012/05/31/nyregion/bloomberg-plans-a-ban-on-large-sugared-drinks.html.

2. Rhona Applebaum, "Coca-Cola Rep: Physical Activity Key," CNN, June, 1, 2012, https://www.cnn.com/videos/bestoftv/2012/06/01/exp-early-applebaum-sugary-drinks.cnn; Bill Clinton, "The President Will Win," CNN interview with Harvey Weinstein (guest hosting for Piers Morgan), May 31, 2012, https://www.cnn.com/videos/bestoftv/2012/05/31/piers-morgan-harvey-weinstein-bill-clinton-barack-obama.cnn.

3. The Coca-Cola Company, Transparency Research Report, April 21, 2021, https://www.coca-colacompany.com/content/dam/journey/us/en/policies/pdf/research-and-studies/transparency-research-report.pdf.

CHAPTER 14

1. N. C. Aizenman, "A Former Coke Exec's Take on Firm's Marketing," *Washington Post*, June 8, 2012, https://www.industrydocuments.ucsf.edu/docs/#id=xkfm0229.

2. Mickey Gramig, "Coca-Cola Offers Discounts on Fun," *Atlanta Journal Constitution*, March 14, 1998.

3. N. C. Aizenman, "A Former Coke Exec's Take on Firm's Marketing," *Washington Post*, June 8, 2012.

4. Robert Pear, "Senator, Promoting Student Nutrition, Battles Coca-Cola," *New York Times*, April 26, 1994.

5. "School Lunch Programs," C-SPAN, May 16, 1994, https://www.c-span.org/video/?56826-1/school-lunch-programs.

6. Associated Press staff, "Panel OKs Compromise on Junk Food at Schools," *Deseret News*, June 23, 1994, https://www.deseret.com/1994/6/23/19116156/panel-oks-compromise-on-junk-food-at-schools.

7. Fiona Fleck, "WHO Challenges Food Industry in Report on Diet and Health," *British Medical Journal*, March 8, 2003.

8. Caroline Wilbert, "Lawyers Want Vending Banned from All Schools," *Atlanta Journal Constitution*, November 29, 2005.

9. "Let's Clear It Up," AmericanBeverage.org, May 24, 2012, https://www.americanbeverage.org/education-resources/blog/post/lets-clear-it-up/.

CHAPTER 15

1. Vasanti S. Malik et al., "Intake of Sugar Sweetened Beverages and Weight Gain, a Systematic Review," *American Journal of Clinical Nutrition*, August 2006, https://www.ncbi.nlm.nih.gov/pmc/articles/PMC3210834/.

2. Vasanti S. Malik et al., "Sugar Sweetened Beverages, Obesity, and Type 2 Diabetes and Cardiovascular Disease Risk," *Circulation*, March 23, 2010, https://www.ncbi.nlm.nih.gov/pmc/articles/PMC2862465/#!po=20.8333.

3. Qibin Qi et al., "Sugar-Sweetened Beverages and Genetic Risk of Obesity," *New England Journal of Medicine*, October 11, 2012, https://www.nejm.org/doi/full/10.1056/nejmoa1203039.

4. Todd Neale, "Cutting Sugary Drinks Does Cut Weight Gain," *MedPage Today*, September 21, 2012, https://www.medpagetoday.com/meetingcoverage/obesity/34904.

5. American Beverage Association, "For Every Complex Problem . . . ," September 24, 2012, https://www.americanbeverage.org/education-resources/blog/post/for-every-complex-problem/.

6. Sonja K. Billes, "Obesity 2012 Opened with Keynote Debate," *Obesity Society eNews*, October 9, 2012, https://www.multibriefs.com/briefs/tos/100912.html.

CHAPTER 16

1. Kimber L. Stanhope et al., "Consuming Fructose-Sweetened, Not Glucose-Sweetened, Beverages Increases Visceral Adiposity and Lipids and Decreases Insulin Sensitivity in Overweight/Obese Humans," *Journal of Clinical Investigation*, April 20, 2009, https://www.jci.org/articles/view/37385.

2. Vanessa Ha et al., "Fructose-Containing Sugars, Blood Pressure, and Cardiometabolic Risk: A Critical Review," *Current Hypertension Reports*, June 22, 2013, https://www.researchgate.net/profile/Russell_De_Souza/publication/241694067_Fructose-Containing_Sugars_Blood_Pressure_and_Cardiometabolic_Risk_A_Critical_Review/links/55b2856a08ae092e9650a32c.pdf.

3. John L. Sievenpiper and Russell J. de Souza, "Are Sugar-Sweetened Beverages the Whole Story?," *American Journal of Clinical Nutrition*, June 26, 2013, https://academic.oup.com/ajcn/article/98/2/261/4577111.

4. Richard Kahn and John L. Sievenpiper, "Dietary Sugar and Body Weight: Have We Reached a Crisis in the Epidemic of Obesity and Diabetes?," *Diabetes Care*, April 2014, https://care.diabetesjournals.org/content/37/4/957.

5. John L. Sievenpiper et al., "Fructose as a Driver of Diabetes: An Incomplete View of the Evidence," *Mayo Clinic Proceedings*, July 1, 2015, https://www.mayoclinicproceedings.org/article/S0025-6196(15)00371-7/fulltext.

6. Russ Greene, "Coke Transparency Less Clear than Ever," *Keep Fitness Legal*, March 29, 2016, https://therussellsblogdotcom.wordpress.com/2016/03/29/coke-transparency-less-clear-than-ever/.

7. Tom Blackwell, "Canadian Researchers Have Received Hundreds of Thousands of Dollars from Soft Drink Makers and the Sugar Industry," *National Post*, December 6, 2015, https://nationalpost.com/health/canadian-researchers-have-received-hundreds-of-thousands-from-soft-drink-makers-and-the-sugar-industry.

8. Ferris Jabr, "Is Sugar Really Toxic? Sifting through the Evidence," *Scientific American*, July 15, 2013, https://blogs.scientificamerican.com/brainwaves/is-sugar-really-toxic-sifting-through-the-evidence/.

9. Kate Lunau, "Death by Sugar: How the Sweet Killer Is Fuelling the Biggest Health Crisis of Our Time," *Macleans Magazine*, May 6, 2014, https://www.macleans.ca/society/health/death-by-sugar-the-biggest-health-crisis-of-our-time/.

CHAPTER 17

1. George Guerin, "Coca-Cola Addresses the Obesity Epidemic with New 2 Minute Commercial, Draws Criticism," NJ.com, January 16, 2013, https://www.nj.com/healthfit/fitness/2013/01/coca-cola_addresses_the_obesity_epidemic_with_new_commercial_draws_criticism.html.

2. Jim Avila, "Coca-Cola Takes on Obesity," *ABC News*, January 15, 2013, https://www.nj.com/healthfit/fitness/2013/01/coca-cola_addresses_the_obesity_epidemic_with_new_commercial_draws_criticism.html.

CHAPTER 18

1. The Coca-Cola Company, "Warren Buffet on Why He'll Never Sell a Share of Coke Stock," YouTube, July 23, 2013, https://www.youtube.com/watch?v=4p1_5bZ8I4M.

2. Christine Idzelis, "Berkshire Hathaway Bet Big on Dialysis: Jim Chanos Thinks It's a Scam," *Institutional Investor*, December 4, 2019, https://www.institutionalinvestor.com/article/b1j9vtzrv9x0xr/Berkshire-Hathaway-Bet-Big-on-Dialysis-Giant-DaVita-Jim-Chanos-Thinks-It-s-a-Scam.

CHAPTER 20

1. Georgia Shape, Twitter post, May 8, 2013, https://twitter.com/GeorgiaShape/status/332224528350605312.

2. "New CDC Director Has Emory Health Connections," Woodruff Health Sciences Center, July 10, 2017, https://news.emory.edu/stories/2017/07/new_cdc_director/.

3. "RE: Congratulations on Becoming Global President of ILSI," February 3, 2015, Industry Documents Library, USRTK Food Industry Collection, https://www.industrydocuments.ucsf.edu/docs/#id=jxcy0227.

CHAPTER 21

1. "Leading Food and Beverage Companies Announce Reduced Calorie Footprint," BipartisanPolicyCenter.org, May 30, 2013, https://bipartisanpolicy.org/blog/leading-food-and-beverage-companies-announce-reduced-calorie-footprint/.

CHAPTER 22

1. "Email from Theresa Hedrick Regarding Update on Council Activities in Preparation for Dr. Oz Segment on LCS Final Press Release," September 12, 2013, Industry Documents Library, NYT Coca-Cola Collection, https://www.industrydocuments.ucsf.edu/docs/phml0228.

2. The Coca-Cola Company, Transparency Research Report, April 21, 2021, https://www.coca-colacompany.com/content/dam/journey/us/en/policies/pdf/research-and-studies/transparency-research-report.pdf.

CHAPTER 23

1. Touch Medical Media Services, "The Effectiveness of Inexpensive Nonmedical Interventions in Improving Obesity and Diabetes Outcomes," YouTube, October 30, 2013, https://www.youtube.com/watch?v=IhpGeh3gRnY.

2. "Email from Rhona S. Applebaum to James Hill and Colleagues Regarding Save the Dates—Oct 28–29," September 6, 2013, Industry Documents Library, NYT Coca-Cola Collection, https://www.industrydocuments.ucsf.edu/docs/nsll0228.

CHAPTER 24

1. "Update on Moss Book," Kimberly Reed email, February 20, 2013, USRTK.org, https://usrtk.org/wp-content/uploads/2016/09/IFIC_Moss-Book.pdf.

2. Sanjay Basu et al., "The Relationship of Sugar to Population Level Diabetes Prevalence," *PLOS One*, February 27, 2013, https://pubmed.ncbi.nlm.nih.gov/23460912/.

CHAPTER 25

1. "Obesity Issues 2014, Final Report," National Press Foundation, University of Colorado, Industry Documents Library, USRTK Food Industry Collection, https://www.industrydocuments.ucsf.edu/docs/qzcl0228.

2. Chris Snowdon, "Sugar Taxes Have Never Worked Anywhere," Institute of Economic Affairs, March 7, 2018, https://iea.org.uk/sugar-taxes-have-never-worked-anywhere/.

3. Trevor Butterworth, "Can a Soda Tax Really Curb Obesity?," *Forbes*, September 16, 2009.

4. "When Research Should Come with a Warning Label—Trevor Butterworth—Harvard Business Review," Rhona Applebaum email, March 6, 2014, U.S. Right to Know, https://usrtk.org/wp-content/uploads/2016/12/GEBN-Butterworth-march-2014.pdf.

5. National Press Foundation, "The Big Debate: Food or Physical Activity?," YouTube, June 17, 2014, https://www.youtube.com/watch?v=T2LLH8Ptcns.

6. "Email from Arti Arora to Tim Goss Regarding the Participation in the 2012 Coca-Cola Symposium," December 21, 2011, Industry Documents Library, NYT Coca-Cola Collection, https://www.industrydocuments.ucsf.edu/docs/jsll0228.

7. David Olinger, "CU Nutrition Expert Accepts $550,000 from Coca-Cola for Obesity Campaign," *Denver Post*, December 26, 2015, https://www.denverpost.com/2015/12/26/cu-nutrition-expert-accepts-550000-from-coca-cola-for-obesity-campaign/.

CHAPTER 26

1. "Email from Alex Malaspina to John C. Peters Regarding the Tommy Thomson Stealing," May 24, 2014, Industry Documents Library, USRTK Food Industry Collection, https://www.industrydocuments.ucsf.edu/docs/rykk0228.

2. "Email from Alex Malaspina to John C. Peters Regarding the Clyde," June 17, 2014, Industry Documents Library, USRTK Food Industry Collection, https://www.industrydocuments.ucsf.edu/food/docs/#id=gpkk0228.

3. "Email from Alex Malaspina to John C. Peters Regarding the Idea to Take the Company Plane for the Visit," June 17, 2014, Industry Documents Library, USRTK Food Industry Collection, https://www.industrydocuments.ucsf.edu/food/docs/#id=fpkk0228.

4. Anjali Anthavaley, "U.S. Soda Makers Pledge 20 Percent Calorie Cut by 2025," Reuters, September 23, 2014, https://www.reuters.com/article/us-health-soda-clinton/u-s-soda-makers-pledge-20-percent-calorie-cut-by-2025-idUSKCN0HI22K20140923.

5. Stephanie Strom, "Soda Makers Coca-Cola, PepsiCo and Dr Pepper Join in Effort to Cut Americans' Drink Calories," *New York Times*, September 23, 2014, https://www.nytimes.com/2014/09/24/business/big-soda-companies-agree-on-effort-to-cut-americans-drink-calories.html.

6. Michael M. Grynbaum, "New York's Ban on Big Sodas is Rejected by Final Court," *New York Times*, June 26, 2014, https://www.nytimes.com/2014/06/27/nyregion/city-loses-final-appeal-on-limiting-sales-of-large-sodas.html; "New York Court Strikes down the Soda Ban," AmericanBeverage.org, June 26, 2014, https://www.ameribev.org/education-resources/blog/post/new-york-court-strikes-down-the-soda-ban/.

7. "Taxes Do Not Make People Healthy," American Beverage Association, July 30, 2014, https://www.americanbeverage.org/education-resources/blog/post/taxes-do-not-make-people-healthy/.

8. Lisa Beilfuss, "Coca-Cola CEO Muhtar Kent's 2014 Compensation Grew 24%," *Wall Street Journal*, March 12, 2015, https://www.wsj.com/articles/coca-cola-ceo-muhtar-kents-2014-compensation-grew-24-1426179710.

9. "Email from Muhtar Kent to Charles P. Rose Regarding the Exercise for Weight Loss Calories Burned in 1 Hour—Mayo Clinic," October 17, 2014, Industry Documents Library, NYT Coca Cola Collection, https://www.industrydocuments.ucsf.edu/docs/fsll0228.

10. CrossFit, "Dr. Steven Blair of Coca-Cola and ACSM's Global Energy Balance Network," YouTube, September 10, 2015, https://www.youtube.com/watch?v=9xBV_Enlh1A.

CHAPTER 27

1. Sarah Steele et al., "Are Industry-Funded Charities Promoting 'Advocacy-led Studies' or 'Evidence-based Science'? A Case Study of the International Life Sciences Institute," *Globalization and Health*, June 3, 2019, https://globalizationandhealth.biomedcentral.com/articles/10.1186/s12992-019-0478-6.

2. Coca-Cola Transparency Research Report, April 21, 2021, https://www.coca-colacompany.com/reports/transparency-research-report.

3. "Email from John Peters to James Hill and Alex Malaspina," January 23, 2015, Industry Documents Library, USRTK Food Industry Collection, https://www.industry documents.ucsf.edu/docs/qtdl0228.

CHAPTER 28

1. "Global Energy Balance Network Report," March 3, 2015, Industry Documents Library, USRTK Food Industry Collection, https://www.industrydocuments.ucsf.edu /docs/tpdl0228.

2. "Proposal for Establishment of the Global Energy Balance Network," July 9, 2014, Industry Documents Library, NYT Coca Cola Collection, https://www.industry documents.ucsf.edu/docs/#id=glml0228.

CHAPTER 30

1. Edward Archer et al., "45-Year Trends in Women's Use of Time and Household Management Energy Expenditure," *PLOS One*, February 20, 2013, https://journals .plos.org/plosone/article/related?id=10.1371/journal.pone.0056620.

2. Candice Choi, "Emails Reveal Coke's Role in Anti-Oobesity Group," Associated Press, November 24, 2015, https://amp.detroitnews.com/amp/76300478; Anahad O'Connor, "Coca-Cola Funds Scientists Who Shift Blame for Obesity away from Bad Diets," *New York Times*, August 10, 2015, https://well.blogs.nytimes.com/2015/08/09 /coca-cola-funds-scientists-who-shift-blame-for-obesity-away-from-bad-diets/.

CHAPTER 31

1. Greg Glassman, personal communication (he attended the event and tweeted about the soda links).

2. Murray Carpenter, "Mr. CrossFit vs. Big Soda," *Washington Post Magazine*, July 13, 2017.

3. CrossFit, "Glassman on D.C. Licensure: 'They Want to Control You,'" YouTube, August 16, 2015, https://www.youtube.com/watch?v=GeWqqYQvPLI.

4. CrossFit, "Greg Glassman on Exercise is Medicine," YouTube, August 20, 2015, https://www.youtube.com/watch?v=buo8ib3Uau4.

5. Russ Greene, "Coke 'Transparency': Less Clear than Ever," Keep Fitness Legal, March 29, 2016, https://therussellsblogdotcom.wordpress.com/2016/03/29/coke -transparency-less-clear-than-ever/.

CHAPTER 32

1. "Heads Up," August 8, 2015, Industry Documents Library, USRTK Food Industry Collection, https://www.industrydocuments.ucsf.edu/docs/fllk0228.

2. "FDA Roundtable Opportunity," July 29, 2015, Industry Documents Library, USRTK Food Industry Collection, https://www.industrydocuments.ucsf.edu/docs /#id=sklk0228.

CHAPTER 33

1. Anahad O'Connor, "Coca-Cola Funds Scientists Who Shift Blame for Obesity away from Bad Diets," *New York Times*, August 10, 2015.

2. Maira Bes-Restrollo et al., "Financial Conflicts of Interest and Reporting Bias Regarding the Association between Sugar-Sweetened Beverages and Weight Gain: A Systematic Review of Systematic Reviews," *PLOS Medicine*, December 31, 2013, https://journals.plos.org/plosmedicine/article?id=10.1371/journal.pmed.1001578.

3. Muhtar Kent, "Coca-Cola: We'll Do Better," *Wall Street Journal*, August 19, 2015, https://www.wsj.com/articles/coca-cola-well-do-better-1440024365.

4. Russ Greene, "Coke 'Transparency': Less Clear than Ever," Keep Fitness Legal, March 29, 2016, https://therussellsblogdotcom.wordpress.com/2016/03/29/coke-transparency-less-clear-than-ever/.

5. Vasanti S. Malik and Frank B. Hu, "Fructose and Cardiometabolic Health: What the Evidence from Sugar-Sweetened Beverages Tells Us," *Journal of the American College of Cardiology*, October 2015, http://www.onlinejacc.org/content/accj/66/14/1615.full.pdf.

CHAPTER 34

1. Candice Choi, "Emails Reveal Coke's Role in Anti-Obesity Group," Associated Press, November 24, 2015.

2. David Olinger, "CU Nutrition Expert Accepts $550,000 from Coca-Cola for Obesity Campaign," *Denver Post*, December 26, 2015, https://www.denverpost.com/2015/12/26/cu-nutrition-expert-accepts-550000-from-coca-cola-for-obesity-campaign/.

3. "FW: INFORM—End of Week US Transparency Site Update," March 25, 2016, Industry Documents Library, DC Leaks Coca Cola Emails, https://www.industrydocuments.ucsf.edu/docs/yrcl0226.

CHAPTER 35

1. David Wright, Jackie Jesko, and Lauren Effron, "This Protest Rally Is Brought to You by Big Soda," ABC News, November 3, 2014, https://abcnews.go.com/US/protest-rally-brought-big-soda/story?id=26664314.

2. Anemona Hartocollis, "Failure of State Soda Tax Plan Reflects Power of an Anti-Tax Message," *New York Times*, July 2, 1010, https://www.nytimes.com/2010/07/03/nyregion/03sodatax.html.

3. "FW: INFORM: Dietary Guidelines Article," May 28, 2015, Industry Documents Library, DC Leaks Coca Cola Emails, https://www.industrydocuments.ucsf.edu/docs/qjdl0226.

4. The emails were released as part of DC Leaks, and quickly publicized in a blog post by CrossFit's Russ Greene. Russell Grantham and Rosalind Bentley, "Hacked E-Mails: Coke Tried to Use Pull with Clinton," *Atlanta Journal Constitution*, November 2,

2016, https://www.ajc.com/business/hacked-emails-coke-tried-use-pull-with-clinton/21LRm3IZL5CmuaSxWYPUAP/.

5. Jeff Shields, "Big Beverage Gives $10 Million to CHOP," *Philadelphia Inquirer*, March 16, 2011, https://www.inquirer.com/philly/blogs/heardinthehall/118077483.html.

6. Janie Har, "Sanders Tells Soda Tax Opponents to Stop Using His Name," Associated Press, October 20, 2016.

7. "Coca-Cola, Pepsi Hit with Wave of Punishing Soda Taxes," Bloomberg News, November 9, 2016.

8. Stephanie Strom, "Creeping Progress in Pledge to Cut Calories in Sugary Soda," *New York Times*, November 22, 2016.

CHAPTER 36

1. Alexei Koseff, "Jerry Brown Dined with Soda Industry Representatives Ahead of Tax Ban Deal," *Sacramento Bee*, June 26, 2018, https://www.sacbee.com/news/politics-government/capitol-alert/article213851144.html.

2. "Deceptive Corporate Tax Trick Threatens Quality of Life in Cities, Jeopardizes Local Services," League of California Cities press release, June 14, 2018, https://www.cacities.org/Top/News/News-Articles/2018/June/Deceptive-Corporate-Tax-Trick-Threatens-Quality-of.

3. "California Governor OKs 12-Year Soda Tax Ban," Associated Press, June 28, 2018, https://apnews.com/57e9b3382c16487181b6f2b6ae08adbf.

4. Eric Crosbie et al., "State Preemption to Prevent Local Taxation of Sugar-Sweetened Beverages," *JAMA Internal Medicine*, January 22, 2019, https://jamanetwork.com/journals/jamainternalmedicine/article-abstract/2720759.

5. Jamey Keaten and Maria Cheng, "U.S. Blocks U.N. Panel from Backing Taxes on Sugar Drinks," Associated Press, June 2, 2018, https://apnews.com/article/14c6143cbbec498fa40fd718f05104cc.

CHAPTER 37

1. "WHO Calls on Countries to Reduce Sugars Intake among Adults and Children," World Health Organization press release, March 4, 2015, https://www.who.int/mediacentre/news/releases/2015/sugar-guideline/en/; full report at https://apps.who.int/iris/bitstream/handle/10665/149782/9789241549028_eng.pdf;jsessionid=92D3433B07E0FC8B44EB3DC9C99C6E6F?sequence=1.

2. "E-mail from James Hill to Alex Malaspina Concerning Daily European News Flash," June 25, 2015, Industry Documents Library, USRTK Food Industry Collection, https://www.industrydocuments.ucsf.edu/food/docs/#id=sxyk0228.

3. "Email from Barbara Bowman to Alex Malaspina Re: Meeting," September 24, 2014, Industry Documents Library, USRTK Food Industry Collection, https://www.industrydocuments.ucsf.edu/docs/mncy0227.

4. "RE: News Digest—October 2, 2014," October 2, 2014, Industry Documents Library, USRTK Food Industry Collection, https://www.industrydocuments.ucsf.edu/docs/sncy0227.

5. "Re: Daily European News Flash—25.06.15," June 27, 2015, Industry Documents Library, USRTK Food Industry Collection, https://www.industrydocuments.ucsf.edu/docs/kpcy0227.

6. Carey Gillam, "CDC Official Exits Agency after Coca-Cola Connections Come to Light," *HuffPost*, June, 30, 2016, https://www.huffpost.com/entry/cdc-official-exits-agency_b_10760490.

7. "Atlanta in 50 Objects," AtlantaHistoryCenter.com, accessed April 25, 2021, https://www.atlantahistorycenter.com/explore/online-exhibitions/atlanta-in-50-objects/cdc.

8. Frederick Allen, *Secret Formula: How Brilliant Marketing and Relentless Salesmanship Made Coca-Cola the Best-Known Product in the World* (New York: HarperCollins, 1994), 329.

9. "Letter from CDC Scientists to Carmen Villar re: Current State of Ethics at the Agency," August 29, 2016, Industry Documents Library, USRTK Food Industry Collection, https://www.industrydocuments.ucsf.edu/food/docs/#id=llcy0227.

10. Ursula E. Bauer, "A Word about the Huffington Post blog," June 29, 2016, https://usrtk.org/wp-content/uploads/2016/06/CDC-Ursula-Bauer-email.pdf.

CHAPTER 38

1. David Stuckler et al., "A Textual Analysis of Sugar Industry Influence on the World Health Organization's 2015 Sugars Intake Guidelines," *Bulletin of the World Health Organization*, May 12, 2016, https://www.who.int/bulletin/volumes/94/8/15-165852/en/.

2. Dr. Margaret Chan, "Obesity and Diabetes, the Slow-Motion Disaster: Keynote Address of the 47th Meeting of the National Academy of Medicine," October 17, 2016.

CHAPTER 39

1. Daniel Aaron and Michael Siegel, "Sponsorship of National Health Organizations by Two Major Soft Drink Companies," *American Journal of Preventive Medicine*, December 15, 2016, http://goodtimesweb.org/industrial-policy/2019/PIIS0749379716303312-oct2016.pdf; Lisa Chedekel, "Probing Soda Company Sponsorship of Health Group," *Brink*, October 14, 2016, http://www.bu.edu/articles/2016/probing-soda-company-sponsorship-of-health-groups/.

CHAPTER 40

1. Jennifer Erickson et al., "The Scientific Basis of Guideline Recommendations on Sugar Intake: A Systematic Review," *Annals of Internal Medicine*, December 20, 2016,

https://annals.org/aim/fullarticle/2593601/scientific-basis-guideline-recommendations-sugar-intake-systematic-review.

2. Candice Choi, "Snickers Maker Criticizes Industry Funded Study on Sugar," Associated Press, December 21, 2016, https://apnews.com/article/cb26ddb939114d8ea0c219d27a788482.

3. Anahad O'Connor, "Study Tied to Food Industry Tries to Discredit Sugar Guidelines," *New York Times*, December 19, 2016, https://www.nytimes.com/2016/12/19/well/eat/a-food-industry-study-tries-to-discredit-advice-about-sugar.html.

4. Dean Schillinger and Cristin Kearns, "Guidelines to Limit Added Sugar Intake: Junk Science or Junk Food?," *Annals of Internal Medicine*, December 20, 2016, https://www.acpjournals.org/doi/10.7326/m16-2754.

5. Nina Teicholz, "The Limits of Sugar Guidelines," *Atlantic*, January 17, 2017, https://www.theatlantic.com/health/archive/2017/01/the-limits-of-sugar-guidelines/512045/.

6. Bennett Holman and Justin Bruner, "Experimentation by Industrial Selection," *Philosophy of Science* 84, no. 5 (2017): 1008–1019.

CHAPTER 41

1. CrossFit, "Diet & Cardiometabolic Health: Beyond Calories—Presented by the CrossFit Foundation," YouTube, July 21, 2017, https://www.youtube.com/watch?v=qCyTqQCoqGw.

CHAPTER 42

1. United States Court for the 9th Circuit, "American Beverage Association v. City and County of San Francisco," James R. Browning Courthouse, Courtroom I, San Francisco, California, April 17, 2017, https://www.ca9.uscourts.gov/media/view_video.php?pk_vid=0000011365.

2. *American Beverage Association v. City and County of San Francisco*, Opinion, September 19, 2017, http://cdn.ca9.uscourts.gov/datastore/opinions/2017/09/19/16-16072.pdf.

3. Michael Grynbaum, "New York City Soda Fight, in Court, Tests Agency's Powers," *New York Times*, June 4, 2014, https://www.nytimes.com/2014/06/05/nyregion/soda-ban-new-york-city-in-appeals-court.html.

4. "San Francisco Board of Supervisors Unanimously Passes First in the Nation Legislation to Combat Soda Advertising and Prohibit City Spending on Sugar-Sweetened Beverages," Scott Wiener for State Senator press release, June 9, 2015, https://campaign-scottwiener.nationbuilder.com/san_francisco_board_of_supervisors_unanimously_passes_first_in_the_nation_legislation_to_combat_soda_advertising_and_prohibit_city_spending_on_sugar_sweetened_beverages.

5. *American Beverage Association v. City and County of San Francisco*, Expert Testimony of Dr. Richard Kahn, January 12, 2016, https://ecf.cand.uscourts.gov/doc1/035113769928.

6. Richard Kahn and John L. Sievenpiper, "Dietary Sugar and Body Weight: Have We Reached a Crisis in the Epidemic of Obesity and Diabetes? We Have, but the Pox on Sugar Is Overwrought and Overworked," *Diabetes Care*, April 2014, https://care.diabetesjournals.org/content/37/4/957.short.

CHAPTER 43

1. "AMA Adopts Policy to Reduce Consumption of Sugar-Sweetened Beverages," AMA press release, June 14, 2017, https://www.ama-assn.org/press-center/press-releases/ama-adopts-policy-reduce-consumption-sugar-sweetened-beverages.

2. "The American Medical Association, Helping Defend Patients," AmeriBev.org blog post, June 15, 2015, https://www.ameribev.org/education-resources/blog/post/the-american-medical-association-helping-defend-patients/.

3. Miriam B. Vos et al., "Added Sugars and Cardiovascular Disease Risk in Children: A Scientific Statement from the American Heart Association," *Circulation*, August 22, 2016, https://www.ahajournals.org/doi/full/10.1161/CIR.0000000000000439.

CHAPTER 44

1. Sara N. Bleich et al., "Reducing Sugar-Sweetened Beverage Consumption by Providing Caloric Information: How Black Adolescents Alter Their Purchases and Whether the Effects Persist," *American Journal of Public Health*, October 16, 2014.

CHAPTER 45

1. Casey M. Rebholz et al., "Patterns of Beverages Consumed and Risk of Incident Kidney Disease," *Clinical Journal of the American Society of Nephrology*, January 2019, https://cjasn.asnjournals.org/content/14/1/49.

2. Robert Paarlberg et al., "Keeping Soda in SNAP: Understanding the Other Iron Triangle," *Society*, June 2018.

3. Rick deShazo, "Frozen in Time," TEDx Millsaps College, September 2017, https://www.ted.com/talks/rick_deshazo_frozen_in_time.

CHAPTER 47

1. Steven Garasky et al., "Foods Typically Purchased by Supplemental Nutrition Assistance (SNAP) Households," Prepared by IMPAQ International, LLC for USDA, Food and Nutrition Service, November 2016, https://fns-prod.azureedge.net/sites/default/files/ops/SNAPFoodsTypicallyPurchased.pdf.

2. Tom Farley, *Saving Gotham: A Billionaire Mayor, Activist Doctors, and the Fight for Eight Million Lives* (New York: W. W. Norton, 2015), 181.

3. Alyssa J. Moran et al., "Increases in Sugary Drink Marketing during Supplemental Nutrition Assistance Program Benefit Issuance in New York," *American Journal of Preventive Medicine*, July 2018, https://www.ncbi.nlm.nih.gov/pmc/articles/PMC6128139/.

CHAPTER 48

1. *Lamar, Coates, and Praxis Project v. Coca-Cola and ABA*, Superior Court of the District of Columbia, July 13, 2017.

2. Batsheva Ackerman et al. v. The Coca-Cola Company and Energy Brands, Inc., Second Amended Class Action Complaint, United States District Court, Eastern District of New York, October 6, 2009, https://www.cspinet.org/sites/default/files/2021-11/vitaminwater_filed_complaint.pdf.

CHAPTER 49

1. Jennifer L. Harris, "Increasing Disparities in Unhealthy Food Advertising Targeted to Black and Hispanic Youth," *Rudd Report*, January 2019, https://media.ruddcenter.uconn.edu/PDFs/TargetedMarketingReport2019.pdf.

2. Associated Press, "Coca-Cola Settles Lawsuits over Benzene," May 14, 2007, https://www.nbcnews.com/id/wbna18664391.

CHAPTER 50

1. Bruce Horovitz, "Coke Executive Answers Questions about Sugary Drinks," *USA Today*, June 7, 2012, https://abcnews.go.com/Business/coke-executive-answers-questions-sugary-drinks/story?id=16521709.

2. "FW: INFORM: U.S. Right to Know Letter to FDA," Industry Documents Library, DC Leaks Coca-Cola Emails, July 6, 2015, https://www.industrydocuments.ucsf.edu/docs/#id=tfdl0226.

CHAPTER 51

1. *American Beverage Association v. City and County of San Francisco*, United States Court of Appeals for the Ninth Circuit, September 25, 2018, https://www.ca9.uscourts.gov/media/view_video.php?pk_vid=0000014266.

CHAPTER 52

1. *Lamar, Coates, and Praxis Project v. Coca-Cola and ABA*, Superior Court of the District of Columbia, Order by Judge Elizabeth C. Wingo, October 1, 2019.

2. Candice Choi, "Coke a Good Snack? Health Experts Who Work with Coke Say So," Associated Press, March 15, 2015.

CHAPTER 54

1. The Coca-Cola Co., "'Beverages for Life'—James Quincey," YouTube, November 20, 2017, https://www.youtube.com/watch?v=f8FNwHmsblw.

2. Richard Quest interview with James Quincey, "Coca-Cola Pledges to Tackle Obesity," CNN, May 9, 2013, https://www.cnn.com/videos/bestoftv/2013/05/09/qmb-coca-cola.cnn.

3. Caitlin Dewey, "Why Chicago's Soda Tax Fizzled after Two Months," *Washington Post*, October 10, 2017, https://www.washingtonpost.com/news/wonk/wp/2017/10/10/why-chicagos-soda-tax-fizzled-after-two-months-and-what-it-means-for-the-anti-soda-movement/.

CHAPTER 55

1. HHS Press Office Staff, "Secretary Price Appoints Brenda Fitzgerald, M.D. as CDC Director and ATSDR Administrator," US Department of Health and Human Services Press Office, July 7, 2017, https://public3.pagefreezer.com/browse/HHS.gov/31-12-2020T08:51/.

2. Sheila Kaplan, "New C.D.C. Chief Saw Coca-Cola as Ally in Obesity Fight," *New York Times*, April 17, 2013, https://www.nytimes.com/2017/07/22/health/brenda-fitzgerald-cdc-coke.html.

3. Sarah Karlin Smith and Brianna Ehley, "Trump's Top Health Official Traded Tobacco Stock While Leading Anti-Smoking Efforts," *Politico*, January 30, 2018, https://www.politico.com/story/2018/01/30/cdc-director-tobacco-stocks-after-appointment-316245.

4. Sheila Kaplan, "Dr. Brenda Fitzgerald, C.D.C Director, Resigns over Tobacco, Other Investments," *New York Times*, January 31, 2018, https://www.nytimes.com/2018/01/31/health/cdc-brenda-fitzgerald-resigns.html.

CHAPTER 56

1. Paulo M. Serôdio, Martin McKee, and David Stuckler, "Coca-Cola: A Model of Transparency in Research Partnerships? A Network Analysis of Coca-Cola's Research Funding (2008–2016)," *Public Health Nutrition*, March 21, 2018, https://www.ncbi.nlm.nih.gov/pmc/articles/PMC5962884/.

2. Chris Prentice, "M & M's Maker Publishes Science Policy in Bid to Boost Transparency," Reuters, February 8, 2018, https://www.reuters.com/article/us-mars-science-candy/mms-maker-publishes-science-policy-in-bid-to-boost-transparency-idUSKBN1FP2AO.

CHAPTER 57

1. Edward Archer, "In Defense of Sugar: A Critique of Diet-Centrism," *Progress in Cardiovascular Diseases*, May–June 2018.

2. Larry Husten, "What Role Should Coca-Cola Play in Obesity Research?," *Forbes*, April 27, 2014.

3. Edward Archer, Gregory A. Hand, and Steven N. Blair, "Validity of U.S. Nutritional Surveillances: National Health and Nutrition Examination Survey Caloric Energy Intake Data, 1971–2010," *PLOS One*, October 9, 2013, https://journals.plos.org/plosone/article?id=10.1371/journal.pone.0076632.

4. Edward Archer et al., "45-Year Trends in Women's Use of Time and Household Management Energy Expenditure," *PLOS One*, February 20, 2013, https://journals.plos.org/plosone/article/related?id=10.1371/journal.pone.0056620.

CHAPTER 59

1. UCSF New Food Industry Archives, November 15, 2018, https://sugarscience.ucsf.edu/new-food-industry-documents-archive.html.

CHAPTER 61

1. Andrew Jacobs, "With Obesity Rates Rising in China, Coke Helps Set Nutrition Policy," *New York Times*, January 10, 2019, https://www.nytimes.com/2019/01/09/health/obesity-china-coke.html.

2. Susan Greenhalgh, "Soda Industry Influence on Obesity Science and Policy in China," *Journal of Public Health Policy*, January 9, 2019.

3. David Olinger, "CU Nutrition Expert Who Took Coca-Cola Money Steps Down," *Denver Post*, March 23, 2016, https://www.denverpost.com/2016/03/23/cu-nutrition-expert-who-took-coca-cola-money-steps-down/.

4. "Hill Named Chair of Nutrition Sciences, Director of Nutrition Obesity Research Center," University of Alabama at Birmingham press release, December 4, 2018, https://www.uab.edu/shp/news/home/students-faculty/james-hill-chair-nutrition-and-director-norc.

CHAPTER 62

1. "Pingree, DeLauro to HHS Inspector General: Investigate Coca-Cola's Lobbying of CDC," Congresswoman Chellie Pingree press release, February 4, 2019, https://pingree.house.gov/news/documentsingle.aspx?DocumentID=291.

2. Nason Maani Hessari et al., "Public Meets Private: Conversations between Coca-Cola and the CDC," *Milbank Quarterly*, March 2019, https://www.milbank.org/quarterly/articles/public-meets-private-conversations-between-coca-cola-and-the-cdc/.

3. Alison Kretser et al., "Scientific Integrity Principles and Best Practices: Recommendations from a Scientific Integrity Consortium," *Science and Engineering Ethics*, February 27, 2019, https://link.springer.com/article/10.1007/s11948-019-00094-3.

4. AAAS, "Scientific Integrity Consortium's Nine Best Practices and Steps for Implementation," Washington, DC, February 16, 2019, https://aaas.confex.com/aaas/2019/meetingapp.cgi/Paper/2365.

CHAPTER 63

1. Jay Moye, "'Our Best and Brightest Days Are Ahead': Muhtar Kent Retires as Coca-Cola Chairman," Coca-ColaCompany.com press release, April 24, 2019, https://www.coca-colacompany.com/stories/our-best-and-brightest-days-are-ahead-muhtar-kent-retires-as-coca-cola-chairman.

2. Ray Rogers, "Harrington Investments Recruits Ray Rogers to Introduce Shareholder Resolution," YouTube, June 4, 2019, https://www.youtube.com/watch?v=0DsmrqFYdCc; "The Coca-Cola Company 2019 Proxy Statement," Coca-ColaCompany.com, April 24, 2019, https://www.coca-colacompany.com/content/dam/journey/us/en/private/fileassets/pdf/2019/annual-shareholders-meeting/2019-Proxy-Statement.pdf.

3. Frank Pigott, "Response of the Office of Chief Counsel, Division of Corporation Finance," US Securities and Exchange Commission, February 21, 2019, https://www.sec.gov/divisions/corpfin/cf-noaction/14a-8/2019/johnharrington022119-14a8.pdf.

CHAPTER 64

1. "Adam Rippon: Pence Spat Shouldn't Distract," Associated Press, February 13, 2018, https://www.cdc.gov/nutrition/data-statistics/sugar-sweetened-beverages-intake.html; Getty Images, "United States Figure Skater Adam Rippon speaks during a press conference at the Main Press Centre on February 13, 2018 in Pyeongchang-gun, South Korea" (caption accompanying photograph by Chris Graythen), https://www.gettyimages.com/detail/news-photo/united-states-figure-skater-adam-rippon-speaks-during-a-news-photo/917593102?adppopup=true.

CHAPTER 65

1. Vasanti S. Malik et al., "Long-Term Consumption of Sugar-Sweetened and Artificially Sweetened Beverages and Risk of Mortality in U.S. Adults," *Circulation*, March 18, 2019, https://www.ahajournals.org/doi/full/10.1161/CIRCULATIONAHA.118.037401.

2. Alice Lichtenstein, "Last Nail in the Coffin for Sugar-Sweetened Beverages," *Circulation*, April 29, 2019, https://www.ahajournals.org/doi/10.1161/CIRCULATIONAHA.119.040245.

3. Zachary J. Ward et al., "Projected U.S. State-Level Prevalence of Adult Obesity and Severe Obesity," *New England Journal of Medicine*, December 19, 2019, https://www.nejm.org/doi/full/10.1056/NEJMsa1909301.

4. "State Level Trends in Obesity with Zach Ward," video posted by choicesproject.org, December 19, 2019, https://choicesproject.org/publications/projected-us-state-level-prevalence-adult-obesity-severe-obesity/#video.

EPILOGUE

1. Roy Gentry memo to Edgar J. Forio, March 22, 1949, Robert Winship Woodruff papers, box 44, folder 12, Stuart A. Rose Manuscript, Archives and Rare Book Library, Emory University.

2. Tanya Albert Henry, "Stating Facts on Sugary-Drink Labels Isn't Free-Speech Violation," AMA, April 15, 2021.

3. Naomi Oreskes and Erik M. Conway, *Merchants of Doubt* (New York: Bloomsbury Press, 2010), 24.

4. The Praxis Project press release, "What Has Changed Since We Filed our Lawsuit Against a Beverage Giant, and What Still Must be Changed," February 8, 2021, https://www.thepraxisproject.org/announcements/2021/2/8/what-has-changed-since-we-filed-our-lawsuit-against-a-beverage-industry-giant-and-what-still-must-be-changed.

5. WHO COVID-19 dashboard: https://data.who.int/dashboards/covid19/cases.

6. Zachary J. Ward et al., "Association of Body Mass Index with Health Care Expenditures in the United States by Age and Sex," *PLOS One*, March 24, 2021.

7. Centers for Disease Control and Prevention, "About Type 2 Diabetes," accessed March 11, 2024, https://www.cdc.gov/diabetes/about/about-type-2-diabetes.html.

8. Joel Achenbach, Dan Keating, Laurie McGinley, Akilah Johnson, and Jahi Chikwendiu, "Chronic Illness Is Killing Us Too Soon," *Washington Post*, October 3, 2023.

9. Adam Pope, "We Have a Lot of Lives to Reach," UAB News, May 18, 2023.

10. Derrick Z. Jackson, "The Junk Food President Aims to Ruin American Nutrition," *American Prospect*, August 23, 2019.

11. Brett Pulley, "Coca-Cola Severs Longtime Ties with Pro-Sugar Group," *Bloomberg*, January 13, 2021, https://www.bloomberg.com/news/articles/2021-01-13/coca-cola-severs-longtime-ties-with-pro-sugar-industry-group?srnd=markets-vp.

12. Scott Kaplan et al., "Evaluation of Changes in Prices and Purchases Following Implementation of Sugar-Sweetened Beverage Taxes across the US," *JAMA Health Forum*, January 5, 2024.

13. Lindsey Smith Taillie et al., "An Evaluation of Chile's Law of Food Labeling and Advertising on Sugar-Sweetened Beverage Purchases from 2015 to 2017: A Before-and-After Study," *PLOS Medicine*, February 11, 2020.

14. Senator Bernie Sanders, "We Can't Allow the Food and Beverage Industry to Destroy Our Kids' Health," *USA Today*, December 14, 2023.

15. Heather Norman-Burgdolf et al., "Sugar-Sweetened Beverage Consumption among Adults in Rural Appalachia," *Preventive Medicine Reports*, vol. 21, December 2021.

16. "Get the Facts: Sugar-Sweetened Beverages and Consumption," CDC.gov, accessed March 15, 2024, https://www.cdc.gov/nutrition/data-statistics/sugar-sweetened-beverages-intake.html.

INDEX

ABOUT THE AUTHOR

Murray Carpenter is the author of *Caffeinated: How Our Daily Habit Helps, Hurts, and Hooks Us*. As a print and radio journalist for twenty-five years, primarily focused on environmental and science stories, he has reported for the *New York Times*, the *Washington Post*, and NPR. His work has taken him across the United States and to Guantanamo, the Colombian llanos, and a factory town in China. He lives in Belfast, Maine.